Blue Plaques of Leeds
The Next Collection

More stories behind the famous people, places and events celebrated by blue plaques

By Kevin Grady & Robert Tyrrell

Leeds Civic Trust
2020

Contents

Preface

Leeds Civic Trust Historic Plaques Scheme formally began with the unveiling of the Burley Bar plaque in October 1987. By mid 2001, the number of blue plaques unveiled had reached sixty-six, and the Trust decided that a book should be published to provide more detailed information about the subjects celebrated by each of the plaques. That book, *Blue Plaques of Leeds: The stories behind the famous people and places commemorated for posterity by Blue Plaques*, was written by Peter Dyson and Kevin Grady, and published in 2001.

A second book about the many plaques erected since then has been long overdue. With about six new plaques being unveiled every year, the challenge of producing a book that is completely up to date has proved rather daunting. Finally, it was decided that the remit of this second book would be to cover the ninety-eight additional plaques erected between June 2001 and October 2017, thereby marking the plaques scheme's first thirty years, and the plaques already erected or on the stocks when Kevin Grady retired as Director of the Trust in December 2016.

Plaque texts rarely extend beyond forty-three words, so this book provides its authors with the opportunity to share some of the fascinating information we have gathered about the subjects celebrated by the ninety-eight plaques. It also provides the opportunity to present an overview of all the 164 plaques erected in the thirty years since 1987; the introduction describes the evolution of the scheme. Following the introduction, the plaques are grouped by theme with each plaque receiving one or two pages of text and pictures; at the top of each page in bold is the heading and full text of the plaque concerned. An appendix contains a complete list of all the 179 plaques erected up to the publication of this book.

Acknowledgements

The writing of this book has proved surprisingly complex due to the many and diverse subjects it encompasses. Moreover, compressing the large amount of material collected to fit the format of one page per plaque has proved challenging. The help of Neil Diamond and Jane Taylor in editing down the length of the first draft of the book has been much appreciated. Likewise, has been the help of Steven Burt, John Crossen, Martin Hamilton, Lynda Kitching, Jane Taylor and Heather Tyrrell in proofreading its final draft.

Especial thanks too are due to Dörte Haarhaus, Meleri Roberts, and Deborah Hill, present and past Trust administrators, for their extensive help in word-processing handwritten drafts, and hunting down photographs and a host of other pieces of information held by the Trust. Very particular thanks go to the book's designer, Huw James of Studio Tom, Dick & Harry, for his skill and immense patience and good humour in bringing the design of the book to fruition.

The warmest thanks are due to the many people who provided information about individual plaques. They are too numerous to name individually, but Chris Hammond must have a special mention because he wrote the piece in this book about William Astbury, and Howard Finlay who assisted Robert (Bob) Tyrrell in many ways. The Trust is also very grateful for the assistance it has received in obtaining pictures to illustrate the book.

Hearty thanks are due to the many proposers and sponsors of plaques, and all those people and organisations who have helped in numerous ways to make the blue plaques scheme the success it continues to be. We hope readers will enjoy this book, and that it will enrich their appreciation of the blue plaques schemes and the many fascinating subjects the plaques have encompassed so far.

Kevin Grady & Bob Tyrrell

March 2020

Sources of Illustrations

Most of the modern photographs of buildings and unveiling events were taken by Kevin Grady, but some were also kindly provided by the Yorkshire Evening Post, Dörte Haarhaus, and Clifford Stead. Many of the historic images have been kindly provided by the collections of the Thoresby Society, Leeds Civic Trust, Leeds City Museums and Galleries, and the authors' collections. Other providers of images have been: Queen's College, Oxford; Mount St Mary's Catholic High School; The Times; the Kenneth Armitage Foundation; Yorkshire Country Cricket Club; the University of Leeds; Andrew Turton; the Sue Ryder Prayer Fellowship; Michael Meadowcroft; Bernard Shooman; the Tolkien Society; Stephen Garnett of the Middleton Railway Trust; and Leeds Grand Theatre.

SAMUEL LEDGARD
(1874 - 1952)
Was landlord here 1896-1952.
The renowned private operator of bus and
coach services in Yorkshire, in a remarkable
career he was also a farmer, brewer,
garage proprietor, quarry owner,
haulage contractor and
caterer to royalty and
the nobility.

ELSON INN
QUALITY
BEERS

Samuel Ledgard's granddaughter, Jenny Baron, at the unveiling, 15 April 2003

Thirty Years of Blue Plaques

Leeds Civic Trust's Historic Plaques Scheme was officially launched on 27 November 1987 with the erection of a blue plaque on the Headrow frontage of the Leeds & Holbeck Building Society Headquarters; the plaque highlighted the location of the Burley Bar Stone which once marked one of the boundaries of the medieval town of Leeds. The idea of starting a plaques scheme to promote public awareness of the history and heritage of the city was first developed by Trust Council members Neville Rowell, Tony Moyes and Olav Arnold. It had been decided that the plaques would commemorate 'events, people, institutions and buildings of very special importance in the history, heritage or shaping of Leeds'. The underlying principles were that any subject more than fifty years old qualified as part of 'history'; people needed to have been dead for ten years to be eligible for a plaque; and, following the example of the London blue plaques scheme, apart from in exceptional circumstances, it was taken for granted that there should be a physical association between the structure upon which the plaque was erected and the subject commemorated.

Only three plaques were erected in the first eighteen months of the scheme, but the enthusiasm for the plaques as an aid to promoting city tourism brought forward offers of finance which assisted in twenty-eight being erected in the next three years. The pace slackened in the next six years with about three a year being erected, but thereafter the scheme flourished with around seven being erected each year. The one hundredth plaque – celebrating the historic Whitelocks public house – was unveiled in 2006, and the one hundred and fiftieth – celebrating Alf Cooke's Crown Point Print Works – was unveiled in 2016. The erection of so many plaques has been made possible by the generosity of plaque sponsors and the enthusiasm of the Leeds public and city business for them; and there has been a sustained flow of excellent suggestions for plaques.

The Burley Bar Stone Plaque Unveiling in 1987: (Left to right) Kevin Grady, George Turnbull (President of the Leeds & Holbeck Building Society), Lord George Marshall (President, Leeds Civic Trust), Olav Arnold (Chairman, Leeds Civic Trust), John Finney (Director of Planning, Leeds City Council).

The Louis le Prince Plaque unveiling on Woodhouse Lane in 1988 – plaque number three: (Left to right) Tony Moyes, Doreen Moyes, Sir Richard Attenborough, Kevin Grady, Neville Rowell.

In the early years of the scheme, there was primarily a focus on celebrating historic buildings and fine architecture in the city centre, but as the years have progressed there has been a sustained effort to erect plaques further afield. Of the first 48 plaques, 42 were located in the city centre, but 78 of the next 116 have been placed in the suburbs, outer towns and villages of the Leeds Metropolitan District; places outside the city centre receiving plaques have included Oulton, Crossgates, Bramley, Scarcroft, Armley, Beeston, Chapeltown, Gledhow, Burmantofts, Morley, Roundhay, Fulneck, Harehills, Meanwood, Hunslet, Cookridge, Headingley, Holbeck, and Wortley.

The Subjects Celebrated by Blue Plaques

Over 90 individuals or families associated with Leeds are either the subject of plaques or mentioned on them, ranging from the great names of the sixteenth and seventeenth centuries such as the great woollen cloth merchant and benefactor John Harrison and Leeds' first historian Ralph Thoresby, to some of the great names of Georgian England including the founder of the civil engineering profession, John Smeaton, and the famous scientist and clergyman Joseph Priestley.

Ralph Thoresby (1658-1725).

The great names of the Industrial Revolution and Victorian industry in Leeds have also been celebrated, such as Benjamin Gott and John Marshall – the men who revolutionised Leeds industry with the introduction of factory production of cloth – and outstanding Victorian industrialists and innovators such as John Barran, Joshua Tetley, Colonel T. W. Harding of Tower Works, and the pioneer of cinematography, Louis Le Prince.

Benjamin Gott (1762-1840).

Distinguished Victorians commemorated have included doctors and surgeons such as Sir Clifford Allbutt and Sir Berkley Moynihan, and figures in the arts such as the painter Atkinson Grimshaw. Moving into the twentieth century, plaques have celebrated great Leeds people ranging from dazzling entrepreneurs such as Montague Burton to great sportsmen such as the cricketers Len Hutton and Hedley Verity. In addition, the plaques have noted the great stars who appeared at theatres, and some forty architects (or architectural practices) who designed particularly fine buildings upon which plaques have been erected.

In the early years of the plaques scheme the people commemorated were all men; their number rising to forty when all the plaques included in this book are added to the total. But in 2002 the Trust began to redress the balance when it erected its first plaque for a woman – the art patron and campaigner for women's rights, Ellen Heaton. Taking account of the plaques discussed in this book, the number of women celebrated by plaques rose to ten, and at the date of publication this has risen to fourteen, including Leeds suffragettes such as Leonora Cohen – the woman who smashed the jewel case in the Tower of London; the legendary 'all girls band' leader Ivy Benson; and the cycling legend Beryl Burton.

The subjects of the 164 plaques are remarkably diverse, but grouping them in broad categories highlights the focal points of the scheme.

Table: Plaques by topics from 1987 to October 2017

Subject	No. of Plaques
Industry and innovation	26
Commerce, shops and markets	15
Transport	8
Welfare and social provision	6
Medicine	5
Education	15
Religion	12
Art and culture	12
Leisure and entertainment	12
Sport	10
Houses of notable people	20
Government, politics and society	16
Historic artefacts	7
Total	**164**

Since Leeds from the seventeenth century has been regarded by contemporaries, above all, as a great centre of industry, commerce and innovation, and one greatly advantaged by its market and transport facilities, unsurprisingly plaques celebrating these aspects of its history constitute almost one third of those erected.

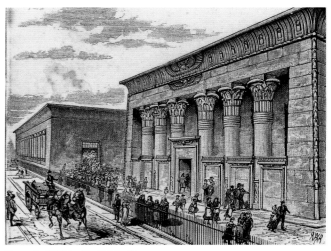

Temple Mill built 1838-43.

Remarkable industrial buildings such as the Egyptian-style Temple Mill and the Moorish-style St Paul's House (a ready-made clothing factory) are featured, while architecturally outstanding commercial buildings such as the Third White Cloth Hall, Kirkgate Market and Leeds Corn Exchange have plaques, as do the Middleton Railway (the world's first commercially successful railway) and the eye-catching Leeds & Thirsk Railway Roundhouse on Wellington Road.

The Corn Exchange erected 1860-63.

The great growth of the parish and borough's population, from around 11,000 inhabitants in 1700 to some 50,000 by 1800, and 430,000 by 1900, required the provision of all manner of new amenities and services in an attempt to meet their needs. Around one-twelfth of the plaques concern health and welfare, including those celebrating institutions ranging from the nationally famous Leeds General Infirmary to the Victorian workhouse, and doctors and surgeons of countrywide repute.

Leeds General Infirmary opened 1869.

Another one-sixth of the plaques are concerned with education and religion: those relating to education celebrate notable schools and colleges ranging from the Leeds Charity School and Richard Kemplay's Academy for Young Gentlemen to Gipton Board School and the Yorkshire College; those relating to religion embrace the Leeds Methodist Pioneers and St Aidan's Church, as well as the Great Synagogue and the city's first mosque.

Kemplay's Academy for Young Gentlemen c. 1830.

Almost a quarter of the plaques celebrate the cultural life and achievements of Leeds and its people, spanning art and literature, leisure and entertainment, and sport. The subjects covered range from the avant-garde Leeds Arts Club to famous authors such as Arthur Ransome and J. R. R. Tolkien; much loved amenities such as the Grand Theatre and the Cottage Road Cinema; as well as the coming of radio broadcasting to Leeds, and sports venues, such as Headingley Rugby Ground; and sporting heroes.

The Victoria Hotel plaque unveiling with Tetley's shire horses in 1989: (left to right) the pub landlord, John Power, Olav Arnold, and Tetley's Finance Director.

The governing of the city and the political campaigning of Leeds people for the rights of individuals are the concern of another twelfth of the plaques. Finally, almost one-sixth of the plaques are in the great 'Queen Victoria slept here' tradition – they draw attention to the houses, both grand and humble, where Leeds people of note and merit have lived. Examples range from architecturally impressive houses set in picturesque grounds, such as Elmete Hall (the home of the Kitsons) and the Mansion at Roundhay Park (the home of the Nicholson family) to the very ordinary homes of suffragettes Leonora Cohen and Mary Gawthorpe. And, indeed a Trust plaque does celebrate a Leeds house where Queen Victoria once slept – Woodsley House (later known as Fairbairn House) on Clarendon Road where, with Leeds in a state of immense excitement, she stayed in 1858 on the eve of opening the city's famous town hall.

Queen Victoria in the grounds of Woodsley House in 1858.

Valerie Ives receiving a gift at City Varieties plaque unveiling in 1997. Trust Chairman Robert Collins and magician Paul Daniels look on.

The Plaques Team

The first plaque was erected shortly after Kevin Grady became Director of Leeds Civic Trust. So extensive was the work leading up to the erection of a plaque that it soon became clear that a keen volunteer was needed to coordinate the scheme if it was to blossom. Miss Valerie Ives took on the role of Plaques Scheme Administrator with gusto, and during her tenure from 1988 to 2006 the plaques increased in number from 3 to 103!

Valerie was succeeded in the role by David Kaye who took the number of plaques to 124 by the time he relinquished the role in 2010. John Crossen succeeded him and continues today as Plaques Scheme Coordinator.

Bob Tyrrell, Kevin Grady and David Kaye (left to right) at the Leonora Cohen plaque unveiling in 2007.

Meanwhile, Kevin Grady and then Kevin Grady and Bob Tyrrell together (from about the seventy-fifth plaque) researched the subjects of the plaques and wrote their texts or edited those submitted by others; Bob Tyrrell also became responsible for the maintenance of the plaques. Michael Pemberton and Roger Garnett became the plaques' skilled erectors; it can be extremely difficult to get plaques level, especially in awkward locations. Invaluable support was also readily given by the Trust's Blue Plaques Group members, Janet Douglas, Veronica Lovell, Steven Burt and Peter Dyson. The administration of the scheme has relied on the work behind the scenes of a succession of Trust administrators – Barbara Stewart, Jayne Harnett, Cath Kelly, Tricia Ryan, Dörte Haarhaus, Deborah Hill and Meleri Roberts.

The Art and Difficulties of Text Writing

The standard circular Trust blue plaques are eighteen inches in diameter and made of cast aluminium. Excluding the title heading, this allows space only for between thirty-eight and forty-three words of text – usually two sentences – in which to communicate what makes the subject so significant and special. After gathering a great deal of information, summarising this in a lively and engaging manner is a big challenge, demanding considerable skill in the art of precis. Sponsors need to be happy with plaque texts, especially if they are going on their buildings, though the Trust has always been the final arbiter on the wording. Agreeing a text can be difficult. In the instance of a plaque telling the story of an ultimately unsuccessful Georgian residential development, the sponsor on whose offices the plaque was to be displayed vetoed the use of the words 'failed' or 'unsuccessful', not wishing to have them associated with his firm. When the physical space to erect a plaque has been limited, for example in the case of the East Bar plaque, smaller fourteen-inch diameter plaques have been used, meaning that texts have had to be much shorter than usual. In one instance where a normal length text was essential, but space was restricted – namely at Whitkirk Manor House – the unprecedented expedient of using a rectangular plaque was adopted. In the year 2000, the Trust departed from its usual eighteen-inch blue and white plaques to erect three twenty-inch blue plaques with gold lettering and borders; these 'millennium plaques' celebrated very special buildings – the Victoria Quarter/County Arcade, Leeds Town Hall and Kirkgate Market; and belatedly Leeds Civic Hall which also received one in 2002.

Michael Pemberton the Trust's first plaque erector.

Plaques Scheme Coordinator John Crossen, Trust Chair Lynda Kitching, and plaque erector Roger Garnett.

The Victoria Quarter unveiling May 2000, one of the blue and gold Millennium Plaques. Left to right: John Bade (Victoria Quarter Manager), Lord Mayor Councillor Keith Parker, John Richards (Civic Trust Chairman).

Sometimes it has been almost impossible to agree a limit to the text with a great enthusiast for a subject, as happened with the plaque for the immensely significant founder of the civil engineering profession, John Smeaton. Since there was ample space at its waterside location and it would not appear excessively large in that setting, the Trust agreed to its biggest plaque ever at twenty-four inches in diameter.

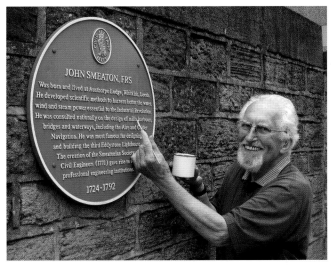

Bob Tyrrell touching up the paintwork on the John Smeaton plaque – the largest Trust plaque.

Above all, the text of a plaque must be factually correct, and many hours are spent researching and checking facts. Though not 'set in stone', the texts are literally cast in aluminium, so mistakes are expensive to rectify. In a handful of instances, incorrect dates have been ground off plaques after manufacture, and replacement dates welded on. A lesson learnt from experience is never to absolutely rely on information about the subject of a plaque provided by applicants, however expert they appear to be. In the case of the plaque for Test cricketer Hedley Verity, for example, only at the very last minute before its manufacture was it spotted that the bowling figures supplied were incorrect. What, we thought, would Geoffrey Boycott have had to say if he had attended the unveiling and spotted a mistake? Over the thirty years of the scheme, the Trust has received excellent service from two highly skilled plaque manufacturers: first the Royal Label Factory, based in Chipping Norton in the Cotswolds until 1998, and thereafter from Leander Architectural, based in Buxton, with which it merged.

The Plaque Unveilings

After the work of researching a subject nominated for a plaque, fundraising, text writing and plaque manufacture, the great day comes – the unveiling.

There have been many memorable and unusual unveilings. Sometimes the excitement has been generated by a star unveiler, such as the actors Sir Richard Attenborough and Maxine Peake, or hearing the startling reminiscences of those involved with the subject, such as the hilarious adventures on tour of the girls in Ivy Benson's Band.

Roger Garnett erecting the Leeds Grand Theatre Plaque.

When the twin sons of Montague Burton unveiled his plaque, they seemed part of living history.

The Burton Twins (Arnold and Raymond) at the Montague Burton unveiling in 2001.

A plaque blessed: the Revd Charles Jenkinson unveiling in 2012.

Often where community groups and organisations have worked very hard to raise funds for plaques celebrating a special subject which is the source of much pride in their localities, really enjoyable bean feasts have often followed the unveilings. When a great assemblage of Methodists from across the world attended the Leeds Methodist Pioneers unveiling, there was a truly international air of joy and celebration.

Some of the quirky features of unveilings stay long in the memory. As incense was wafted over the plaque at St John and St Barnabas Church, Belle Isle, to celebrate the life and work of the Revd Charles Jenkinson, we realised that it was the first plaque to be blessed.

When political banners were raised as Norman Willis, the General Secretary of the Trades Union Congress, unveiled the plaque for the author Arthur Ransome, this became the first unveiling at which there was a political protest. Exhilaratingly, the unveiling of the plaque celebrating Leeds University Refectory as a legendary rock venue by the surviving band members of The Who, Roger Daltrey and Pete Townshend (an altogether remarkable occasion), was followed a couple of hours later by them treating attenders to a full-blown rock concert. Bizarrely, the plaque erected at Leeds Irish Centre, to celebrate it as the birthplace of televised darts, was the first plaque to be initiated by a formal petition from a national newspaper – The Times. And, remarkable to the end, it was the first plaque to be unveiled during a blizzard – the deep snow of which grid locked Leeds and delayed the arrival of the sponsors and unveiler from London by over two hours.

Ongoing Maintenance

The Trust is committed to maintaining its plaques in perpetuity and is grateful to members of the public for reporting damage or wear and tear; several of our earliest plaques have been repainted. Similarly, thanks go to the many Leeds residents who wash and clean their local plaques.

Actress Josephine Tewson unveils the Adelaide Neilson plaque at the West Yorkshire Playhouse in 2008, as theatre director Ian Brown and Kevin Grady look on.

The Value and Importance of the Scheme

Over its first thirty years the Trust's historic plaques scheme has grown astonishingly from one with the limited ambition of erecting thirty plaques to one heading towards attaining two hundred. This achievement is not the result of any diminution in the specialness or importance expected of the subjects chosen for inclusion in the scheme; rather it has much to do with the increased geographical spread and widening of the subject range of the plaques. Moreover, as time has passed, new subjects have become eligible for inclusion in the scheme. But above all it is the enthusiasm of the general public, community groups, and specialist interest groups for the blue plaques scheme which has led to its continued expansion. At the plaque unveiling ceremonies the very great value placed on receiving a Leeds Civic Trust plaque and the appreciation of them by our fellow citizens has been writ large. At these happy occasions it is readily apparent that the importance and value of our blue plaques lies not only in them being a celebration of the history of Leeds and the achievements of its people, but also in them being an affirmation of the value the city places on all sections of its community.

Gertrude Paul's daughter, Heather, speaking at the unveiling of her mother's plaque in 2011.

Derek Rayner, President of LDTEC, Councillor David Congreve and Lynda Kitching at the Fowler Unveiling 4 December 2014

JOHN FOWLER

The Wiltshire-born Quaker engineer erected his Steam Plough Works here in 1861. Some of its buildings still stand opposite on Leathley Road.

He developed the first practical method of mechanical ploughing using a cable system powered by steam engines. This system was exported worldwide

1826 - 1864

Early History

Today the visitor to the thriving city of Leeds can scarcely conceive that once upon a time at its heart was a small medieval manor. In 1086 the Domesday Book tells us that on the manor of Leeds, which stood on the north bank of the River Aire, there were twenty-seven villeins, four sokemen and four bordars, who between them had fourteen ploughs. These men and their families and dependents constituted a population of about two hundred. There was a priest, a church and a water mill, and ten acres of meadow. The manor's agricultural open fields, common land, and waste land extended beyond the small settlement based on Kirkgate to include the areas we know today as Knostrop, Richmond Hill, Burmantofts and Harehills; Quarry Hill, Sheepscar and Chapeltown; Buslingthorpe and Woodhouse Ridge; and a swathe of land, including Woodhouse Moor, which swept down to the River Aire near Kirkstall Road railway viaduct.

But 'Leeds' was more than just a manor. The ancient parish of Leeds, centred on the church at the end of Kirkgate, took in a much larger area including the manors of Allerton, Gipton, Osmondthorpe, Beeston, Hunslet, Holbeck, Ristone (Wortley), Farnley, Bramley, Armley and Headingley-cum-Burley. When Leeds received its borough charter in 1626, the whole parish was included in the borough's boundaries, and the outer manors with their villages became known as out-townships.

The plaques to be described in this section of the book are those which highlight aspects of the story of Leeds from the Middle Ages to the days of Leeds' first historian, Ralph Thoresby (1685-1725). The plaques included in subsequent sections of the book are grouped by theme and encompass the wide span of history during which Leeds developed from being one of the most prosperous market towns in Georgian England, with its prosperity based on woollen cloth manufacture and merchanting, to its growth into an industrial powerhouse and one of the country's great Victorian cities, and then onwards into the twentieth century.

The subjects celebrated by the plaques in this section are Leeds' medieval town bars, Whitkirk Manor House, the manor and out-township of Bramley's village green and pump, Headingley Hall, and finally Weetwood Hall and Cookridge Hall, both of which occupy sites associated with Kirkstall Abbey and were lived in by friends and acquaintances of Ralph Thoresby.

'South East Prospect of Leedes in the County of York', by Samuel and Nathaniel Buck, 1745.

The Medieval Town Bars

The North Bar
The Bar Stone marks the northern boundary of the built-up area of the medieval town of Leeds.

The South Bar
The gate defending the southern entrance to the medieval town of Leeds stood here.

In the Middle Ages the points of entry into the built-up area of the town of Leeds were protected by bars. Leeds was not a heavily defended city like York, so it did not have large stone fortified entrances similar to Bootham Bar and Micklegate Bar. Nevertheless, as John Cossins' Plan of Leeds of 1726 suggests, some, if not all, of the Leeds bars must have been substantial wooden gates, intended to keep out stray cattle, to delay unwanted visitors, and to provide barriers at which tolls could be collected on market days. Perhaps in medieval times, like the bars of the neighbouring town of Wakefield, the Leeds bars were closed every night at eight o'clock, when a curfew rang.

Originally, Leeds had six town bars. These were the North Bar on Vicar Lane, between Lady Lane and Templar Street; the East Bar or 'York Bar', at the end of Kirkgate by the Parish Church; the South Bar on the south side of Leeds Bridge; the West Bar at the west end of Boar Lane; Burley Bar on the Headrow by Albion Street; and, finally, Woodhouse Bar at the bottom of Woodhouse Lane, in what today is Dortmund Square.

As the eighteenth century progressed, gates were no longer required for defensive purposes, but the bars continued to mark important administrative boundaries, and thereafter their position was marked by Bar Stones. In 1755 the Leeds Improvement Act empowered a commission consisting of fourteen principal inhabitants living within the town bars, nominated by the ratepayers, plus the mayor, recorder and Justices of the Peace for the borough, to provide street lighting and paving for the streets 'within the bars' and to ensure that the town was properly cleansed. Under the Act residents within the town bars were required to 'cease throwing ashes, rubbish, dust, timber, dirt, dung, filth, tubs or other annoyances into the streets'. Occupants of houses fronting the street were obliged to 'sweep and clean the street in front of their property between one and three o'clock every Saturday afternoon'. The rapid growth of the town after 1755 made it necessary to extend street lighting, paving and the authority of the street cleaning by-laws beyond the bars. The 1790 Improvement Act, which included provisions to do with water supply, extended the commissioners' jurisdiction to areas 'within 1000 yards of the town bars'. Interestingly, the boundaries denoted by the bars in the early eighteenth century are much the same as those of the present-day Leeds city centre shopping area.

Leeds Workhouse c. 1840: looking north at the junction of Vicar Lane and Lady Lane. The North Bar stood near the white gable end.

The North Bar Stone being cemented into the wall of a new building on Vicar Lane.

Three of the bar stones survive today: the Burley Bar Stone is in a case in the reception area of the Leeds Building Society's Headquarters on Albion Street; the East Bar Stone is set in the wall of Leeds Parish Church precinct; and the North Bar Stone is embedded in the wall of the former West Yorkshire Bus Station on the east side of Vicar Lane, just above Lady Lane. Once Burley Bar and its bar stone had been celebrated as the Trust's inaugural blue plaque in 1987, it became a firm ambition to mark the sites of all the town bars. Plaques were erected for the West Bar in 1989 and the East Bar in 1995. The next two (those highlighted here) were for the South Bar in 2015, and the North Bar in 2017. It is a reminder of the dogged persistence sometimes required to secure the erection of plaques (often delayed by the most peculiar circumstances) that the unveiling of the North Bar plaque marked the thirtieth anniversary of the historic plaques scheme. Attentive readers, however, will have spotted that one bar – Woodhouse Bar – still awaits a plaque; so there is still work to be done.

The plaque highlighting the location of the North Bar Stone is sited at 101 Vicar Lane (LS2 7NL), the former West Yorkshire Bus Station building, which stands just north of Lady Lane. It was sponsored by Professor Neville Rowell and unveiled on 30 October 2017 by James Bailey, General Manager of Victoria Gate, on behalf of Hammerson plc.

The South Bar plaque is situated on the former Aire and Calder Navigation Offices at Bridge End on the south side of Leeds Bridge (LS10 1NB). It was sponsored and unveiled by Professor Neville Rowell on 9 June 2015.

The Aire and Calder Navigation Office on the site of the South Bar, Bridge End.

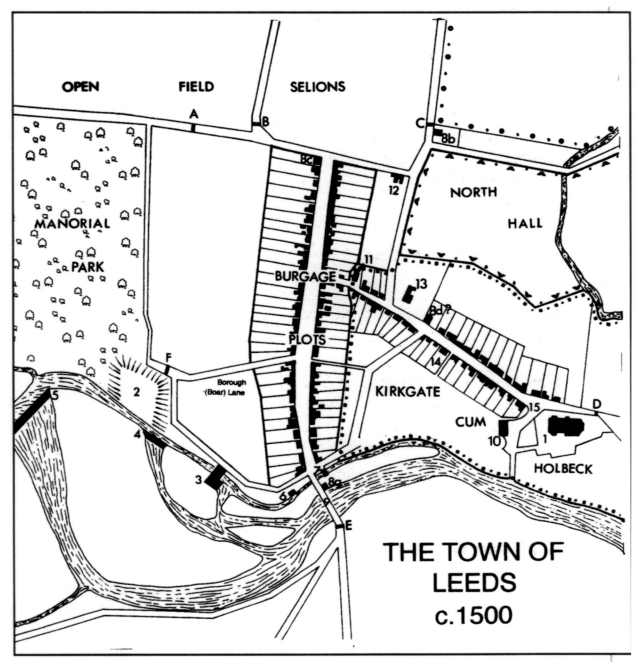

THE TOWN OF LEEDS c.1500

OPEN FIELD SELIONS

MANORIAL PARK

BURGAGE PLOTS

Borough (Boar) Lane

NORTH HALL

KIRKGATE CUM HOLBECK

LEEDS IN THE LATE MEDIEVAL PERIOD.

KEY:

1. St. Peter's — the parish church
2. Castelhyll — site of the former fortified manor house
3. Manorial Corn Mill
4. Bondman Dam
5. High Dam
6. Fulling mill
7. Fulling mill
8. Chantry Chapels:
a. St. Mary's on the Bridge
b. Lady Chapel
c. Sir William Eures' Chapel
d. Thomas Clarell's Chapel
9. Leeds Bridge
10. Tithe Barn
11. Manorial Oven with Hall of Pleas above
12. Rockley Hall
13. The Vicarage
14. The Hospitium.
15. Manor house of Kirkgate-cum-Holbeck.

The Bars — the boundaries of the medieval town
A. Burley Bar.
B. Woodhouse Bar.
C. North Bar.
D. East or York Bar.
E. South Bar.
F. West Bar.

Whitkirk Manor House

The courts of the Manors of Whitkirk and Temple Newsam met here. John Wesley reputedly preached in the garden. Houses in the Manor of Whitkirk were distinguished by a Templar Cross.

The Unveiling: (Left to right) Lynda Kitching (Trust Chair), Ed Anderson (High Sheriff of West Yorkshire), Mrs Desi Abson, Kevin Grady.

This quaint late Tudor-style stone house on Colton Road was built in 1623 and was extended in the early nineteenth century. Stone crosses adorn its gables and the arch around its front door. It was here that the courts of the manors of Whitkirk and Temple Newsam were held in the seventeenth and eighteenth centuries. In the nineteenth century, Michael Scholefield (1762-1842), the steward of the manor of Temple Newsam, lived here. By the late Victorian period the courts were opened at the Manor House, but then adjourned for the conduct of the main business to the Brown Cow Inn. The manor courts were concerned with civil proceedings, transfers of land, conduct of the agricultural system and petty criminal offences. The lordship of Temple Newsam included both the manors of Temple Newsam and Whitkirk, and so the owners of Temple Newsam House and its estate were successive lords of the manor of Whitkirk.

As Whitkirk was originally a manor belonging to the Knights Templar, properties in the manor were marked with Templar crosses. Some of the houses in Whitkirk still bear them today. Although Whitkirk was not incorporated in the city of Leeds until 1927, in the Middle Ages there were over three hundred properties in Leeds township that were part of the manor. They were found in streets such as Briggate, Kirkgate, the Head Row, Templar Street, Mabgate and the Leylands. Residents and tenants of these properties placed Templar crosses on their properties to signify that they were part of the manor. This meant they were exempt from the obligation to grind their corn at the King's mills, the Leeds manorial corn mills on Swinegate.

The miller took approximately one-tenth of the resulting flour as his fee. Even as late as the 1820s residents of the manor of Leeds were prohibited from consuming flour not ground at the King's Mills.

Two of the Templar crosses in Leeds city centre remain today: one on the Pack Horse pub in the yard off Briggate and the other on the building at the corner of Lower Briggate and Call Lane. The association with Whitkirk is also recalled in the name Templar Street.

There is a local tradition that John Wesley preached in the gardens of the Manor House on several occasions; most notably around 25 July 1761.

The plaque is found at Whitkirk Manor House, Colton Road, Whitkirk (LS15 9AA). It was sponsored by Mrs Desi Abson and her late husband and unveiled by the High Sheriff of West Yorkshire, Ed Anderson, on 16 October 2015.

The Manor House in 1892.

Stocks Hill, Bramley

This historic pump and trough are the last reminders of Bramley Village Green which was surrounded by medieval cottages and yards. The Green featured the stocks, pillory and an 8ft pillar which commemorated the holding of Leeds Market here during the plague of 1644-45.

The name Bramley is believed to derive from a Saxon lord called 'bram' together with 'ley', which means a clearing; it was mentioned in the Domesday Book as being a very small area of mostly waste land belonging to the powerful De Lacy family of Pontefract. From 1280 to 1540 the Abbot of Kirkstall was Lord of the Manor of Bramley and subsequently certain Bramley land was owned by Archbishop Cranmer, the Saviles of Howley and the Earls of Cardigan, the latter celebrated by the coaching inn "The Cardigan Arms" in Town Street. Bramley had many woollen mills, tanneries, mushroom farms and a large rhubarb growing area, while the quarries there produced stone for London Bridge (now in the USA), the Houses of Parliament (rebuilt in the 1830s), York Castle Walls, Stamford Bridge, Leeds Central Market and many other public buildings, docks and churches around the country, including the Kent Martello Towers of the Napoleonic era.

Stocks Hill in the late nineteenth century.

On top of Stocks Hill, in Georgian times, stood some handsome three-storey buildings, along with the original 'Old Unicorn' pub, which stood to the left of today's public house of the same name. Today's 'Old Unicorn' was formerly old cottages. Cottages and yards housing various small businesses straddled the hill, but unfortunately were demolished in the 1960s and 1970s. On the right-hand side of the hill could be seen the old steeple of the original Bramley Church of St Margaret's of Antioch built in 1631.

The village stocks stood next to the older public house on a small green.

The oldest known drawing of Stocks Hill is dated 1777 and shows the village pump (replaced in 2008 with a replica), the horse trough and a market cross pillar. That was erected to commemorate the plague that came to Leeds following London's plague in 1644, and the consequent holding of the Leeds market in Bramley on the site of the sloping village green. Stocks Hill remained the meeting place for Bramley people for many years, and Whitsuntide Walks set off from here.

Announcements such as parliamentary election results and information concerning wars were made from the top of the hill, while at Bramley Carnival time the villagers gathered on the hill's top for a wonderful view of the Carnival procession as it travelled along the full length of Town Street.

The plaque is on the stone wall adjacent to the Stocks Hill pump and trough on Town Street, Bramley (LS13 3NA). It was sponsored by the Bramley History Society and unveiled by the Lord Mayor of Leeds, Councillor Frank Robinson on 27 July 2008.

J.H.Barker del.   Published by John Dawson, 1860.   C.Goodall. Engraver.

STOCKS-HILL, BRAMLEY,

SIXTY YEARS AGO.

Stocks Hill c. 1800.

Headingley Hall

The medieval manor house of Headingley almost certainly stood here. The Hall was rebuilt in the 17th century and 1831-6. Residents included John Killingbeck, Mayor of Leeds 1677, George Hayward, Land Agent of the Earl of Cardigan, and his son George J. W. Hayward, born here 1839, intrepid explorer in Central Asia.

The Domesday Book tells us that the Manor of Headingley was held by the De Lacy family based at Pontefract. In 1152 they granted it to the Peitevin family of Altofts. A document in the Bodleian Library Oxford, circa 1200, records that William Peitevin had given the manorial corn mill of Headingley (on Meanwood Beck) to the Knights Templar but he kept the right to have his corn ground for himself and his heirs "living in his capital house or mansion" at Headingley. A fourteenth century survey of Peitevin's land mentions the Ridge, Bentley and the meadow 'next the hall', which suggests that the locality of Headingley Hall was the site of the manorial house.

In 1324 the manorial rights of Headingley were conveyed to Kirkstall Abbey and Headingley Hall became a tenanted farm. In 1539 the abbey was dissolved and Headingley Hall reverted to the crown. In 1564 Queen Elizabeth sold the manor to Robert Savile of Howley, near Morley. His son, Sir John Savile, the first alderman when Leeds received its borough charter in 1626, was a powerful figure in Yorkshire affairs and his son, Thomas, became Earl of Sussex. James Savile, second Earl of Sussex, died without issue and his estates passed to his sister, Frances, who in 1668 had married Francis, Lord Brudenell, son of the second Earl of Cardigan. Thus, Headingley Hall became part of the Cardigan Estate for 200 years.

The keystone above an archway at the hall bears the inscription 'JK 1649', suggesting that part of the existing structure was rebuilt by Alderman John Killingbeck in 1649. His son, John Killingbeck, Vicar of Leeds 1690-1715, was born in Headingley in 1649. In 1832 the hall became the residence of Lord Cardigan's agent. Substantial repairs in 1831-6 gave the hall the form it has today. In 1839 the agent's son, George Jonas Whittaker Hayward, was born; in 1859 Cardigan paid for his army commission and he served in India, after training as a surveyor. From 1865 he undertook journeys of exploration in the wilds of central Asia, reporting back to the Royal Geographical Society and being awarded gold medals for his efforts. He was killed by bandits in 1870 in what today is Pakistan.

From the 1940s the western half of the hall became a separate property called Shire Oak House. Westward Care (Yorkshire) Ltd which acquired the whole building renovated it to create today's residential care home and adjacent care apartments.

The plaque is on the front of the Hall at 5 Shire Oak Road (LS6 2DD). It was sponsored by Westward Care (Yorkshire) Ltd and unveiled on 8 June 2005 by Councillor William S. Hyde, Lord Mayor of Leeds.

Left to right, Peter Hodkinson (Westward Care), Councillor Bill Hyde, and Peter Baker (Trust Chairman).

Weetwood Hall

Rebuilt by Daniel Foxcroft in 1625, his family owned this former Kirkstall Abbey estate for over a century. Later owners and tenants included members of the wealthy Denison, Oates, Marshall and Beckett families. The printer Alf Cooke lived here 1889-1902. It was a University of Leeds women's hall of residence 1919-1991.

The Weetwood, first mentioned in documents in 1240, was a 460-acre woodland owned by the monks of Kirkstall Abbey. It was surrendered to Henry VIII's commissioners in 1539 and granted to Archbishop Thomas Cranmer. By the sixteenth century, much of the woodland had been cleared and it had become a farm. The oldest part of the present-day Weetwood Hall dates from around 1540.

In 1619 Daniel Foxcroft, from the affluent Halifax merchant family, purchased "six cottages and land" at Weetwood (probably the whole estate). He rebuilt Weetwood Hall in 1625. Internally, it has a fine plaster ceiling to which it is thought Daniel added the designs of the Tudor rose, the Lion of England and the Thistle. His son, another Daniel, inherited the property in 1639. He became a trustee of the advowson of Leeds parish church and mayor of Leeds in 1665. His son, Samuel, inherited the property in 1691. The hall was much larger by then, having nine ground floor rooms and eight upstairs. Later deeds mention a brew house, bakehouse, barn, stables, ox house, garden and orchard. In 1741 the family's ownership of the hall ended when it was sold by Francis Foxcroft.

During the mid eighteenth century, the hall and grounds, and 249 acres of farmland, came into the ownership of Lady Ann Denison, who lived there until her death in 1785. The estate then passed to Edmund Beckett on his marriage to the Denison heiress, Maria Beverley, in 1814. In 1821 it was sold to Christopher Beckett and remained in the Beckett family until 1919.

During the Beckett's ownership, the hall had several notable tenants. These included Joseph Oates and Henry Cowper Marshall. The latter, who lived at the hall from the 1830s to 1884, was the fourth son of John Marshall, the flax spinner, and was mayor of Leeds in 1843. Marshall's family remained at the hall until 1889, when the tenancy was taken by Alf Cooke, the illustrious printer (see Crown Point Printing Works plaque, p. 37). The hall's lodges were built during his time. It remained his home until his death in 1902.

During the First World War the hall was used as an Officers' Convalescent Home. Immediately after the war, it was purchased by the University of Leeds, from Sir Henry Hickman Beckett Bacon, for use as a hall of residence for women students. Its buildings were substantially extended in 1925-27, with the addition of a large main block, and it remained a hall of residence until 1991. Recognising the potential and attractiveness of Weetwood Hall, the university decided to retain ownership and gave it a new life as a high-quality conference centre and hotel.

The plaque on Weetwood Hall, which stands by the Lawnswood roundabout at the junction of the Otley Road and the Leeds Ring Road (LS16 5PS), was unveiled on Wednesday, 7 May 2014 by Sheila Griffiths, former Warden of Weetwood Hall.

Cookridge Hall

Built on the site of a monastic grange, this was the home of Thomas Kirke, JP, FRS, 1650-1706, writer, musician, astronomer, churchman, benefactor of parish education, creator of Moseley Wood labyrinth. Remodelled 1754-5 by Sir Charles Sheffield of Normanby Hall, Lincolnshire.

Thomas Kirke was descended from a long line of yeoman farmers and clothiers. The Kirke family lived in the grange throughout the seventeenth century, but when the timber-framed building was replaced by a stone hall with farm attached, the yeomen Kirkes became gentlemen! Thomas Kirke was a man of many talents who became famous for creating the Moseley Wood labyrinth of 120 acres just south-west of the hall. The wood had dozens of intersecting avenues and many different views and visitors from all over the country and Europe came to see it. Street names "Kirkwood" and "Moseley Wood" provide a reminder.

In his day Thomas Kirke owned 1,300 acres in Cookridge and another 200 acres in nearby Eccup and Breary. His substantial income from farm rents allowed him to live the life of a country gentleman, pursuing a wide range of interests. He was a Justice of the Peace and a Fellow of the Royal Society; he wrote with a profound knowledge of birds, insects, trees and wildlife; he composed music, studied astronomy and travelled widely, once to John O'Groats; he wrote articles on his Scottish journey and on algebra and on horsemanship; and his collections included

a display of butterflies and numerous Roman artefacts found on his Cookridge lands. He also acquired an extensive library and was an early local historian, the Leeds historian, Ralph Thoresby, valuing his friendship.

Kirke also invented a perpetual almanac, surveyed local roads and the proposed navigable section of the River Aire, and introduced a new method of recording the parish registers. He was a strong church man with a deep concern for the poor; he made bequests to help fund education in the parish which still benefit children today through "Kirke's Charity".

In 1722 Cookridge Hall was sold to the Sheffields of Normanby, Lincolnshire. The hall was visited once a year by Sir Charles Sheffield, who had it altered to its present style in 1754. Tenants occupied it for most of the eighteenth and early nineteenth centuries, but Richard Wormald, wealthy woollen merchant, bought it in 1820. Major Wormald sold the hall to the Paul family, tanners of Kirkstall, in 1919 and in 1954 it was sold and converted to a home for epileptic patients. Cookridge Hall is now a health club and spa.

This plaque is by the reception at Cookridge Hall, Cookridge Lane (LS16 7NL). It was jointly sponsored by the Trustees of Kirke's Charity, a Leeds City Council Improvement Grant and the Esporta Health and Fitness Club. It was unveiled on 28 November 2003 by Cookridge historian, Don Cole.

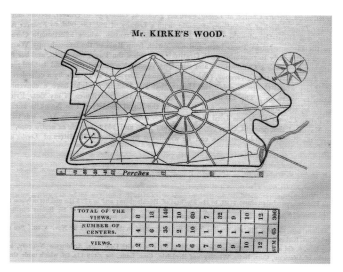

Weetwood Hall 19th and 20th century extensions

Industry and Invention

The prosperity of Leeds was founded on the handicraft cottage-based manufacture and merchanting of woollen cloth, which grew greatly in the seventeenth and eighteenth centuries. The importance of cloth as Leeds' principal industry developed still further in the nineteenth century with the growth of the factory-based woollen and flax industries, and the rapid growth of the ready-made clothing industry pioneered by John Barran. In the twentieth century, the advent of mass-production bespoke tailoring added further to the city's reputation. But in the Victorian period Leeds truly merited its reputation as the 'city of a thousand trades'. In addition to major industries such as brewing, tanning, shoe making, pottery manufacture, and chemicals, engineering came to the fore and, indeed, became the city's most outstanding industry, surpassing textiles as its biggest employer — by 1900 engineering employed one-fifth of the male workforce.

Leeds engineering took many forms, but perhaps its most outstanding success was in the production of steam engines, steam locomotives, steam ploughs, and steam road vehicles. Founded by Matthew Murray in the late eighteenth century with his manufacture of steam engines and steam locomotives, this branch of engineering entered a golden age in the Victorian period with the development of the world-famous 'square half mile' of Hunslet. It had begun to emerge by 1845 when the Railway Foundry was producing main line locomotives at the rate of one per week. In this small area, from mid century, the great locomotive builders Kitson's, the Hunslet Engine Company, Manning Wardle, and Hudswell Clark produced thousands of steam locomotives, exporting them across the world. At the same time, the ingenuity of John Fowler successfully applied steam power to agriculture by manufacturing steam ploughs. Close to his Hunslet works, from the 1870s steam power was also adapted for road vehicles at McLaren's Midland Engine Works, and at the tail end of the century by Mann's Patent Steam Cart & Wagon Company, and the Yorkshire Patent Steam Wagon Company. Their traction engines, steam wagons, and steam rollers were remarkable vehicles. Over at Smithfield Ironworks on North Street (just north of the town centre) in the 1850s, Thomas Green began making his nationally famous lawn mowers and then diversified into producing traction engines, steam rollers and steam trams. Many of these firms endured well into the twentieth century, but some faltered with the advent of petrol and diesel engines.

Leeds in 1858 (Illustrated London News).

Another of the great Leeds industries which grew prodigiously in the later Victorian period was printing. Two of its greatest entrepreneurs were Alf Cooke with his Crown Point Printing Works, and E. J. Arnold who began in Briggate and then moved production to Hunslet.

The genius, critical contribution and achievement of individual engineers and scientists is often forgotten when masked by the fame of the enterprises or institutions in which they worked. But not so in the cases of John Smeaton and William Astbury. In the eighteenth century Smeaton's achievements as a consulting engineer made him the acknowledged founder of the civil engineering profession, while almost two centuries later, Astbury, working at Leeds University, transformed X-ray crystallography into a revolutionary new branch of science that unlocked the secrets of much more complex biological materials, including DNA.

John Smeaton, FRS (1724-1792)

Was born and lived at Austhorpe Lodge, Whitkirk, Leeds. He developed scientific methods to harness better the water, wind and steam power essential to the Industrial Revolution. He was consulted nationally on the design of mills, harbours, bridges and waterways, including the Aire and Calder Navigation. He was most famous for designing and building the third Eddystone Lighthouse. The creation of the Smeatonian Society of Civil Engineers (1771) gave rise to the professional engineering institutions.

John Smeaton's Scottish grandfather set up in business in Leeds, building Austhorpe Lodge in 1698, and his father was an attorney in the town. John attended Leeds Grammar School and delighted at an early age in using tools and making model pumps and windmills. His father wished him to follow him in the legal profession, but John found it so uncongenial that his father eventually allowed him to follow his own choice. He then set up as an instrument maker in London, improving navigational and astronomical instruments. He read his first paper to the Royal Society at 26 and three years later was elected a Fellow. His design improvements to mills were of immense benefit and he was awarded the Copley Medal for his famous paper on the turning of mills by wind and water.

The second Eddystone Lighthouse was destroyed by fire in 1755 and a new one was urgently needed. The President of the Royal Society recommended that Smeaton be commissioned to design and supervise the erection of a replacement. Accepting the commission, he studied previous lighthouse designs and then formulated his own innovative plans, basing the shape on the trunk of an oak tree to give strength and resistance to the wind, and incorporated a lightning conductor.

Constructed of local quarried stone, each piece was dovetailed in place (an idea gleaned from London kerbstones) and the joints were sealed with a specially formulated hydraulic cement. The detailed model which he made is still in Trinity House Museum, London.

Though mainly remembered for the third Eddystone Lighthouse, Smeaton completed a vast range of civil engineering works around the country: the River Calder Navigation; stone bridges at Coldstream, Perth and Banff; the Forth & Clyde Canal; improvements to existing navigations (rivers with canals and locks around weirs and rapids); harbours; fen drainage; more than 50 watermills and several windmills. John Smeaton played a very significant part in the creation of the profession of civil engineering. In 1771 the Society of Civil Engineers was formed, initially as a dining club, providing the opportunity for engineers to meet to discuss their work and many other topics. Smeaton attended the first meeting at the King's Head, High Holborn, and many subsequent gatherings; some years after his death its members began to be called the 'Smeatonians' and the name has stuck ever since.

The plaque was sponsored by the Smeatonian Society of Civil Engineers, and unveiled by their president John McKenzie on 6 October 2005. It is on the towpath wall at Leeds Lock on the River Aire by the Royal Armouries Museum (LS10 1LT).

Sir John Barran MP (1821-1905)

Pioneered the Leeds ready-made clothing industry in the 1850s, introducing the band knife for cutting multiple layers of cloth. In 1887 he added this factory to his others in Park Square. As Mayor he secured the purchase of Roundhay Park for Leeds.

In 1841, at the age of 21, John Barran came to Leeds from London and set up in business as a tailor and clothes dealer at Bridge End. By 1851 he had a shop at No. 2 Briggate and associated workshops producing ready-made garments for sale in his shop and through wholesale distribution to other dealers and outfitters.

Barran pioneered the mass-production ready-made clothing industry in Leeds in the 1850s, utilising the newly invented Singer sewing machine and introducing the band knife for cutting multiple layers of cloth. He built an extensive factory and showroom in Park Square, but it soon became too small and in 1887 he built a huge new factory in Hanover Walk.

This factory was one of the largest clothing factories in the world, covering a ground area of 1,500 square yards and containing five storeys; the immense rooms on each floor were 180 feet long by 60 feet wide. There were special safety measures in case of fire and the whole of the vast pile was splendidly lit, perfectly ventilated and heated, and artificial light was provided by an electric light installation of no fewer than 900 Edison-Swan lamps. Two powerful steam engines drove the machinery. The factory turned out thousands of finished garments daily and the business prospered, continuing to manufacture clothing until the middle of the 1960s.

The plaque is situated by the main entrance to Joseph's Well, Hanover Walk, at the bottom of Clarendon Road (LS3 1AB). It was sponsored by J. Pullan & Sons Ltd, the present owners of Joseph's Well, and unveiled on 4 December 2003 by Brian Walker, Leader of Leeds City Council.

Barran was one of the most influential figures in Victorian Leeds, the founder of one of its greatest industries and a man of great vision. He was very active in politics and was Mayor of Leeds in 1870 and 1871 and Liberal MP from 1876 to 1885. In the 1860s he had the brilliant idea of widening Boar Lane from 21 feet to 66 feet, turning it into one of the most impressive streets in the country. His greatest civic achievement, however, was the creation of Roundhay Park. He was ridiculed in 1871 when he purchased for the town the Nicholson family's 773-acre estate to create the park because many people could not understand how an estate 'so far from Leeds' could ever benefit the people of the town. Today it is one of the greatest jewels in the city's crown.

Part of Barran's factory, now known as Joseph's Well.

Smithfield Ironworks

Built as the Smithfield Hotel in the 1860s to serve Leeds Cattle Market opposite, it later became the imposing frontage of Thomas Green & Son Ltd. Green's made steam and motor rollers, traction engines, steam trams, railway locomotives and grass cutting equipment.

Thomas Green, born near Newark in 1810, served an apprenticeship in joinery and pattern-making in Sheffield before moving to Leeds aged 24. Here he set up a business making woven wire products. In the 1850s he bought a larger site in North Street which became the Smithfield Ironworks. In his foundry he made gates, continuous iron fencing, garden seats and rollers. He gained an interest in the latest invention for cutting grass on lawns (by Edwin Budding of Stroud) and patented improvements to the design. From 1858 Green's produced a range of lawn mowers and horse-drawn mowers which sold steadily well into the twentieth century. In 1863 the firm opened premises in London and by 1887 had a London works at Blackfriars. Thomas died in 1892 at his Roundhay home; from 1886 his two sons, T. W. Green and W. Penrose Green, had been directors of the company and Penrose (Lord Mayor of Leeds 1909-10) became Chairman in 1899.

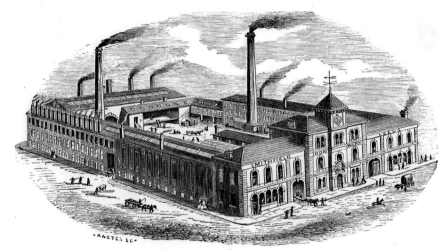

SMITHFIELD IRONWORKS.

After 1892 the Smithfield Ironworks were extended to provide facilities for the increased production of steam tram engines and road steam engines and rollers, including motor rollers. The firm built steam trams for various municipalities and in 1895 it built three tunnel railway locomotives for fairground rides. Between 1874 and 1937 it manufactured some three hundred steam rollers, the final one being supplied to a customer in India. The firm also built narrow-gauge locomotives – a 2-foot example from 1907 can be seen at Armley Mills Industrial Museum.

During the First World War Green's made munitions including bombs, shells, lathes and parts for the Blackburn Aeroplane Company. In the Second World War the firm again made parts for Blackburn's and the lawn mower division made gang mowers for airfields.

Only five of Green's steam rollers now exist in the UK, and only one is currently in working condition – built in 1920 it worked for Leeds Corporation and was found in a scrap yard and restored.

The plaque is on the refurbished Green's office building at 90-94 North Street (LS2 7PN). It was sponsored by the Road Roller Association and unveiled by the Lord Mayor of Leeds, Councillor David Hudson, on 15 July 2001.

A Green's steamroller at the unveiling.

John Fowler (1826-1864)

The Wiltshire-born Quaker engineer erected his Steam Plough Works here in 1861. Some of its buildings still stand opposite on Leathley Road. He developed the first practical method of mechanical ploughing using a cable system powered by steam engines. The system was exported worldwide.

John Fowler was born in Melksham, Wiltshire, on 26 July 1826, the son of a wealthy Quaker merchant. At the age of 16, he was apprenticed to a corn merchant, but he persuaded his father to allow him to pursue an engineering career. In 1847 he joined the Quaker firm of Gilkes, Wilson, Hopkins and Co in Middlesbrough as an apprentice. In 1849 he was part of a Quaker delegation sent to Ireland to see what practical help could be given to aid the population devasted by the potato famine. On his return, he resolved to devote his energies to the development of agricultural machinery which could increase and cheapen food production.

He recognised the immense potential of bringing more land into cultivation by improving its drainage, and set about inventing a ploughing engine that would dig subterranean drainage channels and insert porous drainpipes in them. After much experimentation, with horse power and then steam power, he achieved his goal. His drainage ploughs used a stationary steam engine placed at the corner of a field, with the drainage plough drawn across the field by a series of cables. By 1855, Fowler and his family had moved to London, and he had put up his brass plate as a consulting engineer at 28 Cornhill, London.

John Fowler

His attention then turned to adapting his latest steam drainage plough for normal ploughing — the weight of a steam engine was too great for one to pull a plough across a field without crushing soft ground. By 1858, after several attempts in earlier years, he had succeeded: his steam plough for normal ploughing (again using a cable system, first with stationary engines, and later with traction engines which moved along the edge of the fields) won the much-coveted £500 prize at the Royal Agricultural Society Show in Chester; the judges praised the quality of the ploughing and noted that his engines could be used with other farm tools. Initially, his ploughs were manufactured for him by various engineering firms, including Kitsons in Leeds, but in 1861, in partnership with Kitsons, he built his own dedicated works on Leathley Road, next to their Airedale Foundry. This enabled him to develop his business, manufacturing and supplying steam ploughs worldwide.

Around 1860 he moved to Leeds, living at Denison Hall in Hanover Square. Unfortunately, his health deteriorated due to his excessive hard work, and in 1864 he moved to Prospect House in Ackworth, where he and his family enjoyed the country air

and horse riding. Sadly, later the same year, after contracting lockjaw following a fall from his horse, he died aged only thirty-eight.

Through his prodigious energy and perseverance, he had founded a business which continued successfully for over a century, and diversified into producing a wide range of machinery from locomotives to concrete mixers. During the Boer War, Fowler traction engines were supplied to the British army, and during the two world wars the factory produced a range of munitions, tanks and diesel generators. The Steam Plough Works closed in 1974 and its main buildings were demolished in 1975, but some ancillary buildings still stand on the north side of Leathley Road.

The site of the works is occupied today by Costco's warehouse and car park at the junction of Hunslet Road and Leathley Road (LS10 1BG). The plaque is in the car park, mounted on a plinth made of stones salvaged from the arched entrance to the works. It was sponsored by Leeds and District Traction Engine Club, and unveiled by the Lord Mayor, Councillor David Congreve, on 4 December 2014.

FOWLER'S PATENT STEAM PLOUGH.

Plan of Working.—On the left headland is the Engine and Windlass, and directly opposite to them the Anchor, which is self-moving, and between these th[e] Plough is pulled backwards and forwards, one end of the Plough being alternately in the air and the other in its work, thus avoiding the necessity of turnin[g] at the Headlands. The Plough being constructed with patent slack gear, the rope is lengthened or shortened as the irregularity of the field requires, and [at] the same time both ropes are kept sufficiently tight to prevent them from trailing on the ground, by which means a great saving of draught is effected, th[e] wear and tear (which must necessarily follow from the Rope running on the ground) is entirely avoided without the least diminution of the power of the Engin[e]. Any implement the farmer may deem it expedient to use may be substituted for the Plough with a few modifications.

Hunslet Engine Company (1864-1995)

Was the longest-lived firm in this dynamic area, building over one-third of the 19,000 locomotives produced in Leeds for passenger and freight trains, factories, docks, mines, tunnelling and plantations throughout the world.

By 1845 the Railway Foundry on Jack Lane had become the premier Leeds locomotive builder, producing main-line locomotives at a rate of more than one per week. But in 1858 a shareholders' dispute placed the company in liquidation. From the ashes arose the mainstream industry of five major Leeds firms, one of which was the Hunslet Engine Company, founded in 1864 by John Towlerton Leather, a civil engineering contractor, on part of the Railway Foundry site. James Campbell, its first works manager, and his brother, George, bought the company in 1871. Between 1865 and 1900 annual production rose from around ten engines a year to a maximum of thirty-four. It completed its one thousandth locomotive in 1909.

A Hunslet Engine Company locomotive in Peru in 1982.

The first engine built was Linden, a standard-gauge 0-6-0 saddle tank engine delivered to Brassey & Ballard, a railway civil engineering contractor, as were several of the firm's early customers. Other purchasers included collieries. This basic standard-gauge shunting and short haul 'industrial' engine was the main-stay of Hunslet production for many years. In 1870 the company built its first narrow-gauge engine for a slate quarry in Llanberis and soon established a reputation as a major builder of quarry engines. The first Hunslet engine for export, its No. 10, an 0-4-0ST was shipped via Hull and Rotterdam to Java. By 1902, the company had supplied engines to over thirty countries worldwide.

The company remained in the Campbell family's ownership and management until 1912 when Edgar Alcock became works manager. By then the industry was being asked for far larger and more powerful locomotives. In the 1930s it built its largest locomotives for use in China and India. Throughout the 1930s the company worked on perfecting the diesel locomotive, and after the Second World War an important part of production was flame-proof diesel engines for use in coal mines. In 1958 John Alcock succeeded his father as managing director. The firm's last industrial steam engine was built in 1971, but its diversification allowed it to continue to prosper; in 1982 it and its subsidiaries still employed almost 1,000 staff.

The 'Jack Lane, Hunslet, Leeds' works closed in 1995, the last order being for a batch of narrow-gauge diesel locomotives for tunnelling on the Jubilee Line Extension of the London Underground. Throughout its existence, the firm built 2,236 steam engines and, including diesel engines, in total over 6,000 locomotives. In 2012 the company became part of the Wabtec group of companies. Today, though no longer based in Leeds, it provides bespoke design and manufacturing services for a range of locomotives for the UK and export markets.

The plaque is on the former offices of the Hunslet Engine Company at 125 Jack Lane, Hunslet (LS10 1BJ). It was sponsored by Don Townsley, former General Sales Manager of the company, and unveiled by the Lord Mayor of Leeds, Councillor Neil Taggart, on 21 September 2003.

Hunslet Engine Company offices in Jack Lane.

Midland Engine Works (1876-1959)

J. & H. McLaren produced steam rollers, traction and ploughing engines on this site until 1938. From 1926 they were Britain's first volume maker of high-speed diesel engines, transferring to the Airedale Works, Hunslet Road in 1946. Their products were exported worldwide.

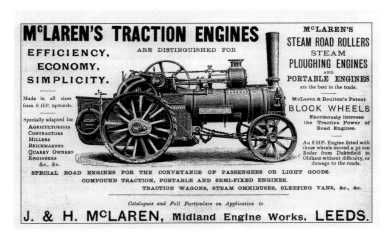

John and Henry McLaren were brought up at Hylton Castle, near Sunderland, and served engineering apprenticeships at Black, Hawthorn and Co., Gateshead. In 1876 the brothers founded their traction engine works in Jack Lane, Hunslet, taking advantage of the large pool of skilled local labour to recruit trained blacksmiths, pattern makers, machinists and fitters. They had the ideal combination of skills as John was a good businessman and Henry an innovative engineer.

In 1877 they published their first catalogue, sold their first 12-nhp traction engine and exported a 6-nhp model to the Sultan of Zanzibar. Gold medals were awarded to McLaren engines at Dumfries, Shrewsbury and Berwick shows. The second catalogue offered a wide range of engines, boilers, winding and hauling engines, air compressing and pumping machinery and ventilating fans.

McLaren's was widely credited with producing some of the finest traction engines in the world: well designed with great attention to detail, built of superior materials and able to command higher prices. John McLaren gave a pep talk to his workforce exhorting them to 'work slowly but surely, steadily and safely. Work should be well done. Everything should go out good and sound – a good traveller, and carry the reputation of the firm.' 125 stationary engines and boilers were produced for use in foundries, breweries, corn mills, saw mills, clothing factories, irrigation works, collieries and peat moss works with many exported to Mexico, Argentina, Australia and New Zealand. One of their forgotten achievements was the invention of the traction centre for driving steam-powered roundabouts.

The development of the oil engine at the turn of the twentieth century started a technical revolution as diesel power gradually replaced steam and petrol engines. McLaren's took on the development of the oil engine and became a major provider of diesel engines for railway traction, power generation, and marine and automotive applications.

During the Second World War McLaren's made auxiliary diesel sets for the Admiralty and generating sets for the RAF. The family relinquished the business in 1943 when it was acquired by Associated British Engineering, which then aimed to strengthen McLaren's by acquiring Kitsons' Airedale works, with its foundries, diverse workshops, and skilled workforce.

The Petter-Fielding (PF) oil engine was made, mainly for export to Asia, the Middle East and South America, to drive pumps and machinery. The mainstay of diesel engine production at Airedale Works was the McLaren-Ricardo (MR) Range of Engines – fifty assembled per week at peak production – used mainly as electricity generators on land and sea.

The plaque is situated on a brick pillar in the grounds of Equinox Ltd in Jack Lane, Hunslet (LS10 1BN), opposite Hunslet Engine Co. It was sponsored by Leeds and District Traction Engine Club and unveiled by Councillor Brian Cleasby, Lord Mayor of Leeds, on 17 June 2007.

The Unveiling: (left to right) Councillor Brian Cleasby, Lynda Kitching, Peter Baker.

Mann's Patent Steam Cart & Wagon Company Ltd (1899-1929)

Steam-powered road vehicles were built here. Previously Mann & Charlesworth Ltd of Dewsbury Road, the company produced unique designs of steam carts, rollers, wagons and tractors.

In the nineteenth century traction engines, ploughing engines, road locomotives, steam rollers and railway locomotives were all produced in the famous 'square half mile' area of Hunslet. The development of steam-powered road vehicles was greatly inhibited by the notorious 'Red Flag Act' of 1865, which directed that all mechanically propelled vehicles on the roads had to have a man walking in front with a red flag. The repeal of the Act in 1896 opened the way for the rapid development of steam-powered road vehicles. Up to this point, traction engines had been used to tow things, but it was considered a revolutionary challenge to produce vehicles that actually carried goods and materials upon their chassis.

One of the Hunslet firms which successfully achieved this was Mann's Patent Steam Cart and Wagon Company Ltd. The partnership of Mann and Charlesworth began in the late 1890s at works in Dewsbury Road, at the junction with Canning Street, where they built traction engines and steam rollers. Success came with the manufacture of steam wagons, and the firm moved to Pepper Road to purpose-built premises which are still standing. To develop design ideas, trials of 'Heavy Motor Cars' had been held in Liverpool and the first steam propelled commercial vehicle was an oil-fired van, Thornycroft No. 1, built in London in 1896. At the third trial in 1901, eight firms entered thirteen vehicles between them; gold medals went to Leyland, Thornycroft and Coulthard, and Mann's received a silver medal.

Mann's made flat-back steam wagons in many body styles, and also made a steam cart with a tipping back to the design of a Wiltshire agricultural engineer, P. J. Parminter. They also made small patching rollers which carried road-making materials within the rear of the body. During the economic depression following the First World War, the firm thoroughly redesigned its wagons and introduced the 'Express' undertype range in 1924 coming, as did Foden's wagon, to almost mirror the style of the very successful Sentinel undertype wagon. The steam wagons and road vehicles produced in Hunslet were exported all over the world as well as being used in this country. But the internal combustion engine was then winning the market war and Mann's ceased production in 1929.

The plaque is on the Pontifex Works in Pepper Road, Hunslet (LS10 2RU). It was sponsored by the Leeds & District Traction Engine Club and unveiled by the Lord Mayor of Leeds, Councillor Neil Taggart on 15 June 2003.

Yorkshire Patent Steam Wagon Company (1900-1971)

Steam road wagons featuring Yorkshire's characteristic traverse-mounted boiler were made here from 1902 until 1937. Later part of the Hestair Group, the firm then specialised in diesel-powered tankers, municipal gulley emptiers and road-sweepers.

In January 1900 the Yorkshire Steam Motor Company began making steam wagons at Ingham Street, across Hunslet Road from Fowler's, in response to an increasing demand for these new self-propelled vehicles. So successful was the firm that it had to move to larger works, but in 1902 it was bought by the Deighton Patent Flue and Tube Company Ltd of Hunslet, and became a branch of this firm under the new name of Yorkshire Patent Steam Wagon Company. It moved to a large works in Pepper Road, and yet again to larger premises nearby.

A unique boiler, having two ends and mounted transversely at the front of the wagon, was a feature of all the company's wagons. Originally chain driven, they went on to shaft drive, and made tippers, tankers and even articulated vehicles, using diesel engines from the 1930s. During the Second World War the firm made aircraft undercarriage components. Subsequently the company specialised in municipal gulley and cesspool emptiers, and mechanical and suction road and precinct sweepers for world markets.

There are only six of the company's steam wagons left in Britain, and one or two 'down under'. Although Mann's and Yorkshire's were relatively minor manufacturers compared to the giants – Foden's and Sentinel's – they nevertheless made a significant and innovative contribution to the market, exporting many

vehicles. There were about eighty recorded manufacturers of steam wagons in the United Kingdom. Production records have disappeared, but it is believed that Mann's produced around 1,750 wagons and Yorkshire's around 2,200. In comparison, Foden's and Sentinel's produced around 6,500 each.

The plaque is on the Pickersgill Kaye works, just off Pepper Road, Hunslet (LS10 2RU). It was sponsored by the Leeds & District Traction Engine Club and unveiled by the Lord Mayor of Leeds, Councillor Neil Taggart on 15 June 2003.

Crown Point Printing Works

Alf Cooke (1842-1902) began printing in 1866. He developed great skills in colour lithography producing art reproductions and portraits of the famous. In 1885 he was awarded a Royal Warrant. Following a fire, in 1895 these works were entirely rebuilt as "the largest, healthiest printing works in the world". Architect: Thomas Ambler.

Alf Cooke was born in Leeds in 1842. His father, John Cooke, kept a shop in Meadow Lane selling newspapers, books and stationery. In 1866 Alf set up his own business in Hunslet renting a shop and house where he sold stationery and newspapers and undertook letter-press printing. Within a year he installed his first lithographic press for colour printing. His business prospered and by the early 1870s he was able to expand into new premises near Crown Point Bridge. All went well until 1880 when a devastating fire gutted his works. Undeterred, he borrowed £31,000 from local banker, William Beckett, to buy a new site in Hunslet and build anew. Within twelve months the new factory, designed by local architect Thomas Ambler, opened, and within four years the loan, capital and interest had been repaid.

He took on all kinds of printing work including wrappers, advertising leaflets and posters, but he became increasingly interested in colour art reproductions, particularly portraits of the great and the good, for which there was a huge demand. He commissioned artists to create the portraits and reproduced them in colour by the hundreds and thousands. In 1885 his portrait of Queen Victoria, framed in a wreath of roses, was a bestseller at home and abroad; 100,000 were distributed in Australia alone with the Sydney Evening News Christmas edition. His colour printing achievements were crowned in 1885 when he was granted a Royal Warrant as 'Chromo-lithographer to Her Majesty'. From then on, he styled himself 'Queen's Printer', and enjoyed his new status to the full, moving to live in the historic grandeur of Weetwood Hall.

In 1894 his printing works were burnt down again. He reorganised his business in a rented warehouse and re-commissioned Thomas Ambler to reconstruct the printing works adding the domed clock tower over the main corner entrance. The grand facade of Crown Point Printing Works is in red brick with stone dressings and has three storeys with a different design to each floor. The ornate corner entrance doorway has pilasters, a broken segmental pediment with scrolls and the monogram 'AC' directly below the domed clock tower. The entrance hall within was originally adorned with hanging baskets of flowering plants and cages of singing birds. The Works housed 300 chromolithographic presses and other machines and employed 600 men.

Following Alf's death in 1902, his son Harry became head of the firm. It subsequently became part of Universal Printers Ltd, but closed down in 2005. The complex's potential and the Works' fine exterior and interior architecture was recognised by the Rushbond Group; it commenced its regeneration and in 2012 sold it on to Leeds City College which occupies it today.

The plaque is on the Hunslet Road frontage of the Leeds City College campus (LS10 1JY), and to celebrate it being the 150th plaque it was sponsored by Leeds Civic Trust. It was unveiled on 25 June 2014 by the Lord Mayor, Councillor David Congreve.

The Print Hall.

Alf Cooke.

E. J. Arnold & Son Ltd

Britain's leading educational suppliers and printers was established in this Georgian merchant's house No. 3 Briggate in 1870. Its warehouse and factory was in Blayds' Yard.

In 1863 Edmund James Arnold, a 23-year old Dorset man, who had served his indentures with a London printer, established in Barnstaple his own business as a printer, publisher and bookseller. In 1870, seeking an area with greater potential, he moved to Leeds and became established at No. 3 Briggate, a merchant's house built in the early eighteenth century. This was a timely move because the Education Act of 1870 established a system of elementary schools supervised by School Boards, and these rate-aided schools had funds to spend on the basic tools of teaching. Henceforward there was a continually increasing demand for school stationery and equipment as the numbers of children in these schools rose from one million in 1870 to six million in 1900.

E. J. Arnold did not neglect the general stationery part of his business but demand from new schools for stationery and school equipment grew so quickly that within twenty years it produced a turnover three times greater than the Commercial Department. By 1876 he had added a factory and warehouse in Blayds' Yard to his original premises, and by 1895 the firm moved to its headquarters in Butterley Street, with a modern printing plant.

By then contracts had been agreed with Education Departments of Leeds, Bradford, Sheffield, Rotherham and Shipley. The schools requisites catalogue of 1890 ran to 264 pages – covering stationery, textbooks, equipment and furniture.

In 1892 E. J. Arnold took his son, Edmund George, into partnership, and in 1903 Harry Wood was also made a director, and the two men worked well together. In one hundred years the company had only four chairmen, passing from father to son – E. J. Arnold to 1918, George Arnold to 1939, Edmund Arnold to 1953, and Martin Arnold to 1982.

The premises at Butterley Street continued to expand, and in 1961 Broadway printing factory was opened in Dewsbury Road to meet the rising demand for all types of school books. Arnold's had a textbook distribution store at White Horse Street; a paper and publications store and modelling materials factory at Airebank Mills; and a woodworking factory at Queen's Road. Some 35,000 schools were customers in the UK. In 1982 the company was sold to Pergamon Press owned by Robert Maxwell. Britain's largest educational supplier merged with Nottingham Handicrafts in the mid 1990s and production in Leeds ceased shortly afterwards.

Edmund James Arnold, the founder.

The plaque is at No. 3 Briggate above the archway leading to Blayds' Yard (LS1 4AF). It was sponsored by the Arnold family and unveiled on 3 July 2002 by Martin and Olav Arnold, great-grandsons of the founder.

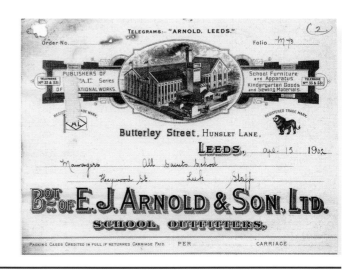

William T. Astbury FRS (1898-1961)

Lived here from 1928 to 1961. His brilliant research at the University of Leeds deduced the chemical composition of hair and wool fibres by X-ray diffraction. In 1938 his team was the first to predict a molecular structure for DNA, which contains the hereditary instructions present in all living organisms.

William Thomas Astbury was born in Longton, Staffordshire. His family was poor, but Astbury's success in winning scholarships provided him with an excellent early education and, ultimately, entry to Cambridge University. His initial studies in mathematics and physics were interrupted by the First World War during which time he served in the X-ray unit of the Army Medical Corps. On his return to Cambridge he began to study the newly-emerging science of X-ray crystallography, pioneered from its beginning in 1912 by William Henry Bragg at Leeds University.

In 1921, having obtained a first class degree, Astbury joined Bragg's newly-formed research group at University College, London, which in 1923 relocated to the Royal Institution. The major redirection of his life's work into macromolecular structures came about in 1926 as a result of a request from Bragg that he take some photographs of fibres which Bragg wished, if possible, to make use of in one of his Royal Institution lectures. Astbury was so successful in applying X-ray techniques to the study of cellulose, silk and wool fibres that in 1928 Bragg recommended him for the post of Lecturer in Textile Physics and Director of the Textile Physics Research Laboratory at Leeds University. Here Astbury made rapid progress in distinguishing the chain structures characteristic of cellulose and silk and the more complex protein structure of keratin – the basic material of wool and hair fibres. He showed, in wool, that the keratin polypeptide chains occurred in two forms: a folded form which he called alpha-keratin and an extended form, beta-keratin- a discovery of enormous scientific and technological importance in understanding the extensibility of wool fibres and the processing of woollen fabrics.

Astbury with the electron microscope.

In 1935, together with a research student, Florence Ogilvy Bell, Astbury began to study the structure of nucleic acids and in 1938 they published the first X-ray diffraction photograph (or fibre diagram) of a nucleic acid and attempted, unsuccessfully, to interpret its structure.

In 1945 Astbury was appointed to the newly-founded Chair of Biomolecular Structure which he occupied until his early death. His great legacy is his early scientific stimulation to so many students to work in the field of molecular biology and the founding of a leading research institution: The Astbury Centre for Structural Molecular Biology at Leeds University.

The plaque is on the front of William Astbury's former home, 189 Kirkstall Lane (LS6 3EJ). It was sponsored by the Thackray Medical Museum, and unveiled on 26 November 2010 by Professor Adam Nelson, Director of the Astbury Centre at the University of Leeds.

Transport

ALL GOODS CARRIED AT OWNER'S RISK.

Estimates given for any class of haulage

Any weight or distance

Telephone No. 25661.

Telegrams: "Ledgard, Armley."

Customer's Machines driven by our staff at customer's own risk.

Samuel Ledgard,
PETROL OR STEAM MOTOR
Haulage Contractor,

CHARS-A-BANCS, Etc.

ARMLEY ROAD, ARMLEY,

LEEDS, Dec 14/23 192

From the days of packhorses and carts, goods transport has been vital to the growth of towns and cities. Roads were poor during the seventeenth and eighteenth centuries, and so Leeds merchants and men of business financed making the River Aire navigable to the River Ouse in 1700, and decades later backed the building of the Leeds and Liverpool Canal, completed in 1816, which made Leeds the centre of a waterway network reaching right across the country. But in the nineteenth and twentieth centuries it was railway, road and air transport which came to the fore.

Plentiful supplies of coal were required to enable Leeds and its industries to grow rapidly. In 1758, to help meet this need, a wagonway was built from Middleton Colliery to the town. From 1812, however, steam locomotives replaced horses as the means of drawing the wagons, and thereby it became the world's first commercially successful steam railway.

The railway age truly arrived in Leeds in 1834 with the opening of the Leeds to Selby Railway. Other railway companies soon built lines linking Leeds to the south, west and north. This led to the creation of Central Station on Wellington Street, whose surviving wagon hoist is an impressive reminder of the enormous volume of goods, as well as passengers, carried by the Victorian railways. The Railway Roundhouse, near Wellington Bridge, which provided accommodation for twenty locomotives belonging to the Leeds & Thirsk Railway, is also a great reminder of the early railways.

Throughout the nineteenth century, however, horses were the mainstay of local transport. William Turton, who commenced in business running a corn and hay provender business, successfully moved into horse-drawn omnibuses, and later became chairman of the Leeds Tramway Company, which operated using horses until electric trams took over in the 1890s. With the arrival of petrol and diesel engines, motor buses gradually took over public transport in Leeds. Without doubt, the most legendary bus and coach operator was Samuel Ledgard.

Leeds was in the forefront of the early aircraft industry. Aviation pioneer Robert Blackburn designed many early aircraft, and manufactured monoplanes in Leeds for service in the First World War. Indeed, he ran pioneering passenger flights from Soldiers' Field in Roundhay Park to London and Amsterdam in 1919.

All these subjects have been celebrated with blue plaques.

The Middleton Railway

Began nearby in 1758 to carry coal from Middleton Colliery to Leeds by horse-drawn wagon. The world's first commercially successful steam locomotives, designed and built by Matthew Murray and incorporating John Blenkinsop's patented rack wheel, started work here on 24 June 1812.

The Middleton Railway was built by the Brandling family, owners of Middleton Colliery, in 1758 to carry coal from the colliery to Leeds Bridge. An Act of Parliament was required to safeguard the right to run the wagonway over other people's land. It had rails made of wood with the wagons pulled by horses. The coal provided the rapidly growing town with a cheap and plentiful supply of fuel, but it was also carried further afield via the Aire and Calder Navigation. The wooden rails were replaced in 1807 by iron ones, which with modification later enabled it to carry the early steam locomotives being developed in Leeds.

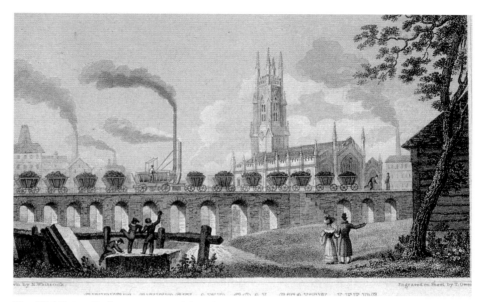

The Middleton Railway approaching the Meadow Lane coal staithe in 1829.

In 1812 the Salamanca steam locomotive was used to tow a load of coal on the railway, which was the first commercially successful use of a steam locomotive in the world. It marked the development of a new method of transport and the beginning of the long-term decline of canals as Britain's major bulk goods transport system. The Salamanca was designed by Matthew Murray, the father of the Leeds engineering industry, who used John Blenkinsop's patented rack and pinion system. It was built at the Round Foundry in Holbeck; four more of Murray's locomotives worked between Middleton and Leeds for more than 20 years and the design was exported to Belgium and Germany.

In the following decades Holbeck and Hunslet in south Leeds became a centre of steam locomotive production recognised the world over. In its heyday, seven companies in Leeds manufactured locomotives and two more produced rolling stock and diesel engines. The Middleton Railway continued in commercial use until its closure in 1959. But in the same year, Middleton Railway Trust was founded by the late R. F. Youell, who re-opened the line in June 1960, backed by a team of enthusiastic volunteers. Today the Middleton Railway is a celebrated part of Leeds' industrial heritage. It is also a leisure and educational asset,

operating meticulously-maintained steam and diesel locomotives, and running a locomotive museum at its Moor Road headquarters.

The plaque is on the Engine House at the Middleton Railway, Moor Road, Hunslet (LS10 2JQ). It was sponsored by Middleton Railway Trust and unveiled on 27 March 2004 by Councillor Neil Taggart, Lord Mayor of Leeds.

A Middleton Railway locomotive pulling a passenger train into the platform of the Moor Road station in 2019.

The Railway Roundhouse

Was built in 1847 to accommodate 20 locomotives for the Leeds and Thirsk Railway. The adjacent crescent-shaped repair shop, forges and fitting shops were used to build and maintain locomotives until 1904. No comparable group of railway buildings now survives in this country. Designed by Thomas Grainger.

The Leeds and Thirsk Railway was planned to join the Great North of England Railway at Thirsk, and was incorporated in July 1845. The main impetus for its construction was the stranglehold exerted by George Hudson, "the Railway King", who was funnelling all traffic to the north and east through York. The civil engineering works on this 39-mile railway were of the highest standard. The line was opened in July 1849 but in 1851 it became the Leeds Northern Railway and later amalgamated into the North Eastern Railway and then the LNER in 1923. Its engineer was Thomas Grainger, a pioneer Scottish railway engineer, and a contemporary of George and Robert Stephenson.

The Railway Roundhouse was a red brick single-storey polygon with gritstone and sandstone dressings and a roof of slate; the bricks were made at William Wilks Brickworks in Kirkstall and the stone was from Bramley Fall or Horsforth quarries. Internally the building contained a central turntable 42½ feet in diameter, open to the air, from which radiated twenty stabling roads with pits. The main access was from the east by way of a stone elliptical arched doorway. All the locomotive bays were closed off to the weather by large timber doors – one pair remains. The roof trusses are made of massive 55-foot timbers, supported by cast iron corbels in the outer walls and by the arcaded brick wall at the inner ends, which contain the arches through which the locomotives passed. The Roundhouse was designed by Thomas Grainger, assisted by resident engineer John Bourne, and represents the best practice of the day. The concept originated with Robert Stephenson, whose most famous roundhouse is that surviving at Chalk Farm, London (1838).

The Roundhouse was the main N.E. Railway shed for Leeds until it was supplanted in 1898 by the newly built Neville Hill shed because, due to its design, it could not be expanded to take more or longer locomotives. Contemporary with the Roundhouse is the range of buildings alongside the Leeds and Liverpool Canal, used as major repair shops for the Leeds and Thirsk Railway equipped with machine tools and forge hearths. Brick arched windows are in the same style as the Roundhouse. The semi-circular "locomotive shed" was built around 1850; it is now believed that it was used to build locomotives and carry out heavy repair work using an overhead travelling crane. The North Eastern Railway left this site around 1904. Various subsequent tenants included the West Leeds Motor Company and Thomas Marshall Engineers. Leeds Commercial Van and Truck Hire moved into part of the building in 1969, expanding into the rest of it when Marshalls left.

The plaque is by the front entrance to the Roundhouse on Wellington Road (LS12 1DR). It was sponsored by Leeds Commercial Ltd and unveiled by Paul Kirkman, Director of the National Railway Museum, on 20 November 2012.

Central Station Wagon Hoist

This steam-powered railway wagon hoist was one of a pair that stood on each side of the viaduct leading to the station goods warehouse. They raised and lowered wagons between the viaduct and the goods yard below. Built for the Lancashire & Yorkshire and London & North Western Railways in the 1850s, the hoists remained in use until the 1950s.

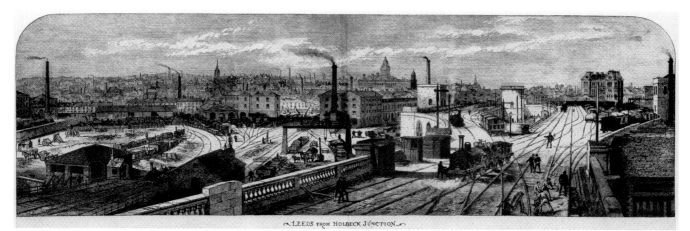

Leeds from Holbeck Junction in 1868 (Illustrated London News). This shows the Central Station and parallel ground level goods stations running along Wellington Street. The surviving wagon hoist is the one on the far left of the viaduct.

In the mid nineteenth century Leeds became an important transport centre as its railway accommodation was greatly improved and extended by the formation of the Wellington and the Central Passenger Stations and the Great Northern and North Eastern Goods Stations, which extended about 700 yards along the south side of Wellington Street. The Central Station was opened in 1854 by the Manchester-Leeds Railway and the London & North Western Railway. In addition to its passenger facilities, a massive goods-handling complex was developed.

A problem encountered in the earliest years of railway building was the difference between road and rail levels at railway termini; there were difficulties moving goods between the levels. The Wellington Street Goods Station engineers solved the problem by using stone hoist towers to transfer wagons between the viaduct leading to the station goods warehouse and the goods yard below. The hoists were made by Richard Kitchin of Warrington and the wagons were rotated on turntables and propelled towards the waiting hoist platforms; each tower was capable of simultaneously handling two wagons, standing in parallel, and they were lowered to ground level where they were run out on to further tracks leading to more wagon turntables. Mineral wagons discharged to dumps on solid ground, and merchandise wagons were propelled into warehousing within the viaduct arches.

Each tower contained two lifting platforms interconnected by gear trains; one platform was at ground level and the other at viaduct track level. If each platform carried an equal wagon load the weights would be counterbalanced and only the power to overcome friction was needed to move the wagons. Steam power was needed for additional lifting power, and a laden wagon could be raised using the engine alone. The steam engine to drive the hoist mechanism was in the central compartment of the power hoist tower, with a long driveshaft to also work the hoist in the north gravity tower. The boiler house to provide steam for the engine was placed within the arch separating the two towers.

When the goods yard closed in the late 1970s, the hoist machinery was scrapped and the warehouse buildings subsequently demolished. The wagon hoists were undoubtedly the last to operate in the country and the one remaining hoist tower is one of the most significant early pieces of railway goods handling equipment to survive anywhere.

The plaque is on the north wall of the Wagon Hoist Tower, which is situated in Wellington Place, off Wellington Street (LS1 4AJ). It was sponsored by MEPC and unveiled by the Lord Mayor of Leeds, Councillor Revd Alan Taylor, on 25 July 2011.

William Turton (1825-1900)

Corn and hay merchant here at Turton's Wharf and warehouse rebuilt 1876. He pioneered horse drawn tramways across northern England. From 1866 he ran omnibuses in Leeds, becoming a founding director, then chairman, of Leeds Tramways Company 1872-1895. Councillor and Poor Law Guardian.

William Turton was born in Leeds in the East Street area and served an apprenticeship as a machine maker before setting up his own business as a hay merchant at the age of 19. He became a leading corn and hay merchant and in 1866 bought into, and then bought out, Atkinson Brothers' horse-drawn omnibus company, which had been running since the 1830s. Turton became one of Leeds' principal omnibus owners, with both monopoly and shared routes and had offices in Briggate and elsewhere.

The Government Tramways Act of 1870 and Leeds Tramways Act of 1871 enabled Daniel Busby, of Liverpool, to begin the development of tramways for Leeds. Trams were basically omnibuses on rails – they were faster, having less friction, and better on hills but required much more infrastructure. Turton opposed competition from the new trams, but accepted compensation for some of his omnibus routes, and when the Leeds Tramways Company was formed in 1872 he was one of six founding directors. He became chairman in 1877, a position he held until the company was transferred to Leeds City Council in 1895. Although direct and blunt, he was an astute, diplomatic and likeable chairman, regarded with esteem and gratitude by the shareholders. In addition, for nearly 30 years he worked with Daniel Busby to introduce and develop horse-drawn tramway systems throughout the North and Midlands. Meanwhile, he also developed his corn and hay business at Crown Point, rebuilding his premises in 1876. This riverside property was perfect for receiving corn, hay and oats from the fields of Yorkshire and Lincolnshire, and later coal into which he diversified. He processed agricultural products here and sold

them on wholesale and retail. The horse was, of course, the essence of transport at this period for private carriages, omnibuses, hauliers' wagons, pit ponies, and military purposes.

Horses were central to William Turton's career and he had a good eye for selecting them for the transport of goods to railheads and to pull trams. But he also contributed in other ways to the public life of Leeds: in 1869 he was elected councillor for Leeds East Ward, continuing until losing his seat in 1878. He was also elected as a guardian of the Leeds Union Workhouse, and would have attended meetings at the workhouse, which later became part of St James's Hospital and is now the Thackray Medical Museum.

Turton's Wharf was used by a successor company until the late 1960s. It was converted into flats circa 1985, and listed Grade II in 1996.

The plaque is positioned beside the high archway entrance in The Calls adjacent to Crown Point Bridge (LS2 7EF). It was sponsored by the Turton family and unveiled by John Turton on 28 September 2007.

Bill head dated 1881 showing Turton's Corn Provender Mill in The Calls.

Samuel Ledgard (1874-1952)

Was landlord here 1896-1952. The renowned private operator of bus and coach services in Yorkshire, in a remarkable career he was also a farmer, brewer, garage proprietor, quarry owner, haulage contractor and caterer to royalty and the nobility.

Born and brought up in the East End Park area, Samuel Ledgard attended York Road Board School. His ambitious father, William, left his job as a pithead engine driver to take over The Shepherd Inn on Pontefract Lane in 1883 and then bought a bottling plant in central Leeds. Aged ten Samuel began to help out in the pub brewery after school. On leaving school in 1889 he worked in the bottling plant by day and as a waiter at The Shepherd in the evenings, earning four shillings per night, a princely sum then! William sold The Shepherd and leased The Angel Hotel in Briggate where Samuel learned how to manage a pub with a clientele of beggars, pickpockets and meat traders. In 1896 he noticed that The Nelson Inn at 212 Armley Road had come on the market; his father bought it for him and he stayed there for the rest of his life. When he took it over, he had £24 to his name; when he died in 1952 he left £129,491.

Outside catering is a familiar concept nowadays, but was rare in the 1890s and it helped to make Ledgard rich. He began modestly, offering organisers of outside events an improved quality of catering. To get to agricultural shows etc. he needed transport and bought a horse and cart. As business boomed he bought more horses and carts and also began making tents and marquees. In 1906 he moved into mechanised transport, buying a steam-powered lorry which allowed him to take on more catering jobs much further away from Leeds.

Prior to the First World War, Samuel had also started to run charabancs to Scarborough and Blackpool, mostly on day-trips, but also offered transport for those wishing to stay for a week. From 1912 he ran the Ledgard bus company. Its distinctive blue and grey buses were part of Leeds life up to the 1960s and at its peak the company had 112 of them. Ledgard's buses had a reputation for 'getting through' when fog, snow, blizzards and even floods halted competitors. It once ran a service on a spectacular route from Guiseley to Otley via The Chevin. The company continued for fifteen years after Samuel's death, until in 1967 it was taken over by the publicly owned West Yorkshire Road Car Company, its former rival. This flamboyant entrepreneur has a street named after him in Armley, Ledgard Way, near the site of his Armley bus depot.

This plaque is on the wall of the former Nelson Inn, Armley Road, Armley (LS12 2LS) and was sponsored by the Samuel Ledgard Society and the Ledgard family. It was unveiled by the Deputy Lord Mayor of Leeds, Councillor Michael Fox, on 15 April 2003.

Samuel Ledgard aged 24 in 1898.

Samuel Ledgard with one of his charabancs.

The Olympia Works (1914-1932)

Robert Blackburn – aviation pioneer – built aircraft here including over 100 BE2C army and navy biplanes and the famous Kangaroo, Swift and Sopwith Baby planes. He test flew the BE2Cs on Soldiers' Field and from there, in 1919, operated passenger flights to London and Amsterdam.

In addition to its great tradition in engineering, Leeds was also a nursery for the development of mechanical flight. Robert Blackburn, son of a Yorkshire engineer, took an early interest in aviation and was one of its pioneers in England. In 1909 he designed, built and flew his first motor-powered aircraft along the Yorkshire coast sands near Filey. Between 1909 and 1914 he produced numerous monoplanes, operating from small factory premises in Benson Street, Balm Road, and other premises in Leeds. Blackburn aeroplanes were already demonstrating their qualities all over the country.

In 1914 Blackburn formed the Blackburn Aeroplane and Motor Company Ltd with its headquarters at the Olympia building (formerly a roller-skating rink) on Roundhay Road. He then began to make rapid progress in the design and construction of many types of aircraft. With the outbreak of war in 1914 he received his first major government commission from Winston Churchill, then Admiralty Secretary, to produce BE2C monoplanes for the army and navy. Vast numbers of land and sea planes were produced by the company for war purposes, but it later specialised in sea planes, facilitated by the acquisition of premises at Brough on the River Humber for testing them. The company also designed some of the country's earliest civil passenger aeroplanes, including the Kangaroo which operated flights to London and Amsterdam from Soldiers' Field at Roundhay Park in 1919. In the early 1920s it was also commissioned by the Greek government to construct its first national aircraft.

The Olympia X523 sea plane.

The Olympia Works was abandoned in 1932 because of limited space and testing facilities. Thereafter the company continued to expand its manufacture of aeroplanes in Yorkshire, especially at Brough and Sherburn-in-Elmet, and also at Dumbarton on the River Clyde. The Olympia Works, however, was temporarily reopened to meet wartime needs from 1936 to 1946, making parts for the Swordfish and the Blackburn Skua dive-bomber, and was subsequently demolished. Until his death in 1955, Robert Blackburn produced many more famous aircraft, including the Swordfish ('Blackfish'), the Beverley, and the Buccaneer, his last major commission.

The plaque is by the entrance door to the Tesco Supermarket at Roundhay Road, Oakwood (LS8 4BU). It was sponsored by Dr Philip Snaith and unveiled by Professor Robert Blackburn, grandson of the aviation pioneer, on 26 May 2004.

Robert Blackburn

Central Station Wagon Hoist

Commerce

In the nineteenth century Leeds became a great Victorian city famed for its many industries, but it was also a great commercial centre noted for its markets, shops and financial institutions. During the eighteenth century the town's provision of covered markets was limited to its cloth halls, but in the next century it extended to retail and wholesale market halls. In the 1860s Leeds Corporation erected the fine Corn Exchange designed by Cuthbert Brodrick, which enabled Leeds to become one of the leading corn trading centres in Great Britain. Significantly, it was to be in the first Kirkgate Covered Market erected in 1857 that Michael Marks had his first market stall. Nearby, at Isaac Dewhirst's warehouse, he met cashier Tom Spencer with whom he was to create the now world-famous retailer 'Marks & Spencer'. Amongst the specialist services which Leeds provided were those of estate agents, surveyors and auctioneers; perhaps the most famous of them all were the Heppers. The fine Hepper House built in East Parade in 1863 is a monument to the firm's skill and longevity.

The Victorian age saw the rise of 'self-help'; importantly, this philosophy extended beyond individualism to individuals grouping together in joint endeavours to improve the lot of the working classes and the lower middle classes. The rapidly growing working-class population of Victorian Leeds wanted wholesome food and good housing. In response to problems with unscrupulous tradesmen selling adulterated flour, in 1847 a group of workmen set up an organisation to rent a mill to provide pure good quality flour. This initiative blossomed into the Leeds Cooperative Society which diversified into supplying all manner of goods and services and became one of the largest cooperatives in the country. In the same decade a group of more affluent workers set up a building club to enable them to build their own houses; this was to evolve into the Leeds Permanent Building Society, one of the city's greatest financial institutions.

The Main Banking Hall

Board Room

Leeds Permanent Building Society Banking Hall and Board Room in 1948.

Leeds Corn Exchange

This magnificent building was designed for Leeds Corporation by Cuthbert Brodrick. Its ingenious roof gave an even northern light for the careful inspection of grain by merchants and factors from all over England and Scotland who occupied its 59 offices and the 170 stands on its trading floor. Trade continued strongly until the 1950s but, as it declined, a new use was needed. Imaginatively remodelled it re-opened in 1990 as a unique speciality shopping centre. Erected 1861-63.

For centuries farmers and merchants attending Leeds corn market had stood near the market cross at the top of Briggate but by the nineteenth century the growth in the town's population, and the importance of Briggate as a thoroughfare, made its use as a marketplace increasingly difficult. New buildings were erected for other market trades and the corn factors and farmers wanted to have their own modern premises. A purpose-built corn exchange was opened in 1828 on the north side of the Headrow facing down Briggate, and significantly increased the volume of trading. However, the new exchange was only for selling corn by sample; and farmers selling grain in sacks were still obliged to trade in the open air.

Traders in the Corn Exchange, c. 1930.

The exchange soon proved to be too small and in 1859, after receiving repeated petitions, the Council decided to erect a new Corn Exchange to house both the sack market and the sale of grain by sample. Cuthbert Brodrick won the competition with a design modelled on the Halle au Blé in Paris. The elliptical building is one of the finest examples of Victorian commercial architecture in the country.

Business prospered throughout the nineteenth century and by 1901 the exchange attracted 160 traders, some from as far away as Liverpool, London and Glasgow. Leeds had developed into a grain trading centre of national importance. As well as being used for corn trading on Tuesdays, the exchange was also used for leather markets from 1903. It continued to trade well in the first half of the twentieth century, but in the 1960s the number of traders declined significantly and by the 1980s few traders occupied the offices around the trading floor. It was clear that a new use was needed for the building and Leeds Civic Trust produced proposals for converting it into a concert hall. This initiative came to nothing, but in 1988 the Council gave a 999-year lease to the London firm Specialty Shops plc which converted the building into a high-quality shopping centre, opening up the basement area by cutting a large hole in the floor of the building. Corn trading continued alongside the new shops and restaurants but came to an end around 1994. Since then the building has undergone various transformations, but remains a centre for specialist shops.

The plaque is inside the building close to the main entrance on Call Lane (LS1 7RB). It was sponsored by Zurich Assurance and unveiled on 16 July 2013 by former corn trader Mark Cockerill.

The Corn Exchange design in The Builder magazine in 1860.

Dewhirst's and Marks & Spencer

This was the warehouse of Isaac Dewhirst, wholesale haberdasher and manufacturer of hosiery, pinafores, underclothing and aprons. Obtaining supplies here, the Polish immigrant pedlar, Michael Marks, met Dewhirst's cashier Tom Spencer. In 1894 they formed the most famous partnership in British retailing.

Michael Marks was born in 1863 in Bialystok in Russian Poland and, following the increasing outbreaks of anti-Semitism and pogroms after the assassination of Tsar Alexander II in 1881, emigrated to England in the early 1880s, moving from London to Leeds in 1884. One day Isaac Dewhirst, the wholesale haberdasher, met a man in Kirkgate who spoke the word 'Barons', but had no understanding of English. A colleague who spoke Yiddish discovered that Michael Marks was a Polish refugee looking for the tailoring firm of Barran's, known to give work to refugees. Dewhirst took him to his office and, on learning that he was looking for work, offered him £5 to get him started. Marks asked if he could use it to buy goods from the warehouse, which was agreed, and he then steadily built up his peddling business, carrying his goods on his back around the dales of the West Riding. He sold buttons, mending wools, pins, needles, tapes, tablecloths, woollen socks and stockings.

Within a year Marks took a stall in Kirkgate Open Market, later graduating to a permanent stall in the Covered Market, where he displayed the same merchandise he had sold as a pedlar. He next employed assistants to run similar stalls at

markets throughout Yorkshire and Lancashire and as far south as Cardiff. His stalls acquired a unique character when he introduced the concept of the Penny Bazaar, and the slogan: 'Don't ask the price, it's a penny'. This simple phrase proved to be a marketing masterstroke that corresponded to the popular needs of working-class customers. He had the gift of sympathy and imagination which enabled him to understand the needs and wants of his customers and always offered the best possible quality goods for the Penny Bazaar. The establishment of permanent stalls allowed him to expand the range of items sold to include earthenware crockery, hardware tools and tins, household goods of all sorts, and stationery, as well as the haberdashery. Isaac Dewhirst continued to take an interest in his business and when Marks was looking for a partner to provide administrative help and capital he suggested that his cashier, Tom Spencer, might be interested. Spencer was an excellent book keeper and in 1894 agreed to go into partnership with Marks.

Michael Marks (1859-1907).

Tom Spencer (1852-1905).

This plaque is on the former warehouse of I. J. Dewhirst on the corner of Kirkgate and Harper Street (LS2 7EA). It was sponsored by the Urban Edge Group who renovated the building and converted it to apartments and shops. The plaque was unveiled by Timothy Dewhirst, Chairman of Dewhirst Group and great-grandson of Isaac Dewhirst, on 21 October 2003.

Isaac Dewhirst's Warehouse at the junction of Kirkgate and Harper Street.

Leeds Co-Operative Society

Was founded in 1847 when workers at Holbeck's Benyon & Co. flax-spinning mill initiated the raising of funds in instalments from working class families to rent a mill on this site. 'The People's Mill' provided them with wholesome, reasonably priced flour. By 2007 co-operatives had spread worldwide with 700 million members – but Leeds Co-operative Society was still the oldest in existence.

The co-operative movement originated with the Rochdale Pioneers in 1844 and a number of co-operative societies were soon formed across Britain to better the lot of working-class people. In 1847 the Leeds working classes knew they were being exploited by unscrupulous mill owners charging exorbitant prices for flour which was mixed with impurities such as plaster of Paris. The situation was so bad that seven workmen in Benyon's Flax Mill decided to act, and issued posters calling a meeting in the 'room behind the Union Tavern' on 1 March to discuss the setting up of a combination for the purpose of renting a mill to supply them with unadulterated flour, and asking each family to pay 20 shillings in weekly instalments. Over one hundred people attended the meeting and over one thousand attended a second meeting in the Tabernacle schoolroom in Meadow Lane. Thousands of families subscribed and the Leeds Co-operative Society was born. By July 1849 it was renting a corn mill off Wellington Street and before long it was so successful that its members were able to erect their own mill, 'The People's Mill', off Water Lane, Holbeck.

This mill enterprise was to burgeon into the Leeds Industrial Co-operative Society Ltd with a huge workforce and a turnover to match. By the 1860s it was the country's largest co-operative society, and it became the city's biggest retailer and largest employer. The society soon diversified into food and non-food retailing, producing most of the goods it sold, and was involved in businesses as diverse as making boots, providing dairy produce, a laundry, coal delivery, cabinet-making

Leeds Co-op Central Stores, Albion Street in 1897.

and millinery services. In 1884 the Co-op opened its new central stores in Albion Street, complete with a 'People's Hall' for concerts and lectures. It continued to grow and expand and by the late 1940s it had a massive portfolio of businesses including 130 grocery branches, 101 butchery departments, 21 drapery outlets, 17 boot and shoe stores, 10 pharmacies, 2 laundries, a bakery producing 95,000 loaves a week, 4 tailoring shops, several farms, a dairy with 250 milk rounds, and a coal service.

In 2007 Leeds Co-op became part of United Co-operatives, based in Rochdale, and it operated food stores, travel agencies, funeral homes, opticians, pharmacies and Sunwin Motors.

The plaque is on a gatepost in Marshall Street, Holbeck (LS11 5JJ), opposite Temple Mill. It was sponsored by Leeds Co-operative Society and unveiled on 1 March 2007 by David Schofield, its last President.

The People's Flour Mill.

Permanent House

Was built on the newly created Headrow in 1930 as the Headquarters of Leeds Permanent Building Society. Its grandeur befitted Leeds' greatest financial institution which from 1848 enabled generations to fulfil the dream of buying their own home. Architect: G. W. Atkinson.

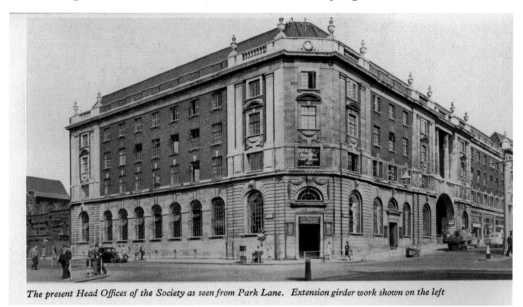

The present Head Offices of the Society as seen from Park Lane. Extension girder work shown on the left

Permanent House in 1948.

In 1848 Leeds possessed a flourishing building club, known as the Leeds Building and Investment Society, which was being conducted on the 'terminating principle'. A group of people wanting houses had clubbed together to buy a piece of land and build the houses. Everyone kept paying subscriptions until every member was housed then the society would be terminated. At a meeting in November that year it was resolved to form a new society, but this time upon the 'permanent principle'; it was to be known as the Leeds Permanent Second Benefit Building and Investment Society, and acquired offices in Exchange Buildings on Lands Lane. Under its rules new members could be freely enrolled, the issue of mortgages was no longer confined to investing members, and members were not obliged to purchase property. Its promoters had philanthropic as well as financial motives. Seeking to promote higher standards for housing, the society drew up five sets of plans to recommend to housebuilders and their purchasers.

In 1852 the society's name was shortened to Leeds Permanent Benefit Building Society, and in 1858 it moved to 32 Park Row now claiming to be the 'largest building society in the world'. In 1862 at the society's Public Tea and Demonstration, a Mr Holmes pointed out to the working classes that for £200 they could own a house 'with a kitchen, parlour, three bedrooms, a backyard and a garden in front'; much larger sums, he added, were 'expended in extravagant living, betting and dissipation'. Just over £1 million was advanced in the first twenty years and in 1878 new offices were established at 18 Park Place.

Following the First World War the Government pledged to build 'homes fit for heroes'. From 1923, under the Housing Act, subsidies were provided and Leeds City Council also provided finance. New estates were built with houses from £350. Leeds Permanent participated in the new building programmes and in 1927 had resources of £9 million and was advancing £2½ million per annum. The society's magnificent new headquarters, Permanent House, was completed in 1930 as part of the city centre's grand Headrow scheme.

By 1950 the Leeds Permanent was the fifth largest building society in the country. It grew from 37 branches in 1960 to 424 branches in 1990 with assets of £14 billion. In 1993 the Head Office moved to Lovell Park Road and Permanent House was vacated. Finally, in 1997 the society merged with the Halifax Building Society, and so the identity of a great Leeds institution was lost. Permanent House was later renovated as part of The Light shopping centre and its banking hall became Brown's Restaurant.

The plaque is on Permanent House at the corner of The Headrow and Cookridge Street (LS1 8EQ). It was sponsored by Brown's Restaurant and unveiled on 16 January 2002 by Mr Arnold Ziff, a former President of the Leeds Permanent Building Society.

Hepper House

Was built in 1863 as auction rooms and offices for John Hepper & Sons, the premier auctioneers and estate agents in 19th and 20th century Leeds. Its architect, George Corson, lavished its frontage and vestibule with an eclectic mix of Romanesque and Byzantine, French and English Gothic styles.

In 1862 the Hepper brothers bought a site at 17a East Parade and erected purpose-built offices and salesrooms to the designs of the noted Leeds architect, George Corson. They moved in on 9 November 1863. The East Parade building has a handsome stone frontage in modified Venetian Gothic style which includes Peterhead granite columns and elaborately carved natural forms in the decoration. There were four well-appointed offices on the ground floor, two for the clerks and two private offices, and two large auction rooms with splendid glass roof lights. Upstairs there was a large estate saleroom and at the back a covered yard with extensive storage accommodation, access for which was from Park Cross Street.

In 1866 Hepper's 'Yorkshire Horse and Carriage Repository' was built with frontages to both Park Place and York Place. Initially Joseph Hepper was responsible for the Repository which continued until 1916. The large yard had boxes for fifty-six horses, galleries to hold eighty carriages, harness showrooms, a saddle room, a shed for cows or extra horses, a large hydraulic lift, offices and a groom's house. It was recognised as one of the most complete repositories in the North of England, and the lettered tiles giving its name are still visible in York Place.

In 1902 the son of John Hepper, John Hepper II, became the President of the Auctioneers Institute of the UK (later to become the Royal Institution of Chartered Surveyors).

To the businessmen of Yorkshire the name of John Hepper stood for all that was 'sound, sagacious and straight as a die'. The business of buying, selling, valuing and estimating the rights and duties of owners or tenants was said to have been raised by Hepper's persevering energy 'to an exact science'. He was all but a final court of appeal on points relating to the value of property.

When John Hepper III became a partner in 1947, he was the sixth generation of the family to join the business. By 1970 the firm had fourteen chartered surveyors, ten young men studying for professional examinations, and branches across the country. The third John Hepper was, for many years, the leading light in Leeds Civic Trust, becoming its founder chairman in 1965; he died in 1991. In 1974, Hepper & Sons merged with Watson & Sons to become Hepper Watson and they continued to trade in Hepper House until 1976. The building was then taken over by Phillips Auctioneers until 2001, followed by Bonham's until 2006. It was then empty and falling into disrepair for a period, but in 2016 it was extensively and elegantly refurbished, revealing its true beauty once again as the Ibérica Restaurant.

The plaque is on the front of 17a East Parade (LS1 2BH). It was sponsored by Ibérica Restaurants Ltd and unveiled on 13 September 2016 by Councillor Judith Blake, Leader of Leeds City Council.

John Hepper III.

Houses

In the late seventeenth and early eighteenth centuries the growing wealth of the Leeds woollen cloth merchants enabled them to build fashionable town houses in Briggate, Kirkgate and Boar Lane, close to the cloth markets. But some longer-standing merchant families, such as the Totties of Chapel Allerton Hall, still preferred a rural environment to the bustling character of the Georgian town. By the 1760s Briggate and Kirkgate were losing some of their appeal as the town centre became increasingly crowded; the township's population doubled from around 15,000 in the 1760s to over 30,000 by 1800. In 1764 the growing wealth and social aspirations of Jeremiah Dixon encouraged him to leave his fine town house on Boar Lane for the country setting of Gledhow Hall and its estate. Other well-off but less-rich merchants moved across the town to the new elegant and socially-segregated Park Estate. Too rich for that, in 1786 John Wilkinson, wanting the lifestyle of a country gentleman but the convenience of the town, built Denison Hall just north of the estate.

From the early 1800s, as the town centre became industrialised and smoke-ridden, many wealthy families built or leased large houses to the north of the town in Headingley, Chapel Allerton, Potternewton and Oakwood. John Marshall, the rich flax spinner, moved to The Grange at Far Headingley, while the very wealthy banker, Thomas Nicholson, built a fine mansion and gardens amidst six hundred acres of the former medieval hunting park at Roundhay. Closer to the town in the 1820s, in the area we know today as Chapeltown, Newton House was one of the first houses built on Earl Cowper's genteel 'Leeds New Town' estate. But the ideal for the 'nouveau riche' was a house set in its own grounds. In 1865 the steam locomotive manufacturer James Kitson built Elmete Hall in large grounds at Roundhay. Soon after, Bardon Hill at Weetwood was one of the many large detached houses set in small grounds built for the wealthy middle classes in the later Victorian and Edwardian period.

Gledhow Hall and estate in 1815, based on a painting by J. M. W. Turner.

Chapel Allerton Hall

The Georgian home of the Tottie family, woollen cloth merchants, and then the distinguished botanist R. A. Salisbury 1782-1799. The Nicholsons, later of Roundhay Park, lived here 1799-1815. From c.1845 to 1901, much extended, it was the home of the pioneer of the ready-made clothing industry and Leeds politician John Barran.

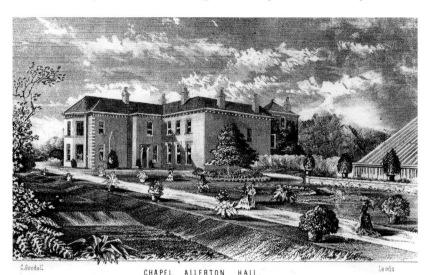

Chapel Allerton Hall.

Chapel Allerton Hall, a Georgian house remodelled in the nineteenth century, has had a series of illustrious owners and tenants. The woollen cloth merchant family – the Totties – were long associated with it. The earliest reference to the hall is in 1672 when Samuel Tottie paid the Hearth Tax on it for four hearths. Another Samuel Tottie bought the house in 1724 and lived there with his family until 1738. In 1743 Richard Tottie, Samuel's cousin, bought the hall, and when he died in 1755, it passed to William Tottie, who ran into debt following loss of trade after the American War of Independence.

In 1781 the house was put up for sale. The advert in the Leeds Mercury announced: 'To be sold situate in Chapel Allerton and Potternewton, a capital mansion with gardens, stables, coach house and about 37 acres in the possession of Mr Tottie and William Dixon'. 'Chapel Allerton', it noted, 'is one of the pleasantest villages in that part of the Country and much resorted to by many families on that account and the goodness of the air.' The following year the purchaser was Richard Anthony Salisbury (formerly Markham), a distinguished botanist who oversaw the garden design at Harewood House and later became first Secretary of the Royal Horticultural Society. He created an extensive collection of rare and exotic plants in the glasshouses in the grounds of his new home. But he too got into financial difficulties and in 1799 the house was sold to the very wealthy Thomas Nicholson.

It was this Thomas Nicholson, together with Samuel Elam, who purchased nearby Roundhay Park from Lord Stourton in 1803. Whilst still living at Chapel Allerton Hall, he began to lavishly develop his Roundhay Park estate, building the present-day Mansion and surrounding it with magnificent pleasure gardens. He died without issue in 1821 and Chapel Allerton Hall passed through the Nicholson family until, following a family dispute, all their properties were put up for auction in 1870. (See the Roundhay Park Mansion and Canal Gardens plaques.)

In 1845 the enterprising John Barran moved to Chapel Allerton Hall, first as a tenant, but then purchasing it in 1870. He lived there until his death in 1901. Significantly, in 1871 he temporarily mortgaged the whole of the Chapel Allerton Hall estate to help raise the funds to purchase Roundhay Park to secure it for the lasting benefit of the citizens of Leeds.

The oldest remaining parts of Chapel Allerton Hall are the stables and coach house dating from the early eighteenth century. The property as a whole was converted into flats in the 1980s.

The plaque is on the wall outside the hall on Gledhow Lane (LS7 4NP). It was sponsored by Gledhow Valley Conservation Group and unveiled by the Lord Mayor, Councillor Judith Chapman on 7 November 2015.

Chapel Allerton Hall Stables.

Gledhow Hall

In 1764 the cloth merchant Jeremiah Dixon bought the estate and hall whose remodelling soon after is attributed to John Carr. Later illustrious residents included: c1817-26 Sir John Beckett, banker, twice Mayor of Leeds, and 1884-1911 Sir James Kitson, industrialist, M.P. and first Lord Mayor of Leeds.

Gledhow meant 'the hill of the kite' from the Old English 'glida'. The land there was gifted to Kirkstall Abbey and on the dissolution of the monasteries it reverted to the Crown. In 1601 the Thwaites family bought the estate from Elizabeth I. John Thwaites's son-in-law, Edward Waddington, inherited the estate and built the curious Gipton Spa House in the grounds.

Jeremiah Dixon (1726-82) was a very successful Leeds cloth merchant who had a long business partnership with Thomas Lee. In 1750 he commissioned the famous Yorkshire architect, John Carr, to build him a fine town house on Boar Lane. In 1763 he sold this to his partner and, with this money and his business profits, he bought the Gledhow Estate in 1764 and remodelled the old hall, the design being attributed to John Carr. Jeremiah also redesigned the surrounding gardens, pleasure grounds, plantations and woods. His initials and the date "1768" are still to be seen on the bridge across Gledhow Lane. On his death in 1782 the estate passed to his eldest son John. At the conclusion of the Napoleonic Wars, however, his interest in the West Yorkshire Militia and Gledhow lapsed and he sold the hall and moved to the other family estate in Norfolk.

Sir John Beckett, Bart. (1743-1826), the distinguished Leeds banker and twice Mayor of Leeds (1775 and 1797), moved to Gledhow Hall around 1817. His wife was the third daughter of Bishop Christopher Wilson of Bristol and the couple founded a dynasty, having eight sons and three daughters. Subsequently, Thomas Benyon, the flax spinner with premises at Meadow Lane, lived there with his family. The property was subsequently bought by James Kitson, later Baron Airedale, head of the Monkbridge Iron and Steel Company and a staunch Liberal. He became the first Lord Mayor of Leeds in 1897 and in 1902 he entertained the Earl of Roseberry at Gledhow, with 200 torchbearers escorting them to the hall. The fine bathroom in Burmantofts faience was designed for him to impress the Prince of Wales who visited in 1885. During the First World War the Kitsons allowed the hall to become a Voluntary Aid Detachment Hospital, almost entirely run by voluntary staff, treating 2,250 wounded up to 1919. Since then the hall has been let as flats.

The plaque is prominent on the hall's boundary wall at the junction of Gledhow Lane and Lidgett Lane (LS8 1PG). It was sponsored by Gledhow Valley Conservation Area Group, and was unveiled by the Lord Mayor of Leeds, Councillor Frank Robinson, on 7 February 2009.

Gledhow Hall in 1878.

Denison Hall

The grandest house ever built in central Leeds was erected in 101 days for John Wilkinson upon inheriting the fortune of his uncle, the cloth merchant, Robert Denison. Its parkland setting reflected his desire for the country gentleman's lifestyle for which he soon abandoned Leeds. Built 1786.

In 1785 the 27-year-old John Wilkinson inherited the fortune of his bachelor uncle, Robert Denison, a rich Leeds merchant, and changed his name to Denison. One of the conditions of his inheritance was that he should continue in business as a merchant in Leeds, so in 1786 he bought nine closes of land in Little Woodhouse ('Claremont' Estate) for £8,500 from John Elam and built Denison Hall there as a merchant's house in the style of a country seat. The house was erected by 60 to 80 stonemasons using 13,680 cubic yards of stone, in 101 days. Its architect is now believed to have been William Lindley of Doncaster, a pupil of John Carr. The finest merchant's house in Leeds, with magnificent views over the Aire Valley, it had a large ballroom with ornate ceiling, billiard room, library, fifteen bedrooms, plus servants' accommodation, coach houses, stabling for fourteen horses, brew house, washhouse and a richly planted 6-acre garden. In spite of his uncle's stipulation in his will, John Denison is thought never to have lived at Denison Hall and, after marrying in 1787, went to live at Ossington Hall on the Nottinghamshire estate, also inherited from Robert Denison.

In 1806 the house was bought by Harry Wormald, partner of industrialist Benjamin Gott, and after his death in 1816 it was let to John Hardy, Recorder of Leeds and later first MP for Bradford. William Hodgson, son of Hardy's coachman, described in his diary the beautiful mansion and large garden and plantation where he went bird-nesting as a child. In the 1820s the house was sold for £11,000 to George Rawson, the wealthy Leeds stuff merchant. In 1862 it was sold to Leeds solicitor William Sykes Ward. Tenants included William Gott (son of Benjamin Gott), whose son John, later Vicar of Leeds and Bishop of Truro, was born there on Christmas Day 1830, and John Fowler, the inventor of the steam plough. Edmund Wilson, Leeds solicitor and founder of the Thoresby Society, bought the house around 1889 and in 1911 it was sold for use as a private nursing home. Leeds City Council purchased it in 1959 and adapted it to accommodate fifty old people. In the late 1990s, Grade II* listed, Denison Hall was developed as thirteen apartments with new buildings to the rear providing more accommodation. Many interior features have been retained, including the vaulted cellars and the beautiful staircase in the central hall.

The plaque is on a gatepost to the east of the hall in Hanover Square (LS3 1BW). It was sponsored by Tandridge Investments Ltd, and unveiled by Mrs Freda Matthews, tireless campaigner for the improvement of Little Woodhouse, on 15 May 2004.

The Grange

Formerly the site of a Kirkstall Abbey farm, the house dates from 1752. John Marshall, millionaire flax-spinner, lived here like a country gentleman from 1804-1818. The banker William Beckett bought the estate in 1834, making major alterations in 1858.

On the dissolution of the monasteries, the Kirkstall Abbey farm of 450 acres, then called New Grange, was bought by the Foxcroft family. In 1590 Judith Foxcroft married Anthony Wade, from Halifax, who took over the estate, and their descendants lived there for the following two centuries. Benjamin Wade, son of Anthony, was Mayor of Leeds (1663) and built a new house in 1626, which historian and diarist Ralph Thoresby referred to as New Grange. The house was rebuilt in 1752 by Walter Wade and there are remnants of this building at the rear of the present house. The last Wade died in 1795, following which the house was occupied by Samuel Buck, Recorder of Leeds, and then from 1804 to 1818 by John Marshall, the highly successful flax spinner. The Marshalls were visited there by friends, Dorothy and William Wordsworth, who were enchanted with the house and its views.

The banker William Beckett bought the house in 1834, carried out extensive alterations and renamed it Kirkstall Grange. The Beckett coat of arms was placed above the central window and bay windows; a single storey extension, balustrades and a new doorway and porch were added. Most of these alterations were made in 1858, when Beckett was MP for Ripon. He had hoped that Queen Victoria would stay at the house when she came to Leeds in September 1858 to open the Town Hall, but she stayed at the home of the Mayor of Leeds, Sir Peter Fairbairn, in Clarendon Road. Nevertheless, Beckett erected a classical archway nearby in Queenswood

to commemorate the Queen's visit. After Beckett's death in 1863, his son built St Chad's Church in the grounds of Kirkstall Grange, and other members of the family continued to live there. In 1874 the title passed to Sir Edmund Beckett Denison QC, later to become the first Baron Grimthorpe.

The family agreed to sell the house and 35 acres of land to Leeds Corporation in 1908. In 1913 the City of Leeds Teacher Training College opened on what was known as the Beckett Park site; it was used as a military hospital during both World Wars. In 1933 the Carnegie College of Physical Training opened on the same site, the two colleges merging in 1968 as the City of Leeds and Carnegie College. In 1976 the college, together with James Graham College, merged with Leeds Polytechnic which had been established in 1970. The college buildings then all became part of Leeds Metropolitan University (now Leeds Beckett University) when it was created in 1993.

The plaque was erected without a ceremony in October 2001. The Grange is approached by St Chad's Drive and stands on the south-west corner of The Acre (LS6 3QX). The sponsors, Leeds Metropolitan University, subsequently wished to celebrate The Grange as it approached one hundred years as an educational establishment, and the plaque was unveiled by Mrs Patricia Lee, wife of Professor Simon Lee, Vice Chancellor, on 7 February 2007.

Kirkstall Grange in the early nineteenth century.

The Mansion

In 1803 the wealthy insurance broker and later banker Thomas Nicholson bought half of the medieval hunting park – 'The Round Hay'. In 1815, after landscaping the park, he moved into this fine new house attributed to architect Thomas Taylor. The estate was purchased for the people of Leeds in 1871.

Thomas Nicholson was born in Chapel Allerton in 1764. A successful Quaker businessman, Thomas married another Quaker, Elizabeth Jackson. He went into partnership with his half-brother, Stephen Nicholson, in 1806, and in 1813 he founded the bank of Nicholson, Jansen & Co. In 1803 he, together with Quaker banker Samuel Elam, bought the 1,300-acre Roundhay Estate for £58,000; Samuel took the land to the south, and Thomas the land to the north where he created a country house estate.

The Mansion was built in ashlar stone in the Greek Revival style, with two storeys and seven bays and an impressive Ionic

THE MANSION, ROUNDHAY PARK, LEEDS.

The Mansion c. 1904.

portico. It was almost certainly the work of Thomas Taylor, one of the first professional architects to live in Leeds, who designed the Union Bank in Commercial Street for Thomas Nicholson and Partners. The Mansion contained a large central hall, a broad double flight of stairs, library, dining room, drawing room, study and morning room. On the first floor there were seventeen bedrooms, with two water closets. Thomas Nicholson died aged 56 in January 1821, having spent over fifteen years landscaping the grounds and building the Mansion. He had created one of the most picturesque landscapes in the country, with its naturalised features of lakes and clumps of trees set sympathetically within the rolling landform of Roundhay.

As he had no children, Thomas left the bulk of his fortune to his half-brother, Stephen, who built a new Anglican church at Roundhay, which was completed in 1826 to Thomas Taylor's design. He also had a row of almshouses and a new day school built. Stephen Nicholson and his wife, Sarah, also had no children and in 1827 Stephen's nephew, William Nicholson Phillips, changed his surname to Nicholson by Royal Licence, and at the age of 23 became sole heir to the estate, inheriting it in 1858. William died in 1868 and his wife, Martha, died in 1871, following which the whole estate was sold, as William's will had stipulated. At the auction sale in Leeds in October 1871, John Barran, the Mayor of Leeds, believing that it would make a wonderful park for the people of Leeds to enjoy in perpetuity, bid successfully for the estate, paying £139,000. In June 1872 Parliament passed the Leeds Improvement Act which enabled the Corporation to buy the estate and in September 1872 Prince Arthur, Queen Victoria's third son, formally opened Roundhay Park. After a variety of teething problems it truly became the people's park in the 1890s with the introduction of electric tramcars.

The plaque is by the terrace entrance to Roundhay Park Mansion, Mansion Lane (LS8 2HH). It was sponsored by Daniel Gill of Dine and unveiled by Councillor John Procter on Wednesday 27 January 2010.

Leeds. Roundhay Park from Mansion.

We went to see the park when we were in Leeds

View of the park from the Mansion c. 1904.

Canal Gardens

These ornamental gardens were formed from a walled kitchen garden built c.1816 for Thomas Nicholson of Roundhay Park. Inheriting the estate in 1833 his step-brother Stephen added the canal, 350 by 34 feet, spanned by two rustic bridges and terminating in an arbour.

Canal Gardens are much older than they seem, and are formed from a former brick-walled kitchen garden dating from the early nineteenth century and a mid-nineteenth century pleasure garden. Then, as now, an existing stream, marked on old estate plans, provides the source of water to fill the canal.

In 1803 Thomas Nicholson, who was born at Chapel Allerton and made his fortune as a merchant in London, used his wealth to purchase the Roundhay estate. It was then agricultural land, a patchwork of dozens of fields, hedged and fenced, all of which had to be dug up to enable its conversion into a beautiful landscape. There was an existing service road, now known aptly as 'Old Park Road'; otherwise, access was poor, and it was only in 1810 that the Wetherby Turnpike Road was completed, allowing Thomas to access his new Carriage Drive. Thomas did not live permanently at Roundhay until 1815, when he and his wife "settled in their new house", being the handsome Mansion that is so popular with Leeds people today.

In those days, rural estates had to be self-supporting in respect of food supplies, so the Waterloo Lake was constructed in 1815 to be both a scenic feature and a source of fresh fish for its owners. In 1838, the artist J. W. Carmichael made one painting featuring a fishing boat at work on the lake and another depicting a gamekeeper, whose duties included catching small game in the park to give to the cook. The walled kitchen garden was equally essential, being carefully tended by a team of gardeners, supplying fresh fruit and vegetables as required. In addition, somewhere nearer the Mansion, there would have been an ice house sunk into the ground, where food might be stored for a while.

Following Thomas' death in 1821, his widow remained in residence until 1833, when Thomas' half-brother, Stephen, inherited the estate. Among other developments, it was Stephen who created or enhanced the pleasure ground with its delightfully serene canal, adjacent to the walled kitchen garden. In 1871, when the whole Nicolson estate was bought by Leeds Corporation and turned into a public park, the kitchen garden was converted for floral displays, particularly roses, while the glasshouses (since rebuilt) featured displays of exotic plants and flowers. Stephen's pleasure garden, with its long sheet of water, remains delightfully formal. Ruffled gently by waterfowls and flanked by green lawns setting off geometric flowerbeds, the canal provides calm and serenity.

The plaque is on the old kitchen garden wall, next to the archway separating the canal from Tropical World, Princes Avenue (LS8 2ER). The plaque was sponsored by the Friends of Roundhay Park, and unveiled by Mrs Marjorie Ziff, President of the Friends of Roundhay Park, on 27 June 2005.

Newton House

Earl Cowper built this fine house c. 1820 on Squire Pastures Farm, a forerunner of the high-class residential development of New Leeds. In 1843 Hutchinson Gresham, a pawnbroker, purchased the villa. Joseph Linsley, mustard, cocoa and chicory manufacturer lived here in 1851.

Chapeltown has an amazingly rich building heritage. The Newton House plaque is one of a series which the Trust has erected in the area to celebrate its finer buildings and their historic associations. Newton House was built in the 1820s as part of the grand vision of a Hertfordshire aristocrat, Earl Cowper, to create 'The Leeds New Town' — a genteel residential estate on the edge of Leeds. Until then, the land had been occupied by Squire Pastures Farm. The estate was intended for the wealthy middle classes, with large villas and terraces and broad tree-lined streets centred on a large square, in the style of Bloomsbury or Bath.

Unfortunately for the earl, people were very slow to buy the building plots, and it took fifty years for all of them to be sold. Only a few really grand villas were built, and the land was eventually sold for much humbler houses. Nevertheless, Newton House, with its fine late-Georgian style and large front garden, is a wonderful reminder of the original vision. The street layout of the 'New Town' remains today, bounded by Spencer Place, Cowper Street, Leopold Street and Chapeltown Road. The aristocratic associations survive in the street names — Spencer, Cowper, Leopold, Louis and Francis were all Cowper family names.

Newton House was purchased from Earl Cowper in 1843 by Hutchinson Gresham, a wealthy Leeds pawnbroker and silversmith, who had his business in Hunslet Lane. Gresham was a pillar of the community, being a trustee of South Parade Baptist Chapel and a town councillor for South Leeds in the 1840s and '50s; subsequently, he became an alderman. He created part of his wealth as a clothier, and, interestingly, John Barran, when he first came to Leeds, was one of his apprentices. Barran was also a trustee of South Parade Baptist Chapel and lived around the corner in Cowper Street in 1853.

By 1851 Newton House was occupied by Joseph Linsley, aged 50, a mustard, cocoa and chicory manufacturer. Subsequent research has shown that the plaque incorrectly gives his name as Lumley. The household consisted of himself, his wife and daughter, a sister-in-law, one niece and two nephews (the niece and nephews being aged 6, 5 and 2 years respectively). Their affluent lifestyle is demonstrated by the presence of a governess and three servants.

The plaque is at 54 Spencer Place, on the corner of Cowper Street (LS7 4BR). It was sponsored by the Angel Group, and unveiled on 10 September 2003 by Mrs Jean White, Deputy Lord Mayor of Leeds.

Elmete Hall

This fine villa, with its 65-acre estate providing spectacular views over Leeds was built in 1865 for James Kitson the wealthy steam locomotive manufacturer. Extended in brick in 1885, for over two decades from 1957 it was a school for the deaf. Architects: Dobson and Chorley. Renovated 2007.

James Kitson's life (1807-1885) was one of those 'rags to riches' stories so beloved of the Victorians. Born at the Brunswick Tavern in Camp Road, where his father was the publican, after a rudimentary education, he began work in a local dye works. His route to success came through classes at the Leeds Mechanics Institute where reading 'A Practical Treatise on Railways' (1825) inspired him to become an engineer. In 1835 he moved to Hunslet, the centre of the Leeds engineering industry, and soon formed a partnership with Charles Todd (a former apprentice at Matthew Murray's Round Foundry) and David Laird (a relative of Kitson's wife, who provided the capital for the venture). Even before they had properly set up their business in the Airedale Foundry, the firm received an order for six locomotives from the Liverpool and Manchester Railway. They then prospered in the railway boom of the 1840s, specialising in the export of railway engines to the British Empire and South America.

In 1865 Kitson purchased what was to become the Elmete Hall estate for £17,000 from William Nicholson, the owner of Roundhay Park. He commissioned local architects Dobson and Chorley to design a large villa in the fashionable Italianate style set in 65 acres of gardens and parkland. The reception rooms of the ground floor were clearly intended to impress and the drawing room, the morning room and the dining room were fitted out by Gillows, the famous Lancaster firm. James Kitson served as an alderman from

1858-68, was mayor of Leeds 1860-61, chaired the building committee for the new infirmary and was chairman of Leeds Musical Festival. On his death in 1885 Elmete Hall was inherited by his son, John Hawthorn Kitson, a noted mountaineer and collector of alpine plants. He added the splendid circular hall and staircase with stone cantilevered stairs, cast-iron balustrade and stained glass dome.

John Hawthorn Kitson died in 1899. In 1921 the hall became the home of Bertram Redman, a successful stockbroker and financier, and in 1923 it was sold to Sir Edwin Airey, the well-known building contractor. When it became clear that planning permission for building a housing estate would be refused, Airey sold the estate to Leeds City Council for the same price he had paid for it. No tenant could be found and eventually, in 1957, it decided to use the hall as a residential school for the deaf, which ran from 1961 to the 1980s. Fortunately, it was subsequently acquired by the developers, Rushbond plc, who splendidly renovated the building for office use, conserving its best features.

The plaque is near to the main entrance of the hall, Elmete Lane (LS8 2LJ) and was sponsored by the Hester family. It was erected in December 2008. There was no unveiling ceremony.

Bardon Hill Stables

This former stables and coach house was built in 1873-5. In 1902 it was lavishly rebuilt by Thomas Winn for Bardon Hill's new occupant the millionaire racehorse owner Joseph Pickersgill, bookmaker to Edward VII when Prince of Wales. It was renovated and converted to luxury apartments in 2002.

In the early nineteenth century the middle classes of Leeds, wishing to escape the smoke of the town centre, moved to pleasant suburbs to the north and 'respectable' terraces for them were built in Headingley. By the mid nineteenth century, the rich upper middle classes sought the greater social seclusion of very large stone mansions set in substantial grounds in the Weetwood area. The banking family, the Oxleys, for example, had Spenfield and The Elms (now Oxley Hall) built for them, while the Barran family built Quarry Dene on Weetwood Lane.

Thomas Simpson, the wealthy Leeds solicitor, had the Gothic-style Bardon Hill built for him in 1873-75. The sheer size of the building and its grounds is reflected in the fact that for many years they accommodated St Urban's Roman Catholic Primary School. A splendid feature of the complex is the unusually large and lavish stable and coach house block, which was used as the dining room, gymnasium and caretaker's flat of the school. The building had five stables and four loose boxes with tiled walls; its stained glass windows and doors were made of teak; the saddle room had a panelled teak ceiling and teak cupboards.

In 1902 Bardon Hill was acquired by Joseph Pickersgill who extensively altered both the house and the stable block. He was a self-made man who began life as a butcher's boy and, when only a teenager, ran his own butcher's shop in the Shambles off Briggate (now the Victoria Quarter). This was an area of Leeds where 'the race card' was called and betting openly conducted and Pickersgill developed a great interest in horse racing. His 1920 obituary in the Yorkshire Evening Post described him as a 'millionaire racehorse owner and turf-commission agent (bookmaker)', his most notable client being the Prince of Wales, the future King Edward VII. Pickersgill was also a successful property speculator and the financial partner of Robert Chorley in the Leeds printing firm of Chorley and Pickersgill.

In 2002-2003 the stable block was transformed by Cala Homes (Yorkshire) Ltd into nine mews apartments, retaining many of the existing features, set around a private courtyard. It stands as a reminder of the lavish and high-spirited lifestyle of the nouveau riche in Edwardian England.

This plaque is at the end of a long drive within Bardon Hall Gardens off Weetwood Lane (LS16 5TX). Sadly, there is now no public access. It was sponsored by Cala Homes (Yorkshire) Ltd and unveiled on 20 November 2003 by Mrs Jacky Banyard, Sales and Marketing Director.

Education

In the centuries before the State provided a comprehensive system, education was only for the children of affluent families or for poor children who were fortunate enough to gain places at schools run by charitable foundations. In 1552 William Sheafield founded Leeds Grammar School 'to teach and freely instruct young scholars, youths and children'. A century later the village of Wortley was fortunate also to gain its own grammar school by the bequest of Samuel Sunderland.

The need to give the mass of the population at least a basic education in reading, writing and arithmetic became more compelling as the Industrial Revolution got under way. In Leeds the first significant steps were taken with the establishment of Sunday schools from the 1780s, and the monitorial schools founded by the Protestant religious denominations from 1811 onwards. The great influx of Irish immigrants into Leeds, notably in the 1840s and 1850s, prompted the founding of Mount St Mary's Roman Catholic convent, orphanage and school in 1853 to help meet their children's needs.

But the religious and voluntary organisations simply could not adequately provide for the rapidly growing number of children. In 1870 Parliament required local authorities to meet the shortfall; thereafter Leeds School Board provided thousands of elementary school places. Gipton Board School erected in 1897 was one of the finest schools in Leeds. A few years later, Leeds Catholics, conscious of the benefits a Catholic grammar school could bring, built St Michael's College which opened in 1909. Meanwhile, the county's long-standing need for higher education was being addressed by the Yorkshire College opened in the 1870s. In 1904 it became the University of Leeds.

Leeds has experienced waves of Jewish immigration from the 1880s and those of migrants from Commonwealth countries after the Second World War. This has been most evident in Chapeltown where many of the new migrants settled. Accordingly, it was in Chapeltown that the life-saving ORT Technical School, which provided refugee Jewish boys with practical training, was accommodated in the early years of the Second World War. It was also in Chapeltown that the exceptionally gifted and charismatic Gertrude Paul became the first black head teacher in Leeds.

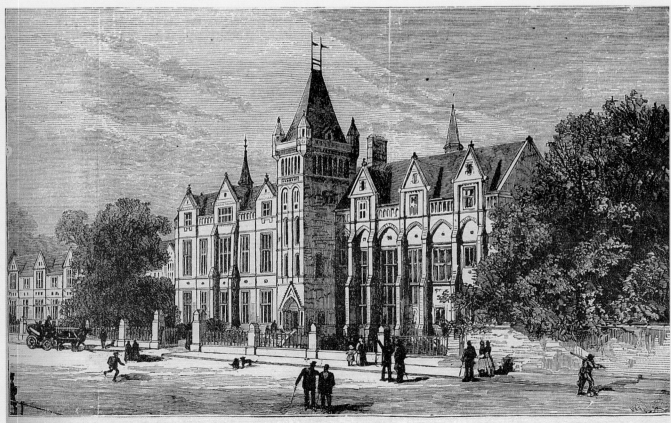

THE YORKSHIRE COLLEGE, LEEDS.

The Yorkshire College c. 1893.

Leeds Grammar School

Was founded in 1552 by William Sheafield chantry priest, Leeds Parish Church. It occupied this building from 1859 to 1997. Famous pupils include: John Smeaton, engineer; G. Studdert Kennedy, 'Woodbine Willie', chaplain; John Ireland, composer; Field Marshal Lord Nicholson of Roundhay. Architect: Edward Barry.

The origins of Leeds Grammar School have been traced back to about 1341, when successive priests of the Clarell Chantry at Leeds Parish Church, in addition to saying prayers to save the souls of their patrons and their families, also taught local boys, probably destined for the priesthood. The Reformation brought the dissolution of the chantries and would have ended the school, but the chantry priest, William Sheafield, left £4-13s-4d in his will of 6 July 1552 to ensure that the school could continue. On his death in 1553 the money was vested with sixteen trustees to provide the salary for a schoolmaster to succeed him and the school was re-established in new premises in The Calls. Known as the Free Grammar School (it only charged for boarders and 'foreigners' – those who lived outside Leeds) it provided lessons in classics and divinity. In 1555 Sir William Ermystead gave some land for a new building on Lady Lane. Sons of artisans were taught there until 1624 when wealthy cloth merchant John Harrison endowed a new school building on his land between New Briggate and Vicar Lane (now at the back of the Grand Theatre). In 1691 Alderman Godfrey Lawson gifted the school a library building.

By 1791 the trustees wanted to introduce subjects other than classics and divinity. The headmaster took them to the Court of Chancery in 1805 which decided in favour of the status quo, but a compromise was agreed allowing modern languages as well as Latin and Greek to be taught. By 1820 the syllabus included religion, Classics, maths, English and foreign languages.

Dr Alfred Barry, son of the architect Charles Barry who had designed the new Houses of Parliament, became headmaster in 1854 and suggested that the school should be relocated to Woodhouse Moor. This was agreed, and his brother, Edward Barry, designed a new school in the fashionable Gothic style, which opened in 1859. The old school was sold to Samuel Denison and used as a foundry until its demolition in 1901. Over the years many buildings were added. By the 1990s the school had 1,370 pupils and, needing new premises, moved to Alwoodley in 1997. In 2008 Leeds Grammar School merged with Leeds Girls High School on the Alwoodley Gates site and is now known as the Grammar School at Leeds.

The plaque is on the former Leeds Grammar School building, Moorland Road (LS6 1AN), now part of the University of Leeds Business School. It was sponsored by Leeds Grammar School, and unveiled on 7 October 2002 by Councillor Bryan North, Lord Mayor of Leeds, with the assistance of Leeds Grammar School pupils Sam Best and Daniel Saffer.

Woodhouse Moor and Leeds Grammar School, c. 1909.

Wortley Grammar School

Was founded in 1677 by the bequest of Samuel Sunderland to teach boys English or Latin. It occupied this new schoolroom from 1814 to 1909 when the school closed. Notable pupils included mathematician and judge C. J. Hargreave, banker and Leeds Mayor, Henry Oxley, and brickworks owner, Joseph Cliff.

commissioner and judge of the Landed Estates Court. Another was Henry Oxley, JP (1803-1890) who became a clerk in the bank of Messrs William Williams Brown, Commercial Street, working his way up to becoming a partner; his son, James Oxley, became head of the firm and lived at Spenfield, Weetwood. Joseph Cliff, JP (1806-79) also went on to great success as the owner of the Sanitation Tube Works, Wortley, Frodingham Ironworks, Micklefield Colliery and Bradford Firebrick Works.

Following a lively ratepayers' meeting in 1896, the school continued in the charge of Mr R. H. Bruce until 1909 when it finally closed, the premises being sold to John Pond, a blacksmith. The income of the foundation was then applied to awarding educational maintenance allowances to Wortley scholarship children and grants to local university or training college students. This successful scheme ran until 2001. The premises were later used as an engineering works, a bakery and a builders, and then restored as offices by Kath Wells, Estate Agent.

The plaque is on the former Wortley Grammar School, now Kath Wells Estate Agency, Lower Wortley Road (LS12 4SL). It was sponsored by Wortley Local History Group and unveiled on 5 June 2009 by the Lord Mayor, Councillor Judith Elliot.

By the will of Samuel Sunderland (formerly of Harden, Bingley, and an Alderman of London), several dwelling houses, cottages, crofts and land in Wortley were conveyed to Joseph Musgrave and four others, upon trust, to employ the rents and profits as directed towards the maintenance of a schoolmaster. He was to be elected by the trustees, and their successors, to teach the sons of the inhabitants of Wortley to read English or Latin. The original school stood at the bottom of Chapel Hill opposite the workhouse. When it became too small for the increasing number of scholars, a new schoolroom and schoolmaster's house beside it were built in 1814 at Town End, Lower Wortley Road.

Mr Joseph Brooke, well-versed in classics and mathematics, was the first schoolmaster in charge of the new building, and served there for over thirty years. His grandson, John Hepper, wrote in 1897: 'He was one of the stern disciplinarian school, who turned out many successful men of business, and taught thoroughly within the then limited area of a practical business education.' Notable scholars included Judge Charles James Hargreave, QC, FRS (1820-66), the eldest son of a woollen manufacturer. He became Professor of Jurisprudence at University College, London, before going to Dublin in 1849 where he served as

Mount Saint Mary's Convent, Orphanage And School

Founded in 1853 by the Sisters of the Holy Family of Bordeaux to serve the Catholic Community displaced from Ireland by famine and which came to live on The Bank, an area of severe poverty and deprivation. Architect: William Wardell. Built 1858.

In the 1820s and 1830s many Irish weavers and 'navvies' left Ireland to seek work in the north of England, settling in Leeds originally in Kirkgate and on The Bank, a high plateau of land once medieval open fields and gardens. During the Industrial Revolution The Bank became an area of foundries, dyehouses and mills powered by coal from nearby mines. Small cottages were built which developed into a warren of courts and alleyways, often unpaved, and without any form of sanitation or drainage – an appalling place in which to live and work. The people suffered typhus and cholera outbreaks.

In the 1840s the Irish potato crop was destroyed by a parasitic fungus leading to around two million deaths from starvation. The infamous 'Great Hunger' during 1846-7 triggered mass emigration, many coming to Leeds. Revd Edward Jackson recalled the scene at The Bank: 'Into these foul streets already supercharged with dirt, disease and every misery, the Irish Famine discharged thousands of gaunt and starving wretches, wild-eyed and in rags, ignorant of the speech of the people they had come among. Where they could they packed into cellars and attics and, if this was impossible, they knocked up shanties in the already abominable streets.' In 1851 the Roman Catholic Oblate Fathers established Saint Mary's Mission to care for the sick and poor of the community,

and later provide education. The Mission Superior looked to the Sisters Oblate of Mary Immaculate to provide teachers and in February 1853 four Sisters arrived from Notre Dame de L'Osier, France. When they first arrived there was no real community on The Bank, just a mass of sick and destitute people.

The Sisters set up St Mary's School for local mill girls, at first as a night school, within their first convent on The Bank in July 1853, using the laundry cellar. Widespread fundraising led to the building of the new convent in 1858 on Richmond Hill, adjacent to the newly built Mount St Mary's Church. The Sisters spent the following years training novices, teaching poor children, instructing converts, visiting the sick and building a large addition to the convent, in which the orphanage was opened in 1863 and new school buildings were opened adjoining the convent. In 1896 St Mary's College was founded as a Pupil Teacher Centre which by 2003 had evolved into St Mary's High School for some 900 boys and girls with nearly 100 staff on a large campus, and a separate Primary School.

The plaque is on the former convent building, within the grounds of Mount St Mary's School, Ellerby Road (LS9 8LA). It was sponsored by Mount St Mary's School, and unveiled on 26 January 2005 by Helen Kennally, historian of the Leeds Irish Community.

Sister Helen Geddes one of the four founding sisters

Gipton Board School

This magnificent building erected by Leeds School Board in 1897 provided an elementary education for boys and girls up to the age of 14. Later known as Harehills Middle School, it closed in 1986 but in 2008 was refurbished as 'Shine', a centre for business, arts and the community. Architect: W. S. Braithwaite.

Leeds' first School Board was elected on 28 November 1870. A census of children showed that 48,787 should be attending school, but there was accommodation for only 27,329. The School Board's response was one of the great achievements of Victorian Leeds. By November 1878, thirty-one large schools, capable of accommodating 19,000 pupils, had been erected in the borough at a cost of £177,000. By the time Walter Samuel Braithwaite was appointed architect to the School Board in 1895, the Board had erected fifty-six schools and a further ten projects were under way.

The population of Leeds had continued to grow dramatically, increasing by more than one-third between 1881 and 1901. The population of the Potternewton area, including Gipton and Harehills, grew from 5,000 to over 26,000 in these two decades, as row after row of back-to-back houses were built to accommodate the working classes. Priority was now being given to sites in the rapidly growing districts of the town.

Gipton Board School was one of the first new schools completed following Braithwaite's appointment. It opened in 1897. Braithwaite's design created a symmetrical, grand, three-storey Renaissance-style building in red brick and ashlar, with carved stone details, arranged in a series of

bays often culminating in Dutch or Elizabethan gables. The symmetry allowed for the provision of separate entrances for boys and girls in projecting bays which contained stairs and cloakrooms, together with towers to conceal ventilation shafts. The accommodation comprised a large central hall, surrounded by lofty and well-lit classrooms.

Later known as Harehills Middle School, the school closed in 1986, but having stood empty for almost twenty years, the building was refurbished by Camberwell, a small social enterprise consultancy committed to helping regenerate deprived areas, such as Harehills, by supporting the development of local entrepreneurs. In 2008, at a cost of £4½ million, the building reopened as the 'Shine' business hub. Today, a hive of activity, it houses a gym, serviced offices used by a range of charities and businesses, conference and meeting rooms, and, at its heart, is a hot-desking hub for aspiring local entrepreneurs.

The plaque was placed on the front of the building, which stands on Harehills Road between Conway Mount and Conway Street (LS8 5HS). It was unveiled by Councillor Judith Blake, Deputy Leader of Leeds City Council, on Wednesday, 28 May 2014.

St Michael's College

Opened in 1909, this Gothic Revival building was the first boys Catholic grammar school in Leeds. Established by the Jesuits, its role was to enable the predominantly working-class Catholic community in the West Riding to raise its social status and material wellbeing.

The architect was Father Benedict Williamson (1868-1948). He studied law and then trained as an architect in the offices of Messrs Newman and Jacques of Stratford. St Michael's is an eccentric but accomplished example of the late Gothic Revival. The building is of significant historical interest as a landmark highlighting the Jesuit education which was largely responsible for the formation of a Catholic middle class in the northern industrial cities. In its layout it encapsulated the broad curriculum of the Jesuits who, at the time of building, were in advance of most secular secondary education establishments.

Despite centralised organisation and shared educational ethos, there was never an ideal physical model for a Jesuit school. Many were established in existing buildings such as stately homes and some were purpose-built. St Michael's is a purpose-built college and could be distinguished in its original layout from contemporary secular schools by the variety of specialised teaching facilities such as the science laboratories. This could be the physical manifestation of the Jesuit tenet that 'God is to be found in all things and therefore that all things are worthy of study' which resulted in a famously broad and progressive curriculum and gave the study of sciences and technology the same status as the liberal arts. The college opened in 1909.

After the 1944 Education Act, its status as a Direct Grant School was confirmed and its growth continued; in the 1970s it had over 600 boys and a sixth form in excess of 120. The college opened up future opportunities in the universities, Colleges of Further Education and in all the Institutes of Further Education; its impact on the Catholic life of the West Riding has been enormous.

After the Jesuits left in 1969 only two Fathers remained to look after the religious education, so the college appointed its first lay headmaster, Mr Morris from St Edward's, Liverpool. In 2005 the college merged with Mount St Mary's

Catholic High School in East Leeds, and closed in July 2008. The building underwent extensive adaptation and refurbishment in 2016 and, now known as 'The Court at Clarendon', provides homes for key workers.

There are two plaques, one situated in the reception hall and the other on the gate post at The Court, Clarendon Quarter, St John's Road (LS3 1EX). The plaques were sponsored by AIG Global Real Estates and unveiled on 27 April 2017 by a past pupil, Robin Smith.

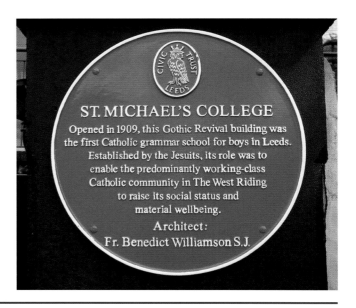

Yorkshire College

These buildings, erected in 1879 with support from the Clothworkers' Company, were the first purpose-built premises of the Yorkshire College (founded in 1874). They comprised the weaving and dyeing sheds and museum of the Textile Department. The College became the University of Leeds in 1904. Architect: Alfred Waterhouse.

The first proposals for what was to become the Yorkshire College came in 1826, when Leeds industrialist John Marshall, one of the founders of London University, introduced a scheme for a 'university' for 16-18 year olds – in effect a good public secondary school. In 1831 the Leeds Medical School was founded and moved to purpose-built premises in Park Street in 1865. Two years later the Paris Universal Exhibition aroused keen interest in scientific training as the basis of industrial efficiency and Leeds engineer James Kitson suggested a Central College for the West Riding to provide technical training. A Technical School was established by Henry and Arthur Nussey and the Yorkshire Board of Education was set up. In 1872 a scheme for a College of Science was proposed, initially with four chairs, and an appeal was launched for £60,000, but only £20,000 was subscribed and the plan nearly foundered. However, success was achieved through the energy of the honorary secretary, Richard Reynolds, and the Nussey family securing an offer from the Clothworkers' Company of London to maintain a department of textile industries.

In April 1874 a constitution for the college was agreed and an executive council set up, with the object of promoting the education of people of both sexes and particularly providing instruction in 'such sciences and arts as are applicable or ancillary to the manufacturing, mining, engineering and agricultural industries of the County of Yorkshire'. In October the college began work in rented accommodation in Cookridge Street. Three professors were appointed initially – Experimental Physics & Mathematics; Geology & Mining; Chemistry – with a fourth, Biology, in 1876. An Arts section was formed in 1877 with professors of classical and modern literature. These were part-funded by Edward Baines, proprietor of the Leeds Mercury newspaper. In 1878 the college became formally known as 'The Yorkshire College'.

In 1876-7 the Beech Grove Hall Estate was purchased for the college and in 1879 the Textile Industries Department was erected, funded by the Clothworkers' Company. The celebrated architect Alfred Waterhouse was invited to design the buildings, which included a lecture room for 90 students, weaving sheds, a museum and a dyehouse opened in 1880.

In 1880 the Victoria University was set up with Owens College, Manchester, as a founder member, followed by Liverpool College in 1884 and the Yorkshire College in 1887. Leeds now had a university college with faculties of Medicine, Science, and Technology, and a faculty of Arts in the making. It became independent in 1904 with the grant of its charter as the University of Leeds.

The plaque is on the Textile Building of the University of Leeds, adjacent to Clothworkers Court on University Road (LS2 9JT). It was sponsored by the University of Leeds and unveiled by John Stoddart-Scott of the Company of Clothworkers on 12 February 2009.

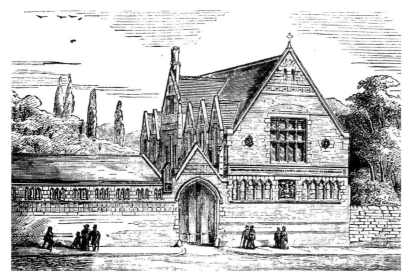

The Textile Department.

The Weaving Shed.

ORT Technical Engineering School

An ORT school was established in Berlin in 1937 to provide a technical education for Jewish boys excluded from state schools. Fleeing the Nazis, in 1939 the school was relocated to Leeds. Most of the 106 boys lived here, while continuing their training at workshops in Roseville Avenue, 1940-42.

Founded in Russia in 1880, ORT stands for Obshestvo Remeslennogo i Zemledelcheskogo Truda sredi evreev v Rossii (The Society for Trades and Agriculture among the Jews in Russia). A British branch was established in 1921. In 1937 a new school opened in Berlin and by July 1938 215 boys from northern Germany were studying there. Although untouched by Kristallnacht, Dr Simon, head of the school, and Colonel Levey, Director of the British ORT, began to discuss moving the school to the UK. The British Ministry of Labour agreed to its relocation to Leeds and the Nazis provided the boys with passports. On 29 August 1939, 106 boys, aged 15 to 17, and seven teachers and their wives left Berlin, with a second group due to leave on 3 September. But with Britain now at war with Germany, the remaining students were denied permission to leave. The Berlin School operated until 1943, when it was closed by the Gestapo, and the students and teachers were sent to concentration camps.

Initially the boys who came to Britain stayed at the Kitchener Camp in Kent whilst the school's workshops at 58 Roseville Road and on Roseville Avenue were completed. The school opened in January 1940 with six houses in Chapeltown rented as hostels for the students. The largest was at 226 Chapeltown Road, where sixty boys lived and ate their meals.

The school had five sections: Welding, Turning and Fitting; Plumbing; Electrical Engineering; Mechanical Engineering; and Carpentry and Joinery. There was also training in Market Gardening. All classes were taught in English and students attended evening classes in English and religious studies, and studied at Leeds School of Technology. Colonel Levey established a strict code of discipline – short hair, hats to be worn outside, coats to be buttoned up and 'no hands in pockets', and boys must not walk in groups of more than three and be in their hostels by 9 p.m. Eager that the school should not offend local opinion, the boys were forbidden from speaking German in the streets. Despite this somewhat militarist regime there were plenty of opportunities for a varied social life – sports, chess, music, film and local dances.

Once qualified, the former students were interned briefly on the Isle of Man, but many went on to serve in the British Army. The Leeds school closed at the end of 1942. After the War, courses for Jewish refugees were organised by British ORT, and today they continue to run courses for those in need all over the world.

The plaque is on a gatepost at 226 Chapeltown Road (LS7 4JE), which is now the New Horizons Independent School for Muslim Girls. It was sponsored by British ORT and unveiled by Sydney Sadler, former pupil of the ORT School on 14 April 2013.

Sydney Sadler, one of the ORT School pupils.

Gertrude Maretta Paul (1934-1992)

Born in St Kitts, she came to England in 1956. She taught at Cowper Street School and in 1976 she was appointed here (then called Elmhurst Middle School) as the city's first black head teacher. She was one of the founders of the West Indian Carnival and a Commissioner for Racial Equality.

Gertrude Paul was born in Parsons Ground Village, St Kitts, the eldest of eleven children. Educated at the Girls Convent Grammar School, she graduated as a teacher in Antigua. She married Lenard Paul in 1955 and taught at Bethel School, St Kitts, before the couple came to England in 1956, where they had two children, Michael and Heather, both born in Leeds. After working as a typist for United Carriers and British Rail, Gertrude became determined to resume her teaching career, and enrolled on a teacher training course in 1959. Two years later she began her first teaching job in Leeds at Clapgate Junior School, Belle Isle. In 1974 she took a postgraduate course in Higher English, and another in Race and Community Studies in the following year.

Gertrude then worked as a senior teacher at Cowper Street School, before in 1976 being appointed Head Teacher at Elmhurst Middle School (now Bracken Edge Primary School) – the first black head teacher to be employed by Leeds Education Authority. Later she became the co-ordinator for the Community Language Team. Her extensive teaching and administrative experience enabled her to launch the first Saturday School at Elmhurst in 1969, and this supported West Indian children in their academic studies, while also teaching them about their cultural and historical roots; it later moved to UCA House.

Throughout her working life in Leeds, Gertrude played an active part in community work. In the 1950s she helped to initiate the Afro Caribbean Asian Association and also to develop the United Caribbean Association (UCA), the International Women's Society, the National Association of Multi-Racial Associations, and the West Indian Centre Committee. She was also a member of the Police Liaison Committee and the Racial Equality Council. In the early 1980s she was appointed a Commissioner for the Commission for Racial Equality by the Home Office (now the Human Rights Commission).

Gertrude Paul put her school at the heart of the local community and was determined to use her skills and influence to make a difference to young people and their families. She hosted youth clubs and summer play schemes as well as initiating the concept of Saturday Schools. As an exceptionally gifted teacher and leader, she made invaluable contributions to the academic, social and spiritual development of her pupils, their families and teachers, and instilled young people with a sense of identity which would equip them to rise above the effects of discrimination and prejudice throughout their lives.

The blue plaque is on the front of Bracken Edge Primary School, Newton Garth, Newton Road, Chapeltown (LS7 4HE). It was sponsored by Chapeltown Townscape Heritage Initiative and unveiled on 21 October 2011 by Gertrude's daughter Heather and grandson Theo.

CIVIC TRUST LEEDS

ORT TECHNICAL ENGINEERING SCHOOL

An ORT school was established in Berlin in 1937 to provide a technical education for Jewish boys excluded from state schools. Fleeing the Nazis, in 1939 the school was relocated to Leeds. Most of the 106 boys lived here, while continuing their training at workshops in Roseville Avenue.

1940-42

Health and Welfare

Leeds has been a centre of distinguished medical practice since the mid eighteenth century. The founding of Leeds General Infirmary in 1767 provided free medical treatment mainly for the working classes, while private medical treatment was given by a growing number of distinguished doctors and surgeons. One of these celebrated by a plaque is Dr John Heaton who worked at the Infirmary as well as the Fever Hospital and the Public Dispensary from the 1840s. Two other internationally famous medical men celebrated by plaques are Sir Clifford Allbutt and Sir Berkeley Moynihan.

Amidst the rapid and chaotic urban growth of Leeds in the nineteenth century, and before the days of the Welfare State, townspeople grouped together to protect their families from the problems of ill health and the risk of destitution. Plaques commemorate notable endeavours in this sphere. The opening of the Leeds General Cemetery in 1835 at Woodhouse offered a private and exclusive burial ground, before the town's first municipal cemetery was created in Beckett Street, Burmantofts, from 1845.

Workers set up Friendly Societies to provide mutual support in hard times; many of these societies were based on particular trades, but the Oddfellows, founded in 1826, took in any workers for whom there was no society specifically catering for their occupation.

Throughout the city's history the people of Leeds have established charities to give support to the less well-off or disadvantaged members of the community. This determination to help others is represented by a plaque for Sue Ryder who sought to help all victims of war by setting up an international charity devoted to the relief of suffering. Today it still renders service to those in need and gives affection to the unloved regardless of age, race or creed.

Leeds General Cemetery Entrance.

John Deakin Heaton (1817-1880)

Eminent physician lived at Claremont, a Georgian merchant's villa from 1856-80. He was a prime mover in the campaign for Leeds Town Hall, and played major roles in the development of Leeds General Infirmary and the Yorkshire College, later the University of Leeds.

John Deakin Heaton, MD (London), FRCP, JP, was an eminent citizen of Leeds in the nineteenth century; he was President of the Leeds Philosophical and Literary Society from 1868 to 1872, and one of the founders of the Yorkshire College of Science (now the University of Leeds). At various times he was physician to the Public Dispensary, the House of Recovery and the Leeds General Infirmary; he was also a lecturer and treasurer at the Medical School. In 1851 he had become the first secretary of the newly created Leeds Improvement Society, which worked to promote architectural and other public improvements. One of his particular projects was to reduce smoke pollution in the city from the many factory chimneys.

John and his sister Ellen (commemorated in a blue plaque in Woodhouse Square) were the children of bookseller and stationer John Heaton and his wife Ann. The family lived in a house attached to his father's bookshop at 7 Briggate, the last house to be lived in at street level in Briggate. From 1843 John lived at 2 East Parade, a house bought for him by his father when he qualified as a doctor. In 1850 he married Fanny Heaton (no relation), the daughter of stuff merchant John Heaton, at St George's Church, Leeds. In 1856 the family moved to Claremont, 23 Clarendon Road, where he added bay windows to some downstairs rooms and enhanced the entrance hall with Minton tiles and a skylight with a coat of arms over the front door. He and his wife and children enjoyed a happy family life at Claremont, welcoming many eminent visitors, as well as large numbers of factory girls and Sunday School scholars invited to enjoy the house and gardens.

Heaton wrote an autobiographical journal which gives a fascinating picture of his life and the great variety of interests and worthy causes that he pursued. He strongly believed in the value of culture and education and his vision for Leeds encompassed the building of the Town Hall, the extensive development of the General Infirmary, the erection of the new School of Medicine in Park Street and the creation of the Yorkshire College. He felt the town and its facilities should be second to none, and strove to persuade his fellow citizens to share his vision.

This plaque is on the wall of Claremont, 23 Clarendon Road (LS2 9NZ). It was sponsored by the Yorkshire Archaeological Society and Mrs I. A. J. Moses, and unveiled by Maurice Beresford, Emeritus Professor of Economic History at the University of Leeds, on 30 October 2002.

Claremont.

Sir Clifford Allbutt (1836-1925)

One of the most widely consulted physicians of his era lived here 1872-81. He was Physician at Leeds General Infirmary 1864-84 and later Regius Professor of Physic at Cambridge. He is best known for inventing the short-stemmed clinical thermometer and revising 'The System of Medicine', the doctor's bible.

Thomas Clifford Allbutt was born in 1836 in Dewsbury, the eldest child of Revd Thomas Allbutt, Vicar of Dewsbury. From St Peter's School, York, he entered Cambridge University to read Classics but, after reading *Philosophie Positive* by Auguste Comte, he changed to Natural Science, gaining a first class degree in 1860. After training at St George's Hospital Medical School, London, and Addenbrookes Hospital, Cambridge, he settled in Leeds because of his family's extensive connections in Yorkshire.

In 1861 Allbutt was elected Physician to the Leeds House of Recovery (a fever hospital) and also held the post of Physician to the Leeds Dispensary. In 1864 he was appointed Physician to Leeds General Infirmary. He was a founder member of the Leeds & West Riding Medico-Chirurgical Society. In 1869 he married Susan England and lived initially at 38 Park Square and then in Lyddon Hall, but moved in 1881 to Carr Manor, Meanwood, (the house now known as the Judges' Lodgings). He knew the writer, George Eliot, and is believed to be a prototype for Tertius Lydgate, the physician in 'Middlemarch'.

In 1867 he invented the short-stemmed thermometer which was made in Leeds and London, and came to be used throughout the world. In 1874 he took consulting rooms at 35 Park Square and rapidly became the region's premier consulting physician from 'Trent to Tees'; it was said that 'no patient could die happy in the belief that everything possible had been done unless they had been seen by Sir Clifford'. In 1878 he became a Member of the Royal College of Physicians, and in 1880 was elected as a Fellow of the Royal Society, the first Leeds General Infirmary physician to be so.

In 1884 Allbutt had to relinquish his post due to the 20-year rule limiting the length of Leeds General Infirmary appointments. Needing a fresh challenge, he was appointed a Commissioner in Lunacy in 1889, having been interested in

psychological medicine throughout his career. In 1892 he was appointed Regius Professor of Physic at Cambridge University and spent eight years editing and writing articles for *The System of Medicine*, probably his greatest service to medicine. During this busy time he made a lecture tour of the USA, Hawaii, Japan and Canada. He was awarded many honorary degrees and was created KCB. In 1915 he published his major work Diseases of the Arteries, including *Angina Pectoris (Hypertension) Arterial Blood Pressure.*

The plaque is on the bay-windowed house adjacent to the main Lyddon Hall building on Leeds University campus (LS2 9JT). It was sponsored by the Faculty of the General Infirmary at Leeds, and unveiled on 7 December 2005 by Dr John Wales, MD, FRCP, retired Consultant Physician and past Chairman of the Faculty.

Sir Berkeley Moynihan (1865-1936)

Inspirational teacher and pioneer in abdominal surgery had his consulting rooms here from 1893-1930. He introduced the wearing of rubber gloves and prized 'caressing the tissues' rather than speed in surgery. President of the Royal College of Surgeons 1926-31. Ennobled 1929.

Berkeley George Andrew Moynihan was born in Malta, where his father was serving in the army. His father had followed his Irish family tradition in joining the army, and, whilst serving in the Crimean War, won one of the first of the newly-instituted Victoria Crosses. After her husband's death of Malta Fever in May 1867, Berkeley's mother was left to bring up her two daughters and a son on £1 per week from the Patriotic Fund as there were no army pensions then for officers' widows. She decided to settle in Leeds, accepting an offer to live with her sister and husband, Police Inspector Alfred Ball, who had no children.

Berkeley wished to follow his father into the army, but his mother hoped he would be a doctor. Happily his two uncles, Mr Ball and his mother's brother, Mr Parkin, paid for his medical training.

He trained in Medicine at the Yorkshire College and Leeds General Infirmary. In 1887, on completing his training in four years, he was appointed house surgeon and three years later became Resident Surgical Officer at the Leeds General Infirmary. In 1895 he married Miss Isabella Wellesley Jessop, daughter of his 'boss'; and in 1896 became Assistant Surgeon at the LGI, making original contributions to surgery, becoming famous in Europe and the USA for many aspects of his work.

Moynihan wrote a series of successful books on abdominal surgery. He was not in favour of speed in surgery, believing it did a lot of damage to the body, advocating 'gentle surgery': 'caress the tissues – don't drag or pull'. He was promoted to full surgeon at the LGI, became professor of surgery at the University of Leeds and was elected to the Council of the Royal College of Surgeons.

During the First World War Moynihan helped to reorganise the British Army Medical Service, taking a particular interest in the surgical problems of chest wounds. In June 1918 he was awarded KCMG for services at home, in France and the USA. Under pressure to move to London, he spent time seeing patients there every week, but it was always his wish to remain based in Leeds, the city that had given him a home as a child. He was made a Baronet, Freeman of the City of Leeds, President of the Royal College of Surgeons for six years, and then elevated to the peerage as Lord Moynihan of Leeds. In August 1936 his wife died and, after writing her life story, Lord Moynihan died six days later. Leeds people lined the streets to see his cortège pass by.

The plaque is at 33 Park Square (LS1 2PF). It was sponsored by the Faculty of Leeds General Infirmary and unveiled by Berkeley Moynihan's grandson, Dr C. B. Wynn-Parry, on 27 January 2003.

Leeds General Cemetery

Alarmed by the insanitary and overcrowded state of the Parish Church graveyard and body-snatching, the Leeds elite bought £25 shares in the Leeds General Cemetery Company. It acquired St George's Fields and created this fine private cemetery, where many Leeds worthies lie. Architect: John Clark. Opened 1835.

The Cemetery Chapel.

In the early nineteenth century interments were often made in family graves that were already full; the gravediggers having to smash earlier coffins and bones to make room. In 1833 the directors of the newly formed Leeds General Cemetery Company purchased ten acres of land on the south side of Woodhouse Moor. The £11,000 to fund the company was raised by selling shares and a public design competition for the cemetery was won by John Clark of Leeds. The cemetery's Ionic temple façade and 'Apollo of Delos' gatehouse look back to the fifth century BC, but its mortuary chapel was plain due, perhaps, to an inability of the Church of England and Dissenters to agree on a design.

The cemetery has a 12-foot-high surrounding wall to deter body-snatchers, although this was rendered unnecessary by the passing of an Act of Parliament in 1832 allowing for the bodies of people dying in workhouses to be donated to medical researchers. There were some five hundred burials per year, and many of the town's early Victorian élite were buried there, including the Baines, Marshalls, Bischoffs, Cawoods, Gotts, Fairbairns, Heatons, Luptons, Rawsons and Nusseys.

In 1968 the cemetery was landscaped, the plain gravestones used to make pathways, and most of the family monuments removed. A few memorials remain, including the Firemen's Memorial, a late Victorian obelisk with fireman's helmet and fire engine, first erected to commemorate fireman James Potter Schofield killed in the Dark Arches fire of 1892, which lasted twenty hours. Another grave of unusual interest is that of Pablo Fanque, the black circus proprietor and his wife. He was an extraordinarily skilled horseman and, in an age when slavery had only recently been abolished, was accepted by the circus fraternity and the public. He is mentioned in the famous Beatles song – Being for the benefit of Mr Kite — which John Lennon based on an old circus poster – 'The Hendersons will all be there, late of Pablo Fanque's fair'. The last burial was in 1978. The cemetery being within the present-day University of Leeds campus, the university took over responsibility for it after its closure. It agreed to make a photographic record of each gravestone and monument available to the descendants of those interred.

The plaque is on the cemetery gatehouse within the University of Leeds campus (LS2 9JT). It was sponsored by Mr and Mrs David Kaye, and unveiled on 24 April 2006 by Dr Julie Rugg, Senior Research Fellow at York University and head of the Cemetery Research Group.

David Kaye, Valerie Kaye and Julie Rugg.

The Leeds Odd Fellows

The 33 lodges of the Leeds District of the Independent Order of Odd Fellows Manchester Unity Friendly Society were administered from here 1910-1979. They offered workers and their families mutual financial protection in times of illness, unemployment and bereavement. Facilities here included meeting rooms, a ballroom and a club. Founded 1826.

regular meetings. The number of members and lodges steadily increased, but eventually there was a consolidation of the number of lodges as members joined the most prosperous ones. All the early lodges were men-only but after 1893 female lodges were founded throughout the city. Between 1911 and 1933 the membership of the Oddfellows doubled. More consolidation followed, with less need for financial protection and more emphasis on social activities and the care and welfare of members. Ten lodges with approximately 2,500 members meet regularly in Leeds today.

The history of societies such as the Oddfellows is unclear because for many years their existence was illegal, so no written records were kept. In the Middle Ages trade guilds were very powerful, controlling all aspects of commerce. Apprentices had the lowest status, above whom were Fellows, paid by the day for work organised by Masters. The Masters controlled the guilds, wearing elaborate and expensive uniforms at meetings, hence the phrase 'livery company'. The Fellows formed their own organisations, banding together in groups of their own trades; those tradesmen who had no colleagues formed groups known as the 'Odd Fellows'.

The Leeds District was administered for many years from premises in Cross Flatts Avenue, Beeston, but in 1910 it bought 2 Queen Square. By 1933, sixteen of the thirty-three lodges in Leeds District met there, the rest meeting in church halls and inns. Parties and other functions were regularly held, especially Christmas parties for the children. The building was sold to Leeds Polytechnic (now Leeds Beckett University) in 1979, and the Leeds District now owns modern premises in Meanwood Road.

Governments were wary of common people organising themselves, for fear of rebellion, so secret signs and codes were introduced for protection. In 1810, the Manchester Unity was formed and the majority of Oddfellows lodges joined it. The Oddfellows developed a sophisticated set of insurance products for working people and when the 1911 National Insurance Act was introduced, Asquith's government used the Oddfellows' experience to decide contributions and it became an administrator of the scheme. In 1948 the NHS took on many of the Oddfellows staff.

The earliest recorded lodge in Leeds is called Loyal Mechanic, founded in 1826, which still has

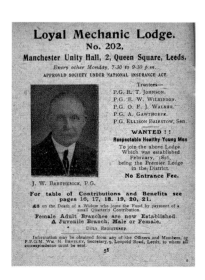

The plaque is on 2 Queen Square (LS2 8AF). It was sponsored by Leeds Oddfellows and unveiled on 20 January 2011 by Bro Alan Cole, Grand Master of the Independent Order of Oddfellows Manchester Unity Friendly Society.

Lady Ryder Of Warsaw (1924-2000)

Sue Ryder grew up here. A committed Christian, in 1953 she established the Sue Ryder Foundation, the international charity devoted to the relief of suffering, rendering service to those in need and giving affection to the unloved, regardless of age, race or creed.

Sue Ryder was born in 1924 at Scarcroft Grange near Leeds, the daughter of Charles Ryder, a farmer and landowner. The Christian faith was central to her upbringing and she learned from her mother especially the value of Christian compassion. In 1939 she joined the First Aid Nursing Yeomanry and was subsequently attached to the newly formed Special Operations Executive, where she worked mainly as a driver and radio operator. Serving in the Polish section, she grew especially close to those from Poland, a country she came to love. She witnessed the full horror of war and the concentration camps, and when the war ended worked in Europe, taking up the cause of people displaced from their homes, often survivors of the concentration camps.

Returning to Britain in 1953, she committed her life to relieving suffering, and established the Sue Ryder Foundation. This was to be a 'living memorial' dedicated to the millions lost in both World Wars. She described it as 'An international foundation devoted to the relief of suffering on the widest scale; which seeks to render personal service to those in need and to give affection to those who are unloved, regardless of age, race or creed, as part of the family of man, and those suffering and dying today as a result of persecution.' She was staunchly supported by her mother, whose home in Cavendish, Suffolk, became the foundation's first home caring for concentration camp survivors. The home was run by volunteers and existed on charitable donations. From these small beginnings, forty years later the Sue Ryder Foundation ran eighty homes in a dozen countries, including twenty-eight in Poland and twenty-two in the former Yugoslavia, and raised funds through a chain of over five hundred charity shops staffed by volunteers. Over its life, the charity – now known simply as 'Sue Ryder'—has widened its work, and in particular today focuses on providing palliative, neurological and bereavement support across the UK and internationally. These specialist services include caring for those with Parkinson's Disease, Huntington's and multiple sclerosis. In Leeds it runs Wheatfield Hospice in Headingley. In short, the charity supports people through the most difficult times of their lives.

In February 1955 Leonard Cheshire VC, founder of the Cheshire Homes for the physically disabled, invited Sue Ryder to visit his new home at Ampthill. Kindred spirits, they became close and married in 1959. Sue Ryder was appointed OBE in 1957 for her work with German prisoners and CMG in 1976; in 1979 she was created a life peer, Baroness Ryder of Warsaw, the title her personal tribute to the people of Poland.

The plaque is on the gatepost of Scarcroft Grange, the first large Georgian-style building on the right as you enter Scarcroft from the direction of Leeds (LS14 3HJ). It was sponsored by the Sue Ryder Prayer Fellowship and unveiled on 25 June 2011 by Sue Ryder's children, Jeromy and Elizabeth Cheshire.

The Unveiling: Left to right: Lynda Kitching, Robert Clifton (Chair of the Sue Ryder Prayer Fellowship), Jeromy and Elizabeth Cheshire, and Sue Doe (SRPF).

The Leeds Fire Brigade Memorial at Leeds General Cemetery

Religion

The Anglican Church dominated religion in Leeds for centuries; in Leeds township the grand old medieval parish church, St Peter's, was complemented by St John's, New Briggate, opened in 1634. In the early eighteenth century a large donation by Lady Betty Hastings enabled the addition of a third church, the impressive Holy Trinity on Boar Lane. With the Declaration of Indulgence in 1672, persecution of Dissenters lessened and they were able to worship more openly. This permitted the building of the Presbyterian Mill Hill Chapel in 1674, the Independent Call Lane Chapel in 1691 and the Quaker Meeting House in Water Lane in 1699.

The coming of the Industrial Revolution saw the rise of Methodism and other denominations. Many merchants and mill owners were attracted to Nonconformity, and the contributions of rich and poor built dozens of chapels. This included Salem Chapel which opened in 1791 and flourished for over two hundred years, reaching out to the local community. In the 1860s the Quakers moved from Water Lane to a purpose-built meeting house and schools on Woodhouse Lane, where they ran educational projects and campaigned against slavery and for peace. From 1859 young men were trained for the Baptist ministry in the rural calm of Rawdon, a startling change from their first premises in an old Bradford weaving shed.

The Victorian era saw a great influx of Irish immigrants who lived at first on The Bank on the east side of the town, where their spiritual and practical needs were initially met by Mount St Mary's Church, orphanage and school. The arrival of many Jewish immigrants from Eastern Europe created the Jewish community in the Leylands, alongside North Street, and saw the establishment of early synagogues in the area. As the Jewish population moved northwards into Chapeltown, the New Synagogue was built on Chapeltown Road in 1931. At the same time nearby a house in Leopold Street was used as a Spanish/Portuguese synagogue and later a Reformed Synagogue. Subsequently, to meet the needs of immigrant Muslim workers from South Asia, it became the first mosque in Leeds.

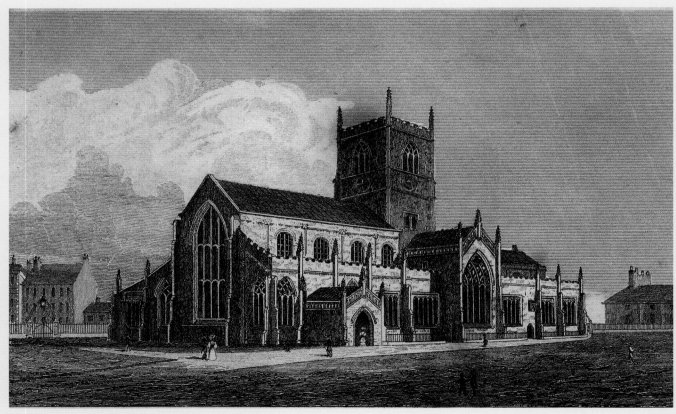

Leeds Parish Church (south side) demolished 1838.

Lady Betty Hastings (1682-1739)

Of Ledston Hall was a lifelong patron of charities for education, the promotion of Christian knowledge and the relief of poverty. In 1721 when the scheme for building this church was revived, her magnificent donation of £1,000 ensured its success.

Lady Elizabeth Hastings was born in London, the eldest daughter of Theophilus Hastings, seventh Earl of Huntingdon, and his first wife Elizabeth, herself the eldest daughter of Sir John Lewis, Baronet, of Ledston Hall, Yorkshire (who had amassed a fortune as a factor in the East India Company). On her father's death in 1701, Lady Elizabeth's brother inherited their maternal grandfather's estate at Ledston, but he bestowed it on her, on condition that she abandon any claim to their father's estate. This generous settlement included an annual income of £3,000. Lady Elizabeth then formed an independent household in 1707 when she took possession of Ledston Hall and its estate.

Lady Betty (as Lady Elizabeth was affectionately known by everyone) was a beauty, as is evident in a portrait by Sir Godfrey Kneller. She was also notable for her intelligence, her pious character, and her support of charitable and religious causes. Ralph Thoresby, the Leeds historian, was a regular visitor to her home, as were many famous theologians and bishops. She made innumerable gifts towards the erection and decoration of local churches; her gift to Holy Trinity Church, Leeds, of £1,000 saved the building scheme from collapse when a wealthy patron failed to honour his promise to endow it. The primary school at Thorp Arch is still called 'Lady Elizabeth Hastings School', one of the five schools that she set up and endowed, the others being the day schools for boys at Ledsham, Aberford, and Collingham, and a boarding school for girls at Ledsham.

She also planned to give grants to students at grammar schools and universities, but later decided to attach her Exhibitions (grants) to Queen's College, Oxford. Lady Betty devised a rigorous system for the selection of five poor scholars to go there every five years. Twelve local grammar schools were asked to select their most distinguished scholars who were required to carry out three classical translations. The Provost and Fellows of Queen's College selected the eight best candidates, from whom five were chosen by lot. The first four years at the college were to be spent studying Arts and Science, and the last year Divinity. These educational grants continue to be paid today by the Hastings Trust and Lady Betty's portrait still looks down on students in Queen's College. In addition senior scholarships are awarded to graduates of the universities of Leeds, Sheffield, Hull, York and Bradford.

Portrait of Lady Elizabeth Hastings. *(Image courtesy of the Provost and Fellows of The Queen's College Oxford.)*

Holy Trinity Church, Boar Lane in 1816.

The plaque is by the entrance to Holy Trinity Church, Boar Lane (LS1 6HW). It was sponsored by Land Securities plc and unveiled on 20 April 2009 by Dr Ingrid Roscoe, Lord Lieutenant of West Yorkshire.

Carlton Hill Friends Meeting House

Erected in 1868 was the principal Quaker Meeting House in Leeds. In 1921 it became Albrecht & Albrecht's clothing factory, the Quaker meetings removing to the schoolroom block to the rear, where worship continued until 1979. From 1933 to 2004 it was the BBC Studios. Architect: Edward Birchall.

London took place at Carlton Hill over a thousand people attended. It was thought to be the largest gathering of Friends since the funeral of George Fox.

Due to declining membership, in 1921 it was decided to sell the two meeting houses to Albrecht & Albrecht, and move the meetings into the schoolroom at the rear. In 1933 the meeting houses were sold to the BBC for radio and later TV studios. With the establishment of Quaker Meetings at Roundhay in 1929 and Adel in 1938, the numbers attending Carlton Hill dwindled and the remaining property was sold to the BBC in 1979. A new meeting house at 188 Woodhouse Lane was opened in September 1987. The last programmes from Broadcasting House were transmitted in 2004. Leeds Beckett University bought it in 2005, refurbished the original meeting house and opened it in 2007 as its flagship 'Institute for Enterprise', renaming the building 'Old Broadcasting House'.

The plaque is on the front of the building at 160b Woodhouse Lane (LS2 9EN). It was sponsored by the Leeds Society of Friends and unveiled on 9 September 2010 by Mary Rowntree, daughter of a long-standing caretaker.

The Quakers were present in Leeds from the seventeenth century, building their meeting house at Water Lane on the riverside site now occupied by ASDA's headquarters. By the mid nineteenth century, Quaker businessmen had prospered and the meeting house, now surrounded by factories, was far from their homes to the north of the river. When the Carlton Hill Estate came on the market in 1864 the Friends immediately purchased it, demolished Carlton House which stood on the site, and erected a new meeting house there.

The Quaker Edward Birchall was chosen as architect. He designed a sober building modelled on the Water Lane meeting house. It accommodated two meeting houses (one each for men and women), a library and reading room, three committee rooms, a stable, and two cottages (one for the caretaker and the other for a visiting Friend). The building cost £14,287; Leeds Friends contributed over £6,000 and generous amounts were sent by Friends' Meetings in Bradford, Darlington, York and elsewhere. The first meeting for worship was held on 19 January 1868.

Leeds Quakers were very active in the nineteenth century, being much involved in the anti-slavery movement, peace movements and adult education (founding, for example, the Swarthmore Education Settlement in Woodhouse Square). When the first annual national Quaker meeting to be held outside

The Friends Meeting House on Water Lane, Holbeck c. 1790.

Salem Chapel

Opened by the Independents in 1791 is the city centre's oldest surviving chapel. Its distinctive bow front was added in 1906. The celebrated ministries of the Revds Parsons, Hudswell, Smith and Wrigley, and Guntrip sustained a vibrant chapel life; closure only came in 2001. Leeds United FC was founded here in 1919.

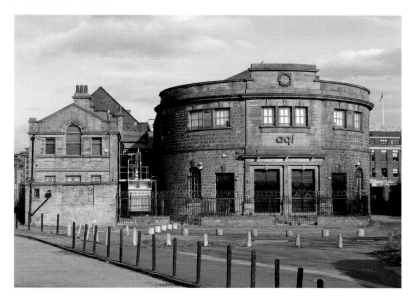

Salem Chapel opened in 1791 and was designed in the fashionable neo-classical style, with high narrow pews to seat a thousand people. The first minister was the Revd Edward Parsons who ministered to the chapel for over fifty years and was, according to a contemporary, 'a man of great energy of character, decidedly evangelical in his views on the gospel yet practical and experimental in presenting and enforcing them'. The congregation was drawn from skilled artisans, shop-keepers and other tradesmen.

In the later years of Parsons' ministry industrialisation resulted in a spate of factory and warehouse building south of the river, and many of those who worshipped at the chapel became men of substance. In response to the chapel's deteriorating location and the fact that four-fifths of the congregation now lived north of the river, in 1838 most of the members decided to move to the more prestigious, newly erected, Albion Chapel in East Parade. Salem was then bought by the Revd William Hudswell, another celebrated Congregationalist preacher who served until 1866 and extended the Day School and Sunday Schools.

After Hudswell's retirement closure threatened, but in 1891 Bertram Smith and Frank Wrigley began their famous dynamic experimental joint pastorate at Salem. They abolished pew rents, organised an Institute for young people, ran various meetings for women, and started a meeting for men on Sunday afternoons. By 1900 the membership of the 'Salem

Brotherhood' reached over a thousand, a figure maintained until 1939. The Institute for Young People began in the Sunday School premises with educational and recreational activities; on every evening of the week Salem was bustling with life. The success of these ventures led in 1906 to the chapel's extension and the erection of an Institute.

Smith and Wrigley retired in 1929, but the congregation continued to flourish under the remarkable Revd Harry Guntrip through whose ministry the chapel began to cater for the special needs of the unemployed, and to promote the discussion of politics, philosophy and psychology. The special role played by Salem, however, eventually came to an end as the slum clearances of the post-war years stripped it of its local community, and it closed in 2001.

A highlight in the chapel's story is that, following the disbandment of Leeds City Association Football Club due to illegal payments made to players during the First World War, the entire playing staff of the club was auctioned off at the Metropole Hotel on 17 October 1919. After the auction more than 1,000 loyal Leeds City supporters met at the Salem Hall and founded Leeds United.

The blue plaque is by the entrance on Hunslet Road (LS10 1JW). It was sponsored by Dr Adam Beaumont of aql, and unveiled on 17 November 2011 by Councillor Revd Alan Taylor, Lord Mayor of Leeds.

BUILT 1791.   RESTORED 1901.

The chapel in 1901 before the front was altered.

Leeds Methodist Pioneers

The first purpose-built Methodist chapel in Leeds, the 'Old Boggard House', was erected here on Boggart Close in 1750-51. A public meeting here on 6 October 1813 led to the formation of the (Wesleyan) Methodist Missionary Society which was highly influential in Methodism becoming a world church.

The religious revival of the mid eighteenth century and the rise of Methodism had its origins in the fervour of John and Charles Wesley, George Whitefield, and Benjamin Ingham — all members of the 'Holy Club' in Oxford. From the mid 1730s, John Nelson, the Birstall stonemason, and Ossett-born Benjamin Ingham both preached and established Methodist societies in the West Riding. Whitefield and the Wesleys began 'field preaching' in the area in the early 1740s. By 1742 Methodism was firmly established in the parish of Leeds, first at Armley. A Methodist society was established in Leeds township in 1743, with worship held at William Shent's barber's shop on Briggate.

Despite John Wesley being pelted by the mob in Leeds in September 1745, the infant Methodist society was not disheartened. It moved its meeting place several times, before settling at the house of Matthew Chippendale, a basket maker, on Boggart Close in 1749. This was a more remote location on the slope of Quarry Hill.

In 1750 the congregation began building their first purpose-built chapel quite literally around Chippendale's house before it was eventually demolished. On 14 May 1751 John Wesley preached in the incomplete shell of what was later referred to as the 'Old Boggard House'. The chapel was rebuilt or much enlarged in 1786. Leeds was now the centre of Methodism for most of Yorkshire, and between 1751 and 1824 the national Methodist Conference met in the town on nineteen occasions.

In 1834 the old chapel was replaced by the adjacent much larger St Peter's Chapel. Methodism had flourished in Leeds, with many new chapels being built. When Walter Farquhar Hook became Vicar of Leeds in 1837, he declared that Methodism was 'the de facto established religion of Leeds'.

By the early nineteenth century some Methodist missionary work had been established in the West Indies, but it was largely reliant on the private initiatives of Revd Dr Thomas Coke. When Coke died at sea, it became clear that Methodist missionary activity needed to be set on a firm financial footing. Leeds took the lead. At a public meeting held at the Boggard House on 6 October 1813, it was decided to establish the Leeds Methodist District Missionary Society. A pamphlet reporting the speeches at the meeting was widely circulated to encourage other Methodist districts to form their own missionary societies.

The growth of these district societies led to the creation of the national Methodist Missionary Society in 1818, with its headquarters in Hatton Garden, London. Its work was highly influential in establishing Methodism as a world church. Though officially founded in 1818, the society held its golden jubilee and centenary celebrations in 1863 and 1913, clearly acknowledging the 1813 meeting at the Old Boggard House in Leeds as the true occasion of its founding.

The plaque is on the left side of Leeds Playhouse 10 metres up from St Peter's Street (LS2 7UP). It was unveiled on Sunday, 6 October 2013 by Revd Ruth Gee, President of the Methodist Conference.

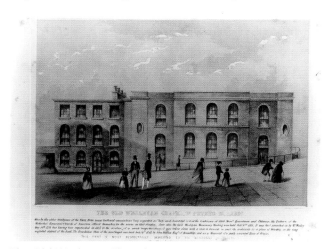

The Old Wesleyan Chapel,
St Peter's Street.

The Unveiling: Revd Ruth Gee, President of the Methodist Conference (third from left).

Rawdon College

From 1859 to 1964 in the peaceful seclusion of this striking Tudor Gothic college, erected by the Northern Baptist Education Society, young men were trained for the ministry of the Gospel. Its library, teaching rooms and Principal's residence occupied the central building with student 'apartments' on either side. Architect: H. J. Paul.

During the eighteenth century Presbyterians and Congregationalists, excluded from the universities, opened their own academies to educate their ministers. There was no ministerial academy in the North of England, however, until 1804 when a Baptist College was founded in an old weaving shed at Little Horton, Bradford. Here the first Principal, William Steadman, sought to identify and train preachers committed to the task of evangelism.

In the 1850s the Northern Baptist Education Society decided to provide a purpose-built college and was offered a woodland site in Rawdon by Robert Milligan, once Mayor of Bradford and a prominent Congregationalist. A building committee was appointed and the design by H. J. Paul of Cardiff was chosen from forty entries to the design competition. The new college was opened on 4 September 1859.

Students had been prepared for taking degrees at London University from 1852, but in 1904 the college became affiliated to the new University of Leeds. At the outbreak of war in 1939 there were thirty men in college but by 1944 just four students remained and it was decided to close it, although correspondence courses were conducted for men in the forces. The college reopened in 1946 with eighteen students. By then the training courses were all biblically based: New Testament Greek, Old Testament Hebrew, Theology and Church History,

RAWDON BAPTIST COLLEGE

with provision also in Homiletics (preaching) and Elocution. Students went out each Sunday, taking services all over Yorkshire and further afield. Football and cricket teams played matches against other colleges and there was close camaraderie for the twenty to thirty men in each year. There were also several medical missionary candidates who lived at Rawdon while doing their medical studies in Leeds and taking an active part in college life.

After several earlier attempts Rawdon was amalgamated with Manchester Baptist College. The united college became the Northern Baptist College. Rawdon College closed in 1964, but from then until 1975 it was used as a hall of residence by students from nearby Trinity and All Saints Teacher Training College. In 1979 it was converted into eighteen residential dwellings with common grounds managed by Craggwood Management Ltd; each of the eighteen owners has one share in the company. The buildings are now known as "Larchwood".

The plaque is placed on a stone wall adjacent to the gateway into Larchwood from Woodlands Drive, Rawdon (LS19 6JZ). The plaque was sponsored by residents of Larchwood and former students of Rawdon College, and was unveiled on 4 September 2010 by the Revd Ernie Whalley, Regional Minister of the Yorkshire Baptist Association.

House of Faith

This house reflects the ever-changing community of Chapeltown. Built soon after 1860 for residents of the affluent middle class suburb, in 1924 it became a Spanish and Portuguese Synagogue, and from 1952 to 1960 the Sinai Reform Synagogue. From 1961 to 1974, as the Jinnah Mosque, it was the first mosque in Leeds.

The Leeds Jewish community, which was established around 1840, lived in and around the Leylands district, gradually moving north to Chapeltown. Most Leeds Jews were Ashkenazim from central and eastern Europe, but there were about forty Sephardi families from Iberia, who opened their own synagogue in Bridge Street in 1915. Nine years later they purchased and converted 21 Leopold Street into a synagogue; this closed in the late 1940s. The Jewish Reform community, which had held services in a private home in Reginald Terrace nearby, bought the house in 1951, and it now became known as the Sinai Synagogue. Opened in February 1952, it had only thirty-seven seats but, although Leeds Jews are largely of the Orthodox persuasion, by 1958 membership had increased to two hundred making the premises far too small. Plans followed for a purpose-built synagogue in Roman Avenue, and the last service in Leopold Street was held on 10 September 1960.

Few people from what was to become Pakistan lived in Leeds until the 1930s. Nur Muhammed Kotia came to Leeds in 1930 and worked as a wholesale clothier. When in 1944 P. G. J. Shah, a civil engineer who worked on Quarry Hill Flats, settled in Leeds his home became a social centre for Leeds Muslims. According to the 1951 Census, there were 145 Pakistanis in Leeds. Two of the early pioneers, Abdul Rahman from Sylhet and Chaudri Bosta Khan of Mirpur, arrived here after working as stokers on British steam ships, and then went into the city's wholesale clothing trade. Together they founded the Leeds Pakistan Muslim Association in 1953. Five years earlier Chaudri Khan was responsible for the purchase of the first Muslim burial plot in the city. It was Abdul Khan who encouraged his fellow Bengali Muslims to raise the money for the purchase of 21 Leopold Street to create the first mosque in Leeds. The whole community in the spirit of Muslim unity rallied to the project; when the Jinnah Mosque, as it was known, opened in June 1961 about five hundred single men from Pakistan and a handful of families lived in Leeds. Many had travelled from their homelands to Bombay (now Mumbai) to work on British ships; settling in Leeds they worked either in textile industries or took on hot and heavy foundry work. The first trustees of the mosque came from both West and East Pakistan (now Pakistan and Bangladesh).

The plaque is at 21 Leopold Street (LS7 4DA) and was sponsored by Unity Housing Association. It was unveiled on 14 March 2012 by Ruth Sterne, life member of the Sinai Synagogue Board and Leeds City Councillor Mohammed Rafique.

The New Synagogue

This fine building was the first Synagogue (1932-1985) of the United Hebrew Congregation formed in 1932. Designed by J. Stanley Wright in a style with a Byzantine flourish, it became the most popular synagogue in Leeds.

After the First World War the movement of the Jewish population to the north of Leeds dictated a move of the synagogue from the centre. The members of the New Briggate Synagogue made unsuccessful overtures to the Great Synagogue in Belgrave Street with a view to amalgamation in a new building. They had already drawn up plans to build in Chapeltown, and Brandsby Lodge, a house belonging to Sir Charles Wilson, MP, with adjoining land located at the corner of Louis Street and Chapeltown Road, was purchased. In 1927 the synagogue building committee appointed local architect, J. Stanley Wright. Unfortunately, money ran out to pay for the ambitious project and the Great Synagogue now agreed to help complete it by amalgamating the two congregations to form the United Hebrew Congregation.

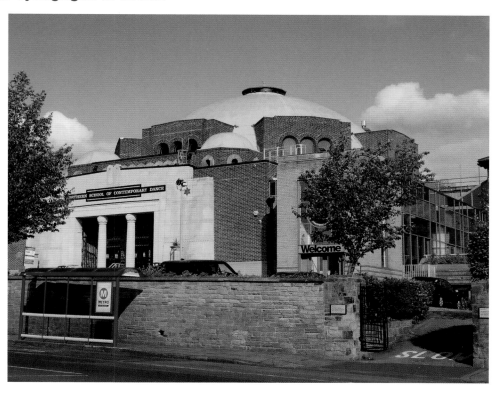

The New Synagogue was an appropriate name and it soon became the most popular synagogue in Leeds. The building, designed in a Byzantine style with a large dome and a minaret, somewhat like an Istanbul mosque but with a classical Greek entrance, represented 'the last flowering of the Islamic Revival style as re-interpreted in the era of Art Deco'. It opened for worship for the High Festivals in 1932. A new chazan (cantor) was sought of a suitable calibre for such a large and prestigious synagogue and Chazan Solomon Stern was selected. He proved to be an inspired choice, and served the congregation for twenty-eight years. His voice and rendering of the prayers are recalled with pleasure by all who heard him. The adjoining Brandsby Lodge became the communal powerhouse, containing the offices of the UHC, Beth Din (Court of Judgement) and the Board of Shechitah (supervision of Kosher ritual slaughter and butchers' shops). The synagogue was filled to capacity for most services in the early years.

In 1942, when it had become plain that millions of Jews had been slaughtered by the Nazis, the Chief Rabbi ordered a day of fasting and prayer for Sunday 13 December; the service in the New Synagogue was packed with more than two thousand worshippers.

Even before the War, Jewish families, many of whom were UHC members, started settling further north in the Moortown area, enabling the Moortown Synagogue to be established.

In the early 1950s Rabbi Solomon Brown was appointed Senior Minister of UHC, responsible for four synagogues. The New Synagogue closed in 1985. The building was purchased by Leeds City Council and is now in use as the Northern School of Contemporary Dance. Listed Grade II, it should long remain as a reminder of the prominent part it once played in Leeds Jewish life.

The plaque is on the front wall of the synagogue beside the main entrance on Chapeltown Road (LS7 4BH). It was sponsored by the United Hebrew Congregation and was unveiled on 14 October 2012 by Judge Ian Dobkin.

Society & Politics

The 1830s saw reform in parliamentary and local government with Leeds gaining its first MPs in 1832 and its first elected municipal corporation in 1835. Whilst borough councils could significantly improve local conditions, it required the lobbying of Parliament to produce major social change. Leeds has produced campaigners in the nineteenth and twentieth centuries whose tireless and brave endeavours improved the condition and rights of men, women and children. These included Richard Oastler in the 1830s and 1840s, and in the years up to the 1930s four redoubtable women – Ellen Heaton, Isabella Ford, Mary Gawthorpe, and Leonora Cohen. Three Leeds political men who drove significant change in the twentieth century were Thomas Edmund Harvey, Sir Charles Wilson and the Revd Charles Jenkinson.

The history of a city's political and governing institutions is often embodied in its buildings. The dominance of the Liberal Party in Leeds politics in the nineteenth century is reflected in the powerful architecture of the Leeds and County Liberal Club, while the ever-growing functions of Leeds City Council in the twentieth century is symbolised by the impressive Civic Hall opened in 1933. The increased strength of trade unions and the Labour Party, especially in local government, is demonstrated by the substantial former Leeds Trades Club building in Chapeltown. In more recent years there has been a very significant increase in the recognition of the rights of gay and transgender people; a building where this is celebrated is the New Penny public house, which has long been a safe haven in what is now the gay quarter of Leeds city centre.

'I am Leeds': Cartoon of Sir Charles Wilson in 1921.

Over the centuries Britain has experienced threats from abroad and, when diplomacy has failed, war has broken out. When the government was alarmed about the growing power and armament of France in the nineteenth century, volunteer regiments and rifle companies were established around the country; the Leeds Rifles was created in 1859 and served with distinction. But over the years the civilians of Leeds have also played their part by making armaments in support of the military; the Barnbow Royal Ordnance Factory opened in 1940 became famous for its manufacture of guns and tanks.

Mary Gawthorpe, centre, leafletting for the WPSU's 'Self-Denial Week', Leeds, February 1908. Illustration courtesy of the Tamiment Library, NYU.

Mary Gawthorpe (centre) during WSPU Self Denial Week in Leeds, 1908.

Richard Oastler (1789-1861)

'The Factory King' was born in St Peter's Square. His 1830 letter to the Leeds Mercury about 'Yorkshire Slavery' began the campaign to reduce the working day of factory children to ten hours. The Ten Hours Act of 1847 owed much to his persuasive writing and compelling oratory.

Richard Oastler was born in St Peter's Square on 20 December 1789, the youngest of eight children. He was educated at Fulneck School in Pudsey, subsequently became a Methodist local preacher, and undertook social welfare work in Leeds. In addition, he supported William Wilberforce and the abolition of slavery in election campaigns. He succeeded his father as steward of Fixby Hall near Huddersfield, where he and his wife lived, and over the years his outlook gradually changed from his upbringing of Radicalism and Wesleyanism to Toryism and Anglicanism. His motto was 'The Altar, the Throne & the Cottage'.

In 1830 he visited his devout Anglican friend John Wood, a worsted spinner in Bradford, who opened his heart to Oastler about the cruelty to children working in the textile mills, likening it to slavery in the West Indies. Children were working from 6 a.m. to 7 p.m. with just one 40-minute break and some were strapped for arriving late or falling asleep. On 16 October 1830 Oastler's letter 'Yorkshire Slavery' was published in the Whig newspaper, the Leeds Mercury, and landed like a bombshell on Yorkshire. He then wrote further letters to the Mercury and put forward the idea of a ten-hour day, while workers organised themselves into 'Short Time Committees' with Oastler as their leader. There followed a period of campaigning in which Oastler developed great powers of oratory and was supported by workers and the doctors who witnessed the ill health of factory employees.

The movement had representation in Parliament. The second reading of a Bill in 1832 was marked by a march of 12,000 men from the West Riding to York. Unfortunately, when a Bill largely concerned

Oastler aged 48.

with children was passed in 1833, it proved unworkable. Oastler became bitter and advocated sabotage, thus alienating himself from friends and his employer. The first Bill limiting factory hours for women and children to twelve hours was passed by Peel's Tory government in 1844 and the Ten Hour Day Act was finally passed in 1847.

Richard Oastler died in 1861 and is buried in St Stephen's Church, Kirkstall, Leeds with his wife and children. In 1869 a bronze statue to his memory was erected in Bradford and unveiled by Lord Shaftesbury; 100,000 people attended the ceremony.

The plaque is sited on the wall of 'The Wardrobe', St Peter's Square, Quarry Hill (LS9 8AH), close to the site of Richard Oastler's birthplace. It was sponsored by Professor Neville Rowell and unveiled on 5 September 2005 by Councillor Andrew Carter, Deputy Leader of Leeds City Council, and Calum Archibald and Olivia Hudson, pupils from Fulneck School.

St Peter's Square showing the three-storey house (third from the left) where Oastler was born.

Ellen Heaton (1816-1894)

Lived in 6 Woodhouse Square from 1859-94. She was an influential Pre-Raphaelite art patron and an active campaigner for women's rights, education, health, environmental issues and anti-vivisection. Her friend, the poet Christina Rossetti, stayed here.

Born in the family home above her father's bookshop on Briggate, Ellen Heaton later lived with her parents at 31 Park Square, but in 1859 moved to her own home at 6 Woodhouse Square, where she died in 1894. The house is now part of Swarthmore Education Centre. For most of her adult life she was a passionate advocate of education. She herself enjoyed a private education, progressing to a 'finishing school' in Mirfield at the time that Charlotte Bronte was a scholar there. She fought for the extension of education to excluded groups, such as girls, women and working-class men. For many years she paid the 3 pence admission fees for working men who wished to attend University 'Extension Lectures', provided 'public teas' for those who wished to attend lectures after a full day's work, and was on the executive committee of the Yorkshire Ladies Council of Education.

A woman of independent means who inherited shares and property from her parents, Ellen Heaton's life story challenges standard pre-conceptions of Victorian spinsters. She was adventurous, intelligent and unconventional, becoming a political activist alongside pioneers campaigning for women's rights. She was a founder member of the Kensington Society, a group of women who agitated for female suffrage, which organised a petition and presented it to Parliament in 1866. Ellen was notable for including working-class women, chars and laundresses, in the campaign. She was mentioned in the letters exchanged between poets Elizabeth Barrett and Robert Browning while they were planning their elopement in 1846, and later visited them in exile in Italy, meeting their avant-garde circle of writers, artists and sculptors. She corresponded regularly with John Ruskin, the art critic and social reformer, who advised her concerning the choice of paintings for her collection, mainly from Pre-Raphaelite artists. Eighteen of her pictures now hang in the Tate Britain Gallery and two in the National Portrait Gallery.

Ellen Heaton in 1849.

In addition to campaigning for equal access to education, she fought for improvements in health care for local women and children, better employment conditions for lace-makers, and environmental protection. She also strongly opposed vivisection. In later years she was an enthusiastic and eccentric proprietor of the Leeds Library in Commercial Street: it was her habit to sit by the library fire with all the daily newspapers, only relinquishing them to other readers one at a time as she finished with them.

This plaque is on Swarthmore Education Centre, Woodhouse Square (LS3 1AD). It was sponsored by the Friends of Swarthmore and the Little Woodhouse Community Association, and unveiled by poet Rommi Smith on 27 February 2002.

Isabella Ford (1855-1924)

Lived here 1865-1922. She founded the Leeds Tailoresses Union and gained a national reputation as a trade union organiser. She spoke widely on socialism and women's suffrage. During the First World War her Quaker background led her to campaign fervently for peace and disarmament.

Isabella Ford was the last of eight children of Leeds solicitor Robert Lawson Ford and his wife, Hannah. Her parents were progressive Quakers, and active supporters of the Liberal Party. They financed and taught in a night school for mill girls on The Bank, where they were later joined by their daughters, Bessie, Emily and Isabella. In 1865 the family moved to Adel where their father built Adel Grange, set in seven acres of landscaped grounds. The girls were educated at home and were taught literature, science, philosophy and became fluent in French and German. One of the reasons Isabella subsequently became a delegate to so many European conferences was because of her linguistic talents. Informally, the girls were exposed to a wide variety of ideas and met many people involved in political activity.

In 1884 Emma Paterson, a friend of Isabella's mother and President of the Women's Protective and Provident League, came to Leeds to support the Tailoresses Society which had recently been formed in the town, and persuaded Isabella to become involved in it. In October 1888, when 200 female weavers at Wilson and Sons went on strike in protest against changes in piece work rates and the system of fines employed by the company, she arranged for leaders of the General Union of Textile Workers to support the strikers and provided £50 a week towards their strike fund. The success of the strike convinced Isabella that the time was ripe to reactivate a Tailoresses Union, which flourished with her support. She was President of the Leeds Tailoresses Union until 1899 and was one of the few who dared to raise the issue of sexual harassment at work. In 1896 she was elected as a delegate to the Trade Union National Congress.

Isabella Ford aged 34.

Her involvement with the workers' struggles brought Isabella into contact with members of the Leeds branch of the Socialist League. Within a month of the founding of the Independent Labour Party (ILP) in Bradford in 1893, she joined the party and for the next ten years combined trade union agitation with campaigning work on its behalf. In 1904 the ILP published her influential pamphlet, Women and Socialism. She argued that women should have the vote not only because of the political power it would give them, but also because it would change the relationship between men and women. She spent the final years of her life campaigning for peace, disarmament and international co-operation.

Adel Grange, Isabella Ford's Home.

The plaque is on the entrance porch of Adel Grange Residential Home, Adel Grange Close (LS16 8HX). It was sponsored by Mike Flynn, the owner of Adel Grange, and unveiled on 6 October 2009 by Frank Ford supported by seven other relatives of Isabella Ford.

Mary Gawthorpe (1881-1973)

Socialist and suffragette lived here 1905-07. Born in Woodhouse, she struggled to achieve financial independence as a school teacher. Inspired by Christabel Pankhurst she was imprisoned in Holloway for her protests at the House of Commons and elsewhere. She was a Women's Social and Political Union organiser and sat on its national committee.

Mary Gawthorpe was born in January 1881 at 5 Melville Street, amidst the red-brick, terraced houses of the working-class district of Woodhouse in Leeds. Her mother had been a mill girl and her father worked in a local tannery. A bright girl, at the age of 13 she became a pupil teacher. Despite difficult family circumstances, and through years of hard work combining teaching and studying, she qualified as a teacher and became an Assistant Mistress at St Luke's Boys School, Beeston Hill. Then aged 21, she rented a house in Fulham Street, Beeston Hill, where for the first time as the householder, she was able to vote in local Council elections.

In Beeston, she joined the Labour Church on Dewsbury Road, and became engaged to Tom Garrs through whose influence she developed an interest in socialist politics and joined the Independent Labour Party. Soon she was writing a women's page for the weekly 'Labour News' and making political speeches. After three years at St Luke's, she transferred to the new Board School in Bramley, where she rented 9 Warrels Mount. Her horizons were broadening, and around this time she became a member of Leeds Arts Club.

Then an event happened that changed the whole direction of her life. On 13 October 1905 Christabel Pankhurst and Annie Kenney were arrested for making a disturbance at a Liberal Party election meeting at Manchester's Free Trade Hall, when demanding votes for women. Inspired, Mary wrote to Christabel Pankhurst in Strangeways Prison telling her that if it was necessary to go to prison to win the vote, she too was ready. She started to write letters to the Leeds press and began her long association with Isabella Ford and the Leeds Women's Suffrage Society. In June 1906 she resigned her teaching post to concentrate on politics, and two months later she became a full-time organiser for the Women's Social and Political Union. On 23 October Mary and a large group of women gathered in the Central Lobby of the Houses of Parliament, awaiting news of whether the government would declare its support for a suffrage bill. When news came that the answer was no, Mary leapt on a chair and began haranguing those present. The police arrived, and arrests were made. Mary was sentenced to two months imprisonment and discovered the appalling conditions in Holloway Women's Prison; she was released after five weeks.

VOTES FOR WOMEN.

Photo. by Schmidt, Manchester.

Miss MARY E. GAWTHORPE,
Organiser, National Women's Social and Political Union, 4, Clement's Inn, Strand, W.C.

In the following years, she campaigned up and down the country, being arrested and imprisoned on many occasions, and quite literally being battered and bruised in the process.

Her efforts in the cause of women's suffrage were prodigious, but she was not in England to see it achieved through the Acts of 1918 and 1928. In 1915 she emigrated to America, where she continued to be active in women's suffrage and labour politics. Married for forty-one years to John Sanders, she died in 1973 aged 91.

The plaque is at 9 Warrels Mount, Bramley (LS13 3NU). It was sponsored by Leeds Civic Trust and Bramley Ward Councillors, and unveiled by Dr Jill Liddington on 30 April 2015.

Leonora Cohen JP, OBE (1873-1978)

Leading suffragette famous for smashing a showcase in the Jewel House at the Tower of London and for her hunger strike at Armley Gaol in 1913. Lived here 1923-1936.

Leonora was born in Hunslet but five years later her father, a skilled stone carver, died leaving her mother to bring up three young children alone, supporting the family by her earnings as a seamstress. Despite ill health and minimal schooling, Leonora made a successful career as a milliner and married Henry Cohen, the couple moving to Harehills. Influenced by her mother's experience of hardship and inability to improve her lot, she contrasted that with drunken men going to vote. She joined the Leeds Women's Social & Political Union.

In 1911 a new Reform Bill was introduced widening the male franchise, but not providing votes for women; this outraged suffragettes. Leonora then became more deeply involved in the campaign, volunteering to attend a meeting of the W.S.P.U. in Caxton Hall, London, where she later took part in smashing government office windows. She was arrested, appeared at Bow Street Magistrates Court and was sent to Holloway Prison for seven days, a transforming moment for her. She now began a new career as a militant suffragette addressing open air meetings which could easily turn violent. Despite continued campaigning,

Asquith's Liberal Government remained unwilling to give women the vote. This led in January 1913 to an outburst of window smashing of central London shops. Leonora was not happy about attacks on civilians' windows, so she looked in the Tourist Guide for a target and decided on the Crown Jewels display in the Tower of London, throwing an iron bar over school boys' heads to smash a glass cabinet. She was at once arrested and sent for trial where she conducted her own defence and was acquitted on a technicality.

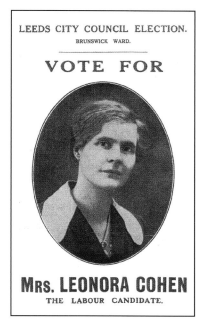

LEEDS CITY COUNCIL ELECTION.
BRUNSWICK WARD.

VOTE FOR

Mrs. LEONORA COHEN
THE LABOUR CANDIDATE.

The Suffragette campaign gathered pace. In November 1913 Asquith was in Leeds for a Liberal rally and Leonora was arrested as she was about to throw a stone at the Labour Exchange and remanded to Armley Prison, where she at once went on hunger and thirst strike. Due to poor health, Leonora was released early from her sentence on licence. On the outbreak of the First World War, suffragette campaigning ceased. Leonora became a munitions worker at Leeds Forge and joined the General and Municipal Workers Union.

In 1918 women over 30 gained the right to vote. By 1922 Leonora was district organiser for the Union. She became the first woman President of the Yorkshire Federation of Trades Councils in 1923 and was appointed a Leeds magistrate, holding office for twenty-five years. Leonora was awarded the OBE in 1928 to recognise 'her contribution to Leeds Public Life'.

The plaque is at 2 Claremont Villas, Clarendon Road (LS2 9NY). It was sponsored by the house's owner, Patrick O'Toole and several others, and was unveiled on 9 June 2007 by Michael Meadowcroft, electoral reformer and former Liberal MP for Leeds West.

T E Harvey (1875-1955)

Leeds born and bred and a profoundly committed Quaker, he was a politician, social reformer, British Museum curator, Warden of Toynbee Hall and a Quaker historian. When Liberal MP for Leeds West (1910-18) he successfully campaigned for the rights of conscientious objectors during the First World War. Lived here 1923-1955.

Thomas Edmund Harvey was born into a prominent Quaker family in Leeds in 1875. Brought up in the city, he received a deeply enriching education successively at Bootham School in York, the Yorkshire College in Leeds, Christ Church College, Oxford, the University of Berlin, and finally at the Sorbonne in Paris. He became committed to a life with a social reforming purpose. After university, he initially worked as an assistant in the Prints Department of the British Museum from 1900 to 1904, while living at Toynbee Hall – the university settlement house, where future leaders could live and work as volunteers amongst the poor of London's East End in the hope that their experience would help bring about radical social change. He remained at the Hall becoming its Warden from 1906 to 1911.

Meanwhile, he began his political career being elected a member of London County Council in 1904 and serving on its Education Committee until 1907. He also served, until 1910, as a member of the Central (Unemployed) Body, the organisation responsible for registering those unemployed men applying for unemployment relief and finding work for them.

In January 1910 he was elected as Liberal MP for Leeds West. As a Quaker he was a pacifist and, along with his brother-in-law Arnold Rowntree, was a staunch advocate in Parliament of the cause of peace throughout the First World War. He took up relief work in France and in Parliament supported the interests of the conscientious objectors to military service under the National Service Acts. He was the author of the amendments which allowed conscientious objectors to undertake work of national importance as an alternative to combatant or non-combative service.

His pacifist stance drew substantial criticism from his constituents, and he stood down at the election in 1918. From 1920 to 1921 he was Warden of the Leeds Swarthmore Settlement, but in 1923 he became Liberal MP for Dewsbury, though losing the seat to Labour the following year. In 1937 he successfully stood as an Independent Progressive candidate for the Combined English Universities seat saying, at the time, that the contest for this should be fought on ideas and not on party political lines. He held the seat until 1945 when he stood down aged 70. Leeds was very much his home from the 1920s. He lived in the impressive villa, Rydal House, on Grosvenor Terrace in Headingley from 1923 until his death in 1955.

Alongside his political career, Harvey wrote many devotional books about the Quakers; his first book, The Rise of the Quakers, published in 1905, is regarded as the most comprehensive modern history of the movement.

The plaque is on the boundary wall of Rydal House, 5 Grosvenor Terrace (LS6 2DY). It was sponsored by Dr Jon Wood and Dr Julia Kelly and unveiled on 6 July 2016 by Michael Meadowcroft, former Liberal MP for Leeds West.

Sir Charles Wilson MP (1859-1930)

Lived here at Brandsby Lodge 1902-27. Through sheer force of personality from 1907 for over 20 years he led Leeds City Council, though his Conservative Party was in the minority. A municipal imperialist, who famously declared 'I am Leeds', he wanted Leeds' fiefdom to extend from the Pennines to the sea.

Charles Wilson was born in Brandsby-cum-Stearsby near Easingwold and worked first as a railway clerk and then as an accountant. A teetotaller and Anglican, he led a young men's Bible class while also soldiering with the Royal Engineers Volunteers. He was a Conservative with a typical Victorian belief in self-improvement through hard work and commitment to personal public service. In 1890 he began his long career in Leeds local government by being elected councillor for the North Ward. In 1904 he became Leader of the Conservatives and when they became the largest party on the Council in 1907, he became an alderman.

A long period of Conservative dominance was maintained by Wilson, as Leader of the Council and also Chairman of its Finance Committee. Extremely adept at political manoeuvring, he maintained control with the support of the declining Liberal party, allowing them a disproportionate share of aldermanships and committee places. He managed to avoid dividing the anti-socialist vote during elections. At the onset of the First World War he and Sir Edward Brotherton took the lead in forming the Leeds Pals battalion. Later on he took command of the Leeds Group of Motor Transport Volunteers.

Wilson was strongly in favour of home ownership, saying in Council that 'people who buy their house turn Tory directly – we shall go on making Tories, and you (Socialists) will be wiped out' (laughter). His 'municipal imperialism' led to the city's acquisition of Shadwell, Roundhay, Crossgates and Seacroft in 1911; Middleton in 1919; Adel in 1924; and Temple Newsam, Alwoodley, Eccup and Austhorpe in 1927. He said 'There is nothing foolish about me

Charles Wilson c. 1923.

saying "I AM LEEDS" because I claim to represent Leeds – the spirit of Leeds – that will not be beaten by anything or anybody.' He was made a Freeman of Leeds and an Hon. LLD of Leeds University, was knighted for his 'public and political services' and in 1923, at the age of 64, entered Parliament as MP for Central Leeds, serving for six years.

In Charles Wilson's time Leeds City Council was a more obvious focal point of the city's life than it is now. He had the energy and political skill to initiate and carry through many projects. He left his mark on Leeds with the Headrow rebuilding scheme, the acquisition of the Temple Newsam Estate and the considerable extensions to the city's boundaries.

The plaque is on the wall in front of Brandsby Lodge, now part of the Northern School of Contemporary Dance on Chapeltown Road (LS7 4BH). It was sponsored by Chapeltown Heritage Advisory Group and unveiled on 18 May 2011 by the Lord Mayor of Leeds, Councillor James McKenna.

Brandsby Lodge.

The Revd Charles Jenkinson (1887-1949)

Vicar of Holbeck, transplanted his congregation here in 1937-1938, having become a Leeds City Councillor in 1930 to drive through a massive and highly controversial programme of inner city slum clearance. He replaced the slums with the world famous Quarry Hill Flats and greenfield Council housing estates at Middleton, Belle Isle, Gipton, Halton, and Seacroft.

for housing reform and in 1933 he and two other Labour councillors issued a report, 'Housing Policy in the City of Leeds', proposing that slum dwellings be cleared at an annual rate of 3,000 up to 1948, that a housing committee be established, and a housing director appointed. These proposals gained wide circulation and provided the blueprint for the brilliant housing programme of the Labour controlled Council in 1933-36. Under his energetic chairmanship the new Housing Committee, with support from R. A. H. Livett, Chief Housing Officer, succeeded in re-housing 6,000 slum dwellers in two years. Plans were made for spacious new estates and Quarry Hill Flats.

Jenkinson lost his seat in 1936 and concentrated on supervising the move of his own congregation from Holbeck to a new estate at Belle Isle. Returning to the Council in 1943, he became Leader of the Labour Group in 1947, and alderman responsible for implementing the city's housing policy. Nationally recognised as a housing expert, he was appointed Chairman of Stevenage New Town Development Corporation in 1948, but within nine months he was dead, at 62, a victim of cancer. His housing reforms were a remarkable feat for a working Anglican priest, demonstrating the public role a strong clergyman could still play within the local community in the 1930s.

Charles Jenkinson was born in Poplar, East London in 1887. His first job at age 14 was in bookkeeping. He joined the Independent Labour Party in 1908. During the First World War, he was a pacifist but served in the Royal Army Medical Corps. From 1919 he studied for a law degree at Fitzwilliam Hall, Cambridge, before entering Ripon Hall, an Oxford theological college. His request to be appointed to 'the hardest parish in the country' was met when he became vicar of St John and St Barnabas, Holbeck, Leeds. Arriving with his wife and son in July 1927, he found a parish of back-to-back slums, public houses and betting shops. Full of energy, he set up a Thursday evening 'Parliament' with rousing debates and visiting speakers, established a Sunday forum and held open-air services with a band.

His greatest challenge was the terribly inadequate and insanitary housing of his parish. Encouraged by growing Anglican concern about the plight of slum-dwellers, in 1930 he gained election to Leeds City Council as Labour councillor for the North Holbeck Ward. He campaigned vigorously

The plaque is on St John & St Barnabas Church, Belle Isle Road (LS10 3DN). It was sponsored by the Diocese of Ripon & Leeds and unveiled on 12 February 2012 by the Lord Mayor of Leeds, Councillor Revd Alan Taylor.

Quarry Hill Flats.

Leeds & County Liberal Club

From parliamentary and municipal reform in the 1830s to 1894 the Liberal Party dominated politics in Leeds. This splendid club in Welsh terracotta opened in 1891. Crowds were addressed from its balcony 'on occasions of political excitement'. Architects: Chorley & Connon.

The dining room provided excellent lunches and dinners for members and their guests and by 1894 the club had 1,650 members paying three guineas a year membership fee.

One of the most interesting features of the building is the large covered balcony, open at the sides, from which crowds in the street could be addressed on 'occasions of political excitement'. Many of the internal features of the club can still be seen today including the five stained glass windows overlooking the grand 7-foot wide oak staircase which include the arms of fourteen Yorkshire towns and cities, emphasising the county element of the club.

With the decline of the Liberal Party the membership of the club fell and by the 1920s part of the building, renamed Quebec House, had been let off as offices. The club continued to occupy part of the premises until 1947, when the property was entirely converted to offices. In the 1950s it was the offices of Leeds Chamber of Commerce and Leeds & District Chamber of Trade. Subsequently, it was acquired by the National Employers' Association and renamed National Employers' House. Today the building is owned by the Norwich Union Property Trust Ltd and in 2002 a lease was taken by the Eton Group which renovated it as the luxurious Quebecs Hotel.

The plaque is on the front of Quebecs Hotel in Quebec Street (LS1 2HA). It was sponsored by the Wainwright family and unveiled on 13 July 2004 by Mrs Joyce Wainwright, widow of Richard Wainwright, former Liberal MP for Colne Valley.

The Liberal Party dominated politics in Leeds for most of the nineteenth century, controlling the Council for the whole period from 1835 to 1894, and in the 1880s and 90s three of the five Leeds MPs were Liberals. In 1880 the Prime Minister, W. E. Gladstone, was elected MP for Leeds, although the seat was taken by his son, Herbert. The party controlled the Council again from 1904 until 1907 but thereafter, with the exception of a short Conservative-Liberal Democrat coalition, the city has been run by either Conservative or Labour administrations.

The Leeds and County Liberal Club was founded in 1881 and moved to its prestigious purpose-built premises in Quebec Street in 1891. Designed by the Leeds architects Robert Chorley and J. Wreghitt Connon (both active Liberals), it was one of a small number of highly distinctive buildings in Leeds city centre made in terracotta brickwork and mouldings supplied by J. C. Edwards of Ruabon in Wales. The facilities of the club were luxurious and included a smoking room, large dining room, reading room, three billiard rooms, grill room, private dining rooms, card rooms, and members' bedrooms.

Leeds Civic Hall

Was erected 1930-1933 by the unemployed building workers of Leeds. Its magnificent accommodation included Lord Mayor's ceremonial rooms, Council Chamber, committee rooms and offices. It was built to serve the 'ever-expanding municipal functions and duties' of Leeds City Council. Architect: Vincent Harris.

The building of the Civic Hall was a magnificent job creation scheme. Leeds Town Hall had been built in 1858 as the centre of local government administration but, as the Council's work rapidly expanded, various departments became scattered around the city. During the Depression of the 1920s unemployment in Leeds was very high, reaching 17% in 1930 and 21% in 1931. The Council seized on an opportunity to both create jobs for unemployed building workers and solve the problem of the inadequate accommodation for its staff. It applied to the Government's Unemployed Grants Committee for a grant towards the building of a Civic Hall and in July 1930 it was successful, subject to the condition that the building work must start by 1st October 1930 and finish within two and a half years. The workforce was to contain mainly workers who were wholly or partly unemployed.

The architect, Vincent Harris (1876-1971), produced a memorable building on an awkwardly shaped site. He had absorbed classical styles of architecture in his Plymouth childhood and his professional studies. His major works included Glamorgan City Hall; Braintree Town Hall; Surrey County Hall, Kingston; and Manchester Central Library. He was later responsible for Sheffield City Hall, also built by many unemployed workers; five buildings on Exeter University Campus; Manchester Town Hall extension; County Hall Trent Bridge; the Council House, Bristol; St Mary's College, Durham University; Whitehall M.O.D. Office Blocks; and Kensington Public Library.

Leeds Civic Hall in 1983.

Building materials and labour were relatively cheap in the 1930s and, with the aid of the large government grant, the Council was able to erect a municipal building with a degree of sumptuousness which we are never likely to see again. The principal effect was to remove both the Lord Mayor and the City Council from the Town Hall to new magnificent accommodation. The Lord Mayor was provided with a splendid suite of rooms, while the Council was provided with a Banqueting Hall, an imposing new Council Chamber and elaborately panelled committee rooms. Other parts of the building accommodated the Departments of the Town Clerk, the City Treasurer, the City Engineer, the Waterworks Engineer, the Sewerage Engineer and the Baths Superintendent. The building was opened by King George V and Queen Mary on 23 August 1933 amidst much pomp and circumstance.

The plaque is by the entrance to the Civic Hall on Portland Crescent (LS1 1UR). It was sponsored by Leeds City Council and unveiled on 10 June 2002 by Mr George Williamson, a former apprentice joiner who worked on the construction of the building.

Architect Vincent Harris.

Leeds Trades Club

Erected in 1934-36 as the Jewish Institute, from 1974 until 1994 this handsomely appointed Art Deco building was the headquarters of Leeds Trades Council. Housing trade union offices, meeting rooms and extensive social facilities, including a lounge and concert hall, it was the vibrant hub of the trade union movement in Leeds. Architect: G. Alan Burnett.

The Jewish Institute had its origins in the Jewish Young Men's Society, founded in 1896 and based in premises on North Street, which provided a range of activities for Leeds Jews. As the community moved out of its Leylands heartland into Chapeltown, there was a need for a new base for the Institute and the new building in Savile Mount was erected. It continued to provide the same social functions as its predecessor and by 1939 had some 3,500 members. By 1970, however, membership had greatly declined as the Jewish community had moved out of Chapeltown and the Institute closed.

In 1974 the building was bought by Leeds Trades Council and reopened as the Leeds Trades Club. The Trades Council had been established in 1860 and by 1868 twenty-seven mainly small local craft-based unions had affiliated to it; a number which grew slowly over the years. The Trades Council met monthly and from its early days considered establishing a trades hall to provide central premises for union activities. It finally achieved this at the turn of the twentieth century when it acquired premises in Upper Fountaine Street, shared with the National Union of Boot and Shoe Operatives and the Gasworkers' and General Labourers' Union. When these premises were demolished the Trades Council moved to Savile Mount, where it was able to establish a social side to its facilities as well as providing meeting and committee rooms and, in the Concert Room, an excellent hall for large meetings. In 1984 Leeds Jazz was established to bring the best of international jazz to the city and the Trades Club Hall was the main venue for these concerts, which are commemorated in the reception area of the building.

In 1994 the Trades Council moved to new premises in North Street as it wished to concentrate on trade union matters. In its heyday while at Savile Mount the Trades Council was a hive of activity playing an important role in the life of busy industrial Leeds, for example sending delegates to sit on many different city committees, both to influence city affairs and to network with influential people.

In 2001 the Trades Club building found new life as the Host Media Centre, a modern multi-media studio space. In 2014 it became the broadcasting studios of the new 'Made in Leeds' TV channel.

The plaque is on the front of the building adjacent to the former main entrance on Savile Mount (LS7 3HZ). It was sponsored by three trade unions; Unite, GMB and Unison, and was jointly unveiled on 1 May 2013 by representatives of the three unions – Dick Banks, Bill Chard and Brian Mulvey.

Left to right: Bill Chard (GMB), Councillor Jane Dowson, Brian Mulvey (Unison), Dick Banks (Unite).

The New Penny

This late Victorian public house was formerly known as the Hope and Anchor. Since 1953 it has provided a safe venue for the Lesbian, Gay, Bisexual and Trans* community both before and following the decriminalisation of homosexuality in 1967. Renamed The New Penny in 1975, it is one of the longest continually running LGB & T* venues in the UK.

Until the 1960s, sex generally was not discussed openly in society, and certainly not homosexuality or lesbianism. When the Wolfenden Report was published in 1957 with the recommendation that 'homosexual behaviour between consenting adults in private should no longer be a criminal offence' attitudes slowly began to change. In 1967 homosexuality was decriminalised, though much prejudice against gay people persisted for several decades. David Thornton, in his *Leeds – A Historical Dictionary* notes that during the years when homosexuality was illegal, casual meetings of men often took place in Leeds, the oldest established meeting place between the wars probably being the Mitre in Commercial Street. Other public houses used by gay men and lesbian women were the King Edward in King Edward Street and the Golden Cock in Kirkgate, whilst bars in the Metropole Hotel and the Great Northern Hotel were used, but by men only. The Royal Hotel in Briggate was where homosexual men and lesbian women met in separate bars, but when these closed the clientele moved to the Hope and Anchor on Call Lane.

The Hope and Anchor, renamed the New Penny in 1975, provided a safe haven for the lesbian, gay, bisexual and transgender community from the 1950s. Though Parliament had decriminalised homosexuality in 1967, the Act had stipulated that homosexual acts must not take place in public places and must not involve more than two people. The Hope and Anchor received national profile on 24 March 1968 when an article appeared in the sensationalist national newspaper *The People* lambasting what it regarded as the lewd and outrageous behaviour of men and women in the pub. 'The Police must put a stop to it', it demanded! This is going on 'not in sinful Soho or permissive Paddington but in the homely, respectable town of Leeds!' It reported that men, 'heavily made up and smelling of perfume were dancing cheek to cheek to the music of a jukebox, and others were kissing passionately on the dance floor and in secluded corners; some wore women's clothes and charm bracelets, and people watched without a murmur! ... Girls too danced together and kissed – many of the girls wore men's hairstyles, suits, shirts and ties.' But the sympathetic and motherly landlady, Cathy Wilson, declared that 'About 90 per cent of my customers are queer or lesbian. They spend all their time and money in here. If I threw them out, where could

they go? They come in here because they regard it as their pub and I get no trouble. I would rather run a pub like this for these people than have a pub full of some of the normal types we have in Leeds. They live in a world of their own and they are no trouble at all. They have really nowhere else to go without getting ridiculed.' 'But', ranted *The People*, 'do we really want pubs like this?'

Fortunately, since those days, a much more enlightened attitude to the lesbian, gay, bisexual and transgender community has developed in Britain. Around 1971 Leeds' first gay club, Charlie's opened in Queen's Court off Briggate, and, in the twenty-first century, Leeds gay village, as it is sometimes referred to, has grown up around Lower Briggate. In 2006 the annual Leeds Pride celebration was launched, and its parade has become bigger and more spectacular every year.

At the unveiling of the New Penny blue plaque, a man of about 65 years old talked very movingly about the social and emotional difficulties of growing up as a young gay man in working-class Hunslet in the 1960s, and how being able to go to the safe haven of the New Penny and meet other gay people had been a turning point in his life – for the first time it made him feel at ease with himself. Hearing him speak, and witnessing the joy of the gay community at the unveiling of the plaque, left absolutely no doubt about the value and importance of including it in the Trust's blue plaques scheme.

The plaque, which is on the front of The New Penny on Call Lane (LS1 7BT), was sponsored by Leeds City Council and unveiled on 19 October 2016 by the Deputy Leader of Leeds City Council, Councillor James Lewis.

Leeds Rifles

A volunteer corps raised by resolution of Leeds Town Council in 1859 when the Government feared the French might invade Britain. This headquarters, Carlton Barracks, was built in 1887 and remained the home of the Leeds Rifles until disbandment in 1969.

Carlton Barracks.

By 1858 relations between Britain and France had become very strained at a time when the French navy was becoming equipped with new ironclad steam-powered warships. Fearing possible invasion when the army was committed to garrisoning the overseas Empire, the War Office authorised Lord Lieutenants to raise a new volunteer force for the defence of Britain, made up of rifle companies throughout the country and artillery volunteers for the defence of coastal towns. The first Leeds company of three officers and one hundred riflemen was formed in September 1859 and by August 1860 there were nine rifle companies at Chapeltown, Monkbridge Ironworks, Wellington Foundry, Greenwood & Batley and Tetley's Brewery, which all became part of 7th Yorkshire West Riding Rifle Volunteer Corps. The Leeds Rifles wore a steel grey uniform, and an 1855-style shako helmet which bore a coiled bugle horn badge bearing 'Leeds Rifles' on a scroll. In 1887 they moved from their Oxford Row Drill Hall to Carlton Barracks and from then on wore Rifleman dark green uniforms.

In 1900 a volunteer Leeds Rifle Company was sent to the Boer War in South Africa, joining the regular soldiers of 2nd Battalion, The Prince of Wales Regiment. Later they manned an armoured train and adopted the continuous blockhouse system. In the First World War the Leeds Rifles had six battalions involved in the action and 2,050 Leeds Riflemen were killed and thousands more were wounded in 43 months continuous service in front line trenches. They fought at Ypres Salient on the Somme and Cambrai, where they supported massed tanks being used in battle for the first time. They took part in the recapture of Bligny Ridge,

following which the Commander of the French 5th Army decorated the Battalion with the 'Croix de Guerre avec Palme en Bronze'.

In the Second World War the Leeds Rifles were split into anti-aircraft gunners and tank regiments. The 45th Tank Regiment fought for five days and nights in the critical battle of El Alamein, helping Montgomery to gain the critical victory against Rommel, but losing three-quarters of their Sherman tanks in the process. The 51st Tank Regiment fought in North Africa in 1943, and in the Italian Campaign on the 'Hitler Line' with Canadian Infantry. With British Infantry they overcame the 'Gothic Line' and 'Rimini Line', and were involved with Polish Infantry in the final battle in Italy.

The Leeds Rifles continued to be a part of the Territorial Army under various units until disbandment in 1969.

The plaque is on a stone column at the entrance to Carlton Barracks, Carlton Gate (LS7 1HE). It was sponsored by the Reserve Forces and Cadet Association, Yorkshire and Humberside, and unveiled on 8 November 2006 by Dr Ingrid Roscoe FSA, Lord Lieutenant of West Yorkshire.

Dr Ingrid Roscoe, Lord Lieutenant of West Yorkshire, and Lieutenant Colonel Gerald Jarrett, the last commanding officer of the Leeds Rifles

Barnbow Royal Ordnance Factory

Was built 1939-40 to make armaments for the Second World War. Employing at its peak 3000 workers, including 2000 women, it provided around 9000 guns, 6 and 25 pounders, 3.7 inch anti-aircraft shells, 40mm Bofors and 17 pounders for Sherman tanks. Between 1945 and closure in 1999, over 4000 Centurion, Chieftain and Challenger tanks were built there.

The names 'Barnbow' and 'Barnbow Lasses' are now most famously associated with the highly-important First World War Leeds munitions factory sited between Cross Gates and Garforth, whose buildings were demolished in the 1930s. In 1939, however, the Ministry of War bought a 60-acre greenfield site at Manston Lane, Crossgates (one mile from the site of the original Barnbow factory), on which it built the Barnbow Royal Ordnance Factory, which became noted above all for the manufacture of tanks.

The new factory was built quickly, and from 1940 production centred on barrels and breech-blocks for light and medium guns, primarily 6, 17 and 25 pounders. By the end of the war almost 9,000 barrels and breech-blocks had been produced for the army and navy. Barnbow's involvement with tanks began just before D-Day with the fitting of a 17-pounder gun to the American Sherman M4 tank, known as the Firefly. The 17-pounder was the final wartime effort to produce a gun effective against German tank armour.

On the battlefields of the Second World War the tank had proved to be the decisive weapon. Thereafter the Cold War soon began and the West needed to counter the threat of Russian armour in Europe. ROF Barnbow was chosen to manufacture Centurion Mark 1 (Cruiser Type) tanks. By 1962 a total of 4,423 Centurions (both Mark 1 and 2) had been built of which 2,392 were made in Leeds.

Tanks ready for transporting from Barnbow.

The Centurion was succeeded by the Chieftain tank which entered army service in 1963. Its specially-designed multi-fuel engine overcame the range limitations imposed on the Centurion by the use of a petrol engine. By the time the Chieftains were withdrawn from service in 1996, 640 of them had been made in Leeds, many for export to the Middle East. The ageing Chieftains were replaced by the Challenger tank which was designed to provide a more stable platform when firing on the move. Barnbow made 243 of them between 1982 and 1990. The Gulf War provided an opportunity to show what Challenger was capable of. The first model was followed by Challenger 2, an altogether more sophisticated tank.

When the Royal Ordnance was privatised in 1986, the Leeds factory was bought by Vickers Defence Systems and new investment was made. But the reduction in demand for tanks due to the end of the Cold War led to a more than halving of its 3,000-strong workforce. The remaining 600 workers were made redundant in 1999. Barnbow's vital contribution to the defence of the nation and another world-famous sector of Leeds engineering had come to an end.

The plaque is on the former factory gates, Austhorpe Road (LS15 8FS). It was sponsored by Bellway Homes and East Leeds Historical and Archaeological Society, and unveiled on 20 April 2015 by Mrs Val Orrell, a former Barnbow employee.

Lynda Kitching, Val Orrell, and Jacki Lawrence.

Art & Culture

Over the centuries Leeds has produced men and women of great intellectual and artistic ability, and has established influential institutions to promote the intellectual and cultural advancement of its inhabitants. During the first fifteen years of the blue plaques scheme, plaques were erected for the Restoration dramatist William Congreve, the children's author Arthur Ransome, and the distinguished artist Atkinson Grimshaw; the importance of Leeds College of Art was also recognised. More recent plaques concerning the sphere of education have been noted earlier in this book. Though the section which follows discusses only seven plaques, the people and institutions which they celebrate span the spheres of philosophy, science, literature, music, and the visual arts of painting and sculpture across three centuries.

Oulton-born Richard Bentley was one of the eighteenth century's most outstanding classical and religious scholars and a philologist; while in 1768 the Leeds Library was founded, now the country's oldest surviving proprietary library. In the early nineteenth century the Leeds elite founded the Leeds Philosophical and Literary Society to be a permanent forum for intellectual and scientific inquiry. Towards the end of the century, Frank

Kidson, a Leeds man of wide cultural interests, achieved distinction as an expert on ceramics but, above all, as a national authority on folk music and popular song.

In the early 1900s a rather bohemian set of Leeds people, some eighty years after the founding of the 'Phil & Lit', established the influential Leeds Art Club which for two decades took an avant-garde interest in politics, philosophy, art and literature. Meanwhile, in the Edwardian period and beyond, the University of Leeds (the renamed Yorkshire College founded in 1874) continued to bring a procession of leading academics to Leeds. In the 1920s, two and a half centuries after Richard Bentley, another renowned philologist and subsequently famous author, J. R. R. Tolkien, came to teach at the university. The association of the sculptors Henry Moore and Barbara Hepworth with Leeds College of Art is very well known, but another of its distinguished alumni was the sculptor Kenneth Armitage, who was brought up in Leeds and whose sculptures adorn the city today.

The Leeds Library, Commercial Street in 1816.

Richard Bentley, FRS, DD (1662-1742)

Born in 4-5 Bentley Square; educated at Wakefield Grammar School and Cambridge; Keeper of the King's Library at St James and Master of Trinity College, Cambridge. His brilliant translations and reappraisal of classical texts made him one of England's greatest and most controversial scholars.

Richard Bentley was born at his maternal grandparents' house in Oulton. He was the second child of Thomas Bentley, yeoman farmer, and his wife Sarah née Willies. In 1676 he enrolled as an undergraduate at St John's College, Cambridge, where he studied logic, ethics, natural philosophy, and mathematics. He was awarded his BA degree in 1680 and MA in 1683. In January 1683 he became tutor to James Stillingfleet, whose father, Edward, was Dean of St Paul's Cathedral. Over the next six years Bentley took advantage of Dean Stillingfleet's outstanding library to consolidate his knowledge of the classics and scripture.

Henry Compton, Bishop of London, ordained Bentley deacon in 1690, and Edward Stillingfleet, now Bishop of Worcester, soon made him his chaplain. In 1691 Bentley wrote a letter in Latin to John Mill, Principal of St Edmund's Hall, Oxford, which instantly made his reputation and was published as a 98-page appendix to the *Histora Chronica* by John Malalas of Antioch (c.480-570). Scholars throughout Europe were impressed. In 1692 Robert Boyle bequeathed £50 per annum for eight sermons 'proving the Christian religion'. Bentley was appointed the first Boyle Lecturer; his first set of sermons were specifically against atheists and they were frequently reprinted. John Moore, Bishop of Norwich, ordained him priest in September 1692. In December 1693 he was appointed Keeper of the King's Libraries, and soon assumed custody of the St James' Palace Library. In 1695 he was appointed Chaplain-in-Ordinary to King William III, and elected Fellow of the Royal Society. In 1696 Bentley was created Doctor of Divinity at Cambridge.

RICHARD BENTLEY

In 1697 Bentley's Dissertation upon Epistles of Phalaris was published in *Reflections upon Ancient and Modern Learning*. He proved that the letters of King Phalaris could not have been written by him for stylistic, historical and chronological reasons and his philology destroyed a complacent humanist illusion of familiarity with the ancient world. In December 1699 he was named Master of Trinity College, Cambridge. He was elected vice chancellor at Cambridge in 1700. Bentley corresponded with continental scholars and worked hard on his new edition of Horace and many other texts. Much of his unpublished work had to wait until nineteenth century scholars took it up. Through the enthusiasm of the German academics the full range of Richard Bentley's work has been understood. His command of Latin, Greek and Biblical Studies was prodigious, and his grasp of critical principles has confirmed him as one of the greatest ever scholars.

The plaque is on the old chapel in Bentley Square, adjacent to the house where Richard Bentley was born, off Calverley Road, Oulton (LS26 8JH). It was sponsored by The Oulton Society, and unveiled by their vice chairman, Malcolm Brocklesby, on 7 June 2006.

Bentley's birthplace.

The Leeds Library

A proprietary subscription library founded in 1768 with Joseph Priestley as Secretary. Since 1808 it has occupied these purpose-built premises designed by Thomas Johnson. The first floor reading room and Thomas Ambler's 'New Room' extension are among the architectural wonders of Leeds.

The Leeds Library is the oldest surviving proprietary subscription library in the British Isles. It was founded in 1768 by 104 affluent townspeople, each subscriber contributing an initial guinea and an annual subscription of 5 shillings. Subscription libraries had been set up from the 1750s in response to an increased interest in reading at a time when there were no rate-supported public libraries. The most famous of the original subscribers was Dr Joseph Priestley, the distinguished scientist and minister of Mill Hill Unitarian Chapel, who came to Leeds in 1767 from Warrington, where he had taken a leading part in developing the Warrington Circulating Library. He was the first Secretary of the Leeds Library, from 1768-9, and elected second President from 1769-73, leaving Leeds in 1773 to take up the post of private librarian and literary companion to Lord Shelburne.

The first librarian was Joseph Ogle, a bookseller whose shop was at 'the Sign of the Dial' at Kirkgate End. The new library occupied a room at the back of his shop. Ogle supplied new books and attended to members. The original collection consisted of 503 volumes, but by the time the decision to move to larger premises was taken in 1781, the library had 319 members and 2,300 volumes. These second premises were also

Leeds Library main room.

in Kirkgate in the grand former home of Sir James Ibbetson. Joseph Ogle's daughter, Mary, had taken over as librarian when her father died in 1774; she married John Robinson, a bookseller, and the couple moved with the library to its second home and ran a new booksellers' shop at the same address.

Requiring much larger premises, in 1806 the library purchased a plot of land in the new Commercial Street where the elegant building, which the library still occupies today, was erected to the designs of Thomas Johnson. The library, which opened on 1 July 1808, had four shops on the ground floor, the rents from which have made a major contribution

to its long survival. When additional space for books was required by the late 1870s, the fine 'New Room' was added to the back of the building to the designs of Thomas Ambler. In 2008 the library's 500 shareholders gave up their proprietary rights so that the library could become a charity. Today it has over 1,000 members and is a thriving cultural hub within the city of Leeds.

The plaque is on the front of the Leeds Library at 18 Commercial Street (LS1 6AL). It was sponsored by the Leeds Library and unveiled on 4 September 2007 by the Deputy Lord Mayor, Councillor Revd Alan Taylor.

The Philosophical Hall

The imposing home of the Leeds Philosophical and Literary Society stood here until 1966. Erected in 1821 it became the centre of scientific and cultural life in Leeds, housing a fine museum conveyed to the City in 1921.

Leeds has a long tradition of scientific investigation. In the 1770s three of the most advanced scientists of their age met together in Leeds: John Smeaton, the civil engineer; William Hey, surgeon and one of the founders of Leeds Infirmary; and Joseph Priestley, minister of Mill Hill Chapel. From the end of the Napoleonic Wars in 1815, the country's economy improved, Leeds industry flourished, and the town grew in size and importance. A letter in the Leeds Mercury of 26 September 1818 from 'Leodiensian' pointed out that there was a great demand for a society to foster scientific and literary development in the town. Correspondence continued and a public meeting was held in the Court House in November 1818 chaired by William Hey, at which a philosophical and literary society was formed to discuss 'all the branches of Natural Knowledge and Literature, but excluding all topics of Religion, Politics and Ethics'.

There were no obvious models on which to base the building which would provide a home for the society. Having consulted widely, the members of the building committee bought the site on Park Row and employed as its architect R. D. Chantrell, who had trained with Sir John Soane. Chantrell produced a dignified design in the Greek Revival style. The basement provided residential accommodation for the curator and cellars; the ground floor housed the vestibule, lecture hall and laboratory; and the first floor became the popular museum, which soon became overcrowded, following the invitation to local collectors to deposit their specimens. In 1861-2 it doubled in size when architects Dobson & Chorley created a new lecture hall, a vast zoology gallery, a library and kitchens. They also remodelled the façades of the whole building in the Italianate manner.

The museum's lecture theatre was the centre of scientific and artistic life in the town for over a century and the collection became one of the finest outside London. Speakers included naturalists, scientists, literary figures, musicians, social reformers and later politicians. In the days before television, radio, cinema, or any northern red brick universities, or popular science journals, there was a hunger for some form of intellectual life. In 1921 the building and its collection were given to Leeds City Council and then became known as the City Museum. In the 1920s and 30s school parties visited the museum. For most children who had never travelled and had no books at home, this museum opened their eyes and rolled back their horizons. The building was badly damaged by bombing during the Second World War and demolished in 1966.

This plaque is on HSBC Bank, 33 Park Row (LS1 1LD). It was unveiled on 28 June 2001 by Dr Peter Evenett of the Leeds Philosophical & Literary Society, and sponsored by the Society.

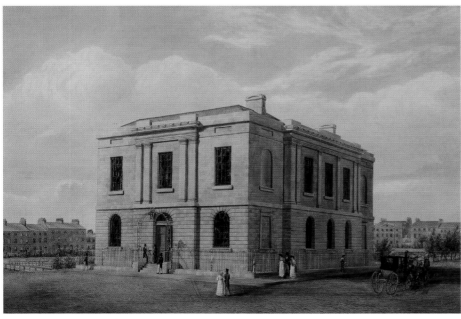

The Philosophical Hall in 1821.

Frank Kidson M.A. (1855-1926)

Musical antiquarian and folk-song collector lived here 1904-1926.

The youngest of nine children, Frank Kidson was born in 1855 at the family home at 7 Centenary Street, close to the future site of Leeds Town Hall. His father, Francis Kidson, was a butcher turned rate-collector. On leaving school, Frank joined his brother, Joseph, who dealt in antiques on Albion Street. After a few years he left Joseph to become a landscape painter. During his travels throughout northern England and the Scottish Borders he was able to develop his early enthusiasm for collecting traditional songs and tunes.

He began to write about painting and music. He wrote two series of articles about folk song for the *Leeds Mercury* and in 1890 published his first book, *Old English Country Dances*, and in 1891 *Traditional Tunes*. In his obituary it was said of *Traditional Tunes* that it was 'of outstanding interest in the history of our folk-song, being the first published collection of non-harmonized, "undoctored", English traditional airs and texts to be accompanied by scholarly notes'. The English Musical Renaissance prompted a growth of interest in traditional song on the premise that composers could use its melodies as source material in creating a characteristically national art music. Kidson was generally accepted by this time as the country's leading authority on traditional song and

he was invited to become a founder member of the Folk Song Society in 1898. He was elected to its committee and was responsible for vetting songs which appeared in the society's journal.

By this time his own interests had expanded to embrace the whole history of English printed music, and his research resulted in the publication of *British Music Publishers* in 1900. He was now regarded as the greatest living authority on early music, and the book his most important publication. In addition, he contributed a remarkable 365 entries to *Grove's Dictionary of Music and Musicians*.

Moving to 5 Hamilton Avenue, Chapeltown, in 1904, he spent the rest of his life working on a second edition, but due to the overwhelming volume of material never completed the task. Nevertheless, his first edition remained authoritative until the publication of *Music Publishing in the British Isles* in 1954.

His interests extended to the history of Leeds and in 1892 he, and his brother Joseph, published *Historical Notices of The Leeds Old Pottery*, until the 1950s the definitive history of the pottery. Frank was a scholar of great modesty and integrity. His considerable achievements were attained without the benefit of any institutional support, but late in his life his work was recognised by the University of Leeds with the award of an honorary MA degree.

This plaque is at 5 Hamilton Avenue, Chapeltown (LS7 4EG). It was sponsored by the Frank Kidson Memorial Fund and unveiled by Dr Vic Gammon, Senior Lecturer in Popular and World Music at the University of Leeds, on 20 May 2003.

The Leeds Arts Club (1903-1923)

A highly influential forum for the avant-garde in politics, philosophy, art and literature met here from 1908. Ground-breaking exhibitions included the 1913 Post-Impressionist show and Cubist and Futurist Art in 1914. Famous speakers included G. B. Shaw and W. B. Yeats.

The Leeds Arts Club was founded in 1903 by Leeds school teacher Alfred Orage and Yorkshire textile manufacturer Holbrook Jackson. It became one of the most advanced modernist cultural centres in Britain before the First World War. The Arts Club placed Leeds in the forefront of modernist thinking by providing a programme which mixed socialist politics, feminism and the spiritualism of theosophy. It also popularised the thought of the German philosopher, Friedrich Nietzsche, helped to develop Guild Socialism and exhibited Impressionist and Post-Impressionist art at a time when such works would never have been accepted at the City Art Gallery. In addition, it was able to attract a host of celebrated speakers, including G. K. and Cecil Chesterton, George Bernard Shaw, Hillaire Belloc, W. B. Yeats, Edward Carpenter, Isabella Ford and Wyndham Lewis.

The club's first home was on the first floor of the Leeds Permanent Building Society, which then stood in front of the Art Gallery. It opened daily 10 a.m. to 10 p.m. with Friday night discussion groups and regular meetings each Saturday afternoon. There were specific groups for music, sketching, poetry and play-reading, a book club and library, and regular exhibitions of architecture, paintings, sculpture, arts and crafts designs, photography, and music recitals. Membership was drawn largely from the local middle classes, including architects, men and women teachers, businessmen and many staff of the newly-established university. In 1907 Orage and Jackson moved to London to edit the influential cultural and political journal, *The New Age*, and in 1908 the club moved to 8 Blenheim Terrace, a roomy three-storey terraced Georgian house, allowing separate sections of the club to meet as required.

From 1912 the club came under the sway of Frank Rutter, the newly appointed Director of Leeds City Art Gallery, and Michael Sadler, the new vice chancellor of Leeds University. Rutter, finding his ambitions to found a modern art collection at the Art Gallery frustrated,

organised a series of avant-garde exhibitions for the club. Jacob Kramer and Herbert Read, who became a major art critic and theorist, also became involved but, by the early 1920s, Rutter, Sadler and Read had left Leeds. Jacob Kramer, returning to the city from London, then became the mainstay of the club in its final years. He organised exhibitions of the Glasgow Boys, a Contemporary Art Society Exhibition turned down by the Art Gallery, and a final exhibition which showed works by Augustus John, Wilson Steer, Spencer Gore and himself.

The plaque is at 8 Blenheim Terrace, Woodhouse Lane (LS2 9HZ). It was sponsored by Mr Ben Read (the son of Herbert Read) and unveiled on 15 May 2012 by Dr Ingrid Roscoe, Lord Lieutenant of West Yorkshire.

J.R.R. Tolkien CBE (1892-1973)

Academic and author lived here between 1924 and 1925. While Reader, later Professor, at the University of Leeds 1920-1925, he collaborated on a new edition of Sir Gawain and the Green Knight. Tolkien went on to write The Hobbit and The Lord of the Rings.

At King Edward's Grammar School, Birmingham, John Tolkien showed a special aptitude for languages and discovered Old and Middle English, Old Norse and Gothic. He won an exhibition (a grant) to Exeter College, Oxford, in 1911, studying classics, and then English. Much concerned with linguistic studies he achieved a first class honours degree in 1915.

After recovering from war service and working with the Oxford English Dictionary, in 1920 Tolkien was appointed Reader in English Language at Leeds University. He lodged initially at 25 St Michael's Road, Headingley. His wife Edith and their infant sons John and Michael joined him in Leeds, and the family rented rooms at 5 Holly Bank, Headingley and then at St Mark's Terrace. University life proved a refreshing change for Edith and the boys. In 1924 the family moved to 2 Darnley Road, West Park, on the edge of the city, where Edith gave birth to their third son Christopher.

George Gordon, Professor of English at Leeds divided the English syllabus into two options; one for studies in post-Chaucerian literature; and the other for studies of Anglo-Saxon and Middle English, which he entrusted to Tolkien. By early 1921 Tolkien had prepared Middle English texts, and a small Middle English dictionary. He now sought a project with greater scope, and collaborated with lecturer E. V. Gordon on a contemporary analysis of 'Sir Gawain and the Green Knight'. Published in 1925 it became the standard college text.

In October 1924 Tolkien was appointed first Professor of English Language at Leeds University, a considerable achievement at age 32. However, in the 1920s the university was still a small institution and Tolkien had his sights upon higher things. In 1925 the Professorship of Anglo-Saxon at Oxford became vacant and Tolkien applied. With support from distinguished colleagues he was successful, and spent the rest of his academic career there. Looking back in 1961 to his time in Leeds, Tolkien said 'I was devoted to the University of Leeds, which was very good to me, and to its students, whom I left with regret.'

A continuing theme in Tolkien's academic work was the conviction that literature and language are not divisible, each informing and illuminating the other. These considerations influenced his growing pre-occupation with early mythology, legends and languages which led to his creation of heroic fantasy – *The Silmarillion* story cycle, the mythological race of hobbits, and the saga of *The Lord of the Rings*, works in book and film that have given great pleasure to millions.

The plaque is at 2 Darnley Road, West Park (LS16 5JF). It was sponsored by The Tolkien Society and the University of Leeds and was unveiled by Dr Kersten Hall on 1 October 2012.

Kenneth Armitage (1916-2002)

Born in Roundhay, he attended Leeds College of Art and the Slade School of Fine Art, London. International recognition followed his selection for the 1952 Venice Biennale. 'Both Arms', 2000, Bronze, was inaugurated by Nelson Mandela in 2001.

Kenneth Armitage was born in Roundhay in 1916. A scholarship from school took him in 1934 to Leeds College of Art. His years there were not fruitful because the college was almost exclusively concerned with painting and graphic work. In 1937 he went on to the Slade School in London where he received proper professional training in sculpture and, influenced by Brancusi, saw himself primarily as a carver, a notion he was later to reject. Like Henry Moore before him he made for the British Museum and was overwhelmed by the Egyptian and Cycladic sculpture.

He served in the British army throughout the Second World War. His final military role as the officer in charge of a course teaching aircraft identification sowed the seed for the work that brought him fame – 'work in which flatness becomes a bulk, an abstraction humanised by the interruption of totemic body parts'.

From 1946-56 he was Head of Sculpture at the Bath Academy of Art, Corsham. The art of bronze casting had been in severe decline because of post-war austerity, but he was instrumental in a foundry being built at Corsham so that work by students and staff could be cast under their own supervision.

At the end of this period he had destroyed all his pre-war carvings and was now finding his mature style to make groups of figures in which a flat membrane envelops upright or buttress supports. 'Two Linked Figures', 'People in the Wind' (now in the Tate Gallery) and 'Friends Walking' are all fine

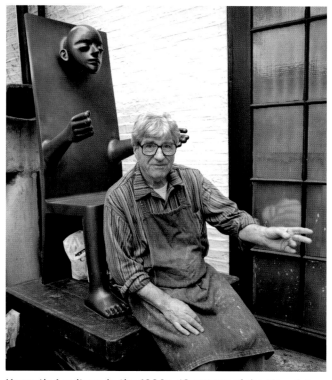

Kenneth Armitage in the 1990s. (Courtesy of the New Art Centre, Roche Court; photographer Anne Purkis).

examples of his most fecund and arguably most expressive period.

He first attracted international attention at the 26th Venice Biennale in 1952. His reputation gathered momentum and was consolidated at the 29th Venice Biennale in 1958 where he won the prize for the best British sculptor under 45.

In 1996 a major show at the Yorkshire Sculpture Park marked his 80th birthday and he accepted an honorary membership of the Royal Academy. Another wonderful year for Armitage was 2001 as it began with a retrospective of his drawings at the Jonathan Clark Gallery and reached a climax with him attending the unveiling by Nelson Mandela of 'Both Arms' as a permanent monument in Millennium Square.

The plaque is on a wall in Nelson Mandela Gardens, Millennium Square (LS2 3AD). It was sponsored by the Kenneth Armitage Foundation and unveiled by the chairman of the Kenneth Armitage Foundation, Robin Hiscox on 5 May 2017.

Legs Walking.

Entertainment

In the eighteenth, nineteenth and twentieth centuries much leisure time in Leeds was spent in inns and alehouses. Whitelocks, the iconic Victorian public house in Turk's Head Yard off Briggate, was popular with many 'Leeds Loiners', notably in the twentieth century when musicians, artists, actors, soldiers and journalists met there regularly. For the Leeds elite the Leeds Club was established in 1852 to bring the sophistication and refinement of a London gentlemen's club to the higher levels of the Leeds business community and society. By the mid nineteenth century popular entertainment in the town was provided by the singing rooms of public houses, and small music halls (the City Varieties was built in 1865), whilst several theatres (largely shunned by the respectable middle classes) were well-patronised. But when the well-named Grand Theatre opened in 1878, it brought both sumptuous style and respectability to theatre-going. At that time, Leeds-born actress Adelaide Neilson was at the height of her international fame – a fame little remembered today because of her early death.

In the early twentieth century the age of mass entertainment began in Leeds with the arrival of cinemas, including the pioneering Cottage Road (1912) and the deluxe Majestic Cinema (1922). Meanwhile, home entertainment was revolutionised by the arrival of the wireless. Local radio broadcasting to the masses began in Leeds in 1924 with the establishment of the Leeds-Bradford Relay Station. The age of the dance hall came in the 1920s and 1930s with the big band swing sound – the mould-breaking Ivy Benson, leader of the famous all-girls swing dance band, came from Leeds. The 1950s and 1960s brought pop and rock music. The most celebrated rock venue in Leeds was the Leeds University Refectory – it was there in 1970 that The Who recorded their now legendary album 'Live at Leeds'. All these places of entertainment and entertainers have been celebrated by blue plaques.

'The Good Old Days' at the City Varieties Music Hall, which received a blue plaque in 1997.

Whitelocks

Occupying a medieval Briggate burgage plot, it was first licensed as the Turk's Head in 1715. Rebuilt by the Whitelock family in the 1880s, it later extended into the row of Georgian working men's cottages. John Betjeman described it as 'the very heart of Leeds'.

Briggate is the focal point of Leeds and reflects the city's evolution over the centuries with its yards, alleys and fashionable Victorian arcades, each of which had a pub in it at one time, or still does. The best-known and best-loved pub in Leeds is Whitelocks in Turk's Head Yard. It opened as the Turk's Head in 1715, catering for merchants who met to do business over a glass of home-brewed ale and a bite to eat. In 1880 John Lupton Whitelock bought the pub and remodelled it six years later, establishing the decor still in evidence today with the long marble-topped bar, mirrors to reflect the warm ambience, polished brass work and cast-iron tables, all contributing to the Victorian atmosphere. John was a showman and astute businessman: he installed electricity in the pub, including a revolving searchlight at the Briggate entrance to the yard. At one time an Irish giant was employed as a doorman to make sure that gentlemen were wearing dinner jackets and ladies sat at tables, while dwarfs were employed as waiters. The pub was run by his descendants until 1944, when Percy Whitelock sold it to Scottish Brewers Ltd.

Whitelocks was a favourite rendezvous with stage stars and Vesta Tilley, Flora Robson, Moira Shearer and Sybil Thorndike all patronised the

Len Hutton (right) being toasted at Whitelocks.

dining room. It even received royal approval when Prince George, later Duke of Kent, entertained a party in a curtained-off section of the restaurant. The Leeds Savage Club met there: a group of writers, artists and musicians, founded by the eccentric Edmund Bogg, a Leeds picture framer and historian who was known as 'T'Owd Chief' because of his idiosyncrasy of wearing a Red Indian chief's headdress. Whitelocks also became a meeting place for military personnel. Former Leeds Lord Mayor Alan Pedley recalled that Whitelocks was renowned throughout the services as the place to go if a soldier, sailor or airman found himself in Leeds.

Whitelocks achieved national fame. It was described by Dr John Rothenstein, Director of the City Art Gallery, as his 'diminutive Bohemia'. He said 'Its seclusion gave it something of the atmosphere of a club. The narrow long dark room, half restaurant and half bar, served as a meeting place for a number of personalities in the artistic, literary, musical and public life of Yorkshire. It also attracted a large number of medical students from Leeds Infirmary, dog fanciers, bookmakers, and the like.'

This plaque is on the wall of Whitelocks First City Luncheon Bar in Turk's Head Yard, Briggate (LS1 6HB). To celebrate it as the 100th plaque erected by Leeds Civic Trust it was sponsored by the Trust. It was unveiled on 23 May 2006 by Sarah Lupton Whitelock, great-great-granddaughter of John Lupton Whitelock.

The Leeds Club

Moved here in 1852. As a prestigious gentlemen's club, it was the meeting place for the town's leading business and professional men. Its lavish classical interior included coffee, smoking and dining rooms, a billiard room, bedrooms and a ballroom. Founded 1849.

The decision to form a committee to set up the Leeds Club was taken at a meeting at the Leeds Court House on 23 March 1849, chaired by Liberal Alderman John Hope Shaw, a solicitor and mayor at the time. The club initially met in rooms within the Stock Exchange in Albion Place, but soon took a lease on two houses on Albion Place built by William Hey (the famous surgeon) but then owned by a Mr Martin. The club purchased the properties in 1861 for £5,300 and began to consider how best to improve them.

Numerous schemes were submitted by eminent architects including Cuthbert Brodrick and Perkin & Backhouse, but none were adopted. There is a curious suggestion in the club's minutes that a scheme submitted by the club's steward was eventually accepted! A mortgage of £9,000 was raised on the security of the building, and the work was supervised by architect Thomas Ambler, (who designed St Paul's House, Park Square, for John Barran). At the AGM in 1864 the alterations were reported as being complete to the general satisfaction of members; the minutes recording that 'the labours have been great and the result of them has provided one of the best club houses in the country'.

The main features of the club building's grand interior remain virtually as they were in 1863 and it has been sympathetically maintained throughout its existence. This Grade II* listed building predates the era of the established political clubs and has seen them all out. Until its closure in 2013 it always asserted its non-political character, and its membership lists included Leeds worthies from both sides of the political divide, as well as many members of no political affiliation. Historically, the club was renowned as a meeting place where business deals were done and decisions made.

The club maintained its prestigious position in Leeds society for over a century but gradual changes in business and social practice had an impact. Fewer business and professional people travelled to 'town' and stayed at their club premises during the week, and the tradition of long lunches began to wane, as did the number of members. In recent years the club reconstituted itself and sought to attract a new generation of members – men and women. However, these efforts came to nothing, and in 2013 the venue ceased to operate as a club. It is now an attractive restaurant, bar and events venue.

The plaque is by the entrance at 3 Albion Place (LS1 6JL). It was sponsored by Mr Bob Isle, Hon. Secretary of the Leeds Club and unveiled on 8 December 2004 by the Lord Mayor, Councillor Chris Townsley.

Leeds Grand Theatre & Opera House

This magnificent theatre opened in 1878. Its transformative renovation in 2005-2008 included the creation of the Howard Assembly Room as an inspiring performance venue. Stars who have appeared here include: Henry Irving, Sarah Bernhardt, Marie Lloyd, Laurence Olivier, Julie Andrews, Margot Fonteyn, Frankie Vaughan, John Tomlinson and Josephine Barstow. In 1978 it became the home of Opera North. Architects: George Corson and James Watson.

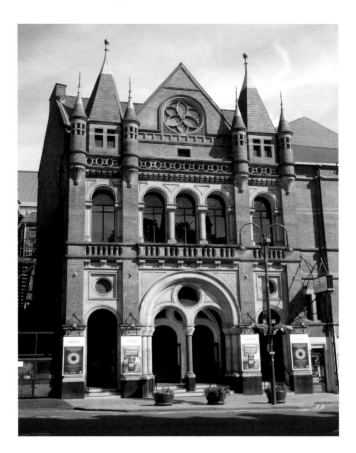

An apparently off-the-cuff remark by Prince Albert, Queen Victoria's consort, inspired the building of the Grand Theatre. Visiting Leeds in 1858 for the opening of the Town Hall, he was told there was not a good theatre in the town and replied 'then you should have one, for nothing is more calculated to promote the culture and raise the tone of a people'. In 1875, the Theatre Royal, Hunslet Lane and the Amphitheatre, Lands Lane burnt down, leaving a cultural vacuum. A meeting of 'influential gentlemen' led to the formation of a company with a capital of £50,000 to build a theatre worthy of Leeds.

George Corson was commissioned to design the theatre. Unusually, it was decided to combine on one site a theatre, an assembly room, a supper room and six shops with frontages to New Briggate. Assisted by James Watson, Corson rose to the challenge, touring major European theatres and opera houses. The heart of the building was from the outset conceived as an opera house. Total seating capacity was 2,600. Until electricity was installed in 1895, gas lit the whole of the Grand, other than the stage, where limelight was used. The height of 30 feet from cellar to stage level came into its own during major productions as a 'good sized castle or ship could be sent up from the regions below'.

The theatre opened on 18 November 1878 with a performance of Shakespeare's *Much Ado About Nothing*. On 4 August 1879 the conjuror Dr Lynn opened the Assembly Rooms, designed to accommodate 1,200 people for many different purposes: bazaars, balls, public meetings, concerts and smaller dramatic performances. In the main theatre, pantomime provided a spectacular offering every festive season. Early programmes for the rest of the year were a mixture of opera, ballet, music hall and plays.

By the 1960s radio and 'the deadlier thrust of television' affected attendances. In 1969 Leeds City Council was discussing plans for an office block on the site, but a widespread campaign against the theatre's closure led to the Council taking a lease and setting up a trust to renovate and operate the theatre. In 1973 the Council bought the Grand and a promise was given that it would remain 'a live theatre, providing the finest touring productions in opera, ballet and drama for the people of Leeds and the West Riding'.

The plaque is on the front of the theatre, to the left of the main entrance, on New Briggate (LS1 6NZ). It was sponsored in memory of Martin Frazer by Richard Adkinson and Martin's family, and unveiled by writer Kay Mellor on 23 July 2013.

Adelaide Neilson (1848-1880)

Renowned international tragic actress was born nearby in St Peter's Square. "Her Juliet was perfect; her Isabella had marvellous earnestness and beauty".

Adelaide Neilson was born in 1848 at 35 St Peter's Square, the daughter of an unmarried strolling player and a Spanish nobleman. As a child she lived in Skipton and then worked at Green Bottom Mill, Guiseley. She was a quick pupil and at an early age recited passages from her mother's playbooks. In 1861 she ran away to London, having apparently learned the secrets of her parentage, and worked as a seamstress and behind the bar in a public house near the Haymarket, where she acquired a reputation as a Shakespearean declaimer. In 1864 she married Philip Henry Lee, who had apparently taken a great interest in her before their marriage and had sent her to a Ladies' Academy.

In 1865 Adelaide made her stage debut at Margate as Julia in Sheridan Knowles' *The Hunchback*, and later made her London debut at the Royalty Theatre, playing the part of Juliet. She was a remarkable beauty of a 'Spanish type' with large dark eyes and a musical voice and her performances made a profound impression on the critics. Over the following years she appeared in many theatres in London, around Britain and across the Atlantic in diverse roles, often creating parts for the first time. Amelia Neville of San Francisco wrote: 'Of all the Juliets I remember leaning over stage balconies, none was so bewitching as Adelaide Neilson, none so moving in later scenes. She was at the height of her fame when she came to San Francisco in 1877. It was a brilliant engagement of adulation and applause.' Adelaide Neilson's last visit to America ended in July 1880 and after her last performance 'she took her final curtain calls with tears in her eyes'.

Her private life was bohemian; she divorced Henry Lee and later became engaged to actor Edward Compton. In August 1880 she and Compton travelled to Paris, possibly to buy their wedding clothes. She drank a glass of iced milk in the Bois de Boulogne, was seized with what was apparently a gastric attack, and died on the same day. She was buried at Brompton Cemetery, leaving an estate of £25,000 which endowed a theatrical charity, the Adelaide Neilson Fund. Joseph Knight, said of her in *The Dictionary of National Biography*: 'As a tragedian she has had no English rival during the last half of the nineteenth century. In comedy she was self-conscious and spoiled her effects by over-acting. The best of her original parts from Walter Scott's novels were Amy Robsart in *Kenilworth* and Rebecca in *Ivanhoe*. It is not easy to see how these could be improved.'

The plaque is by the side entrance to Leeds Playhouse on Quarry Hill. It was sponsored by Professor Neville Rowell, and unveiled by actress Josephine Tewson on 29 January 2008.

Cottage Road Cinema

Opened as the Headingley Picture House on 29th July 1912 by film pioneers Owen Brooks and George Reginald Smith. It occupies a converted motor garage built in 1908 for the owner of nearby Castle Grove. It is the oldest continually operating cinema in Leeds.

in Headingley, followed by the Hyde Park in 1914, and the Lounge two years later. They all prospered because going to the cinema was all the rage. As early films were silent a pianist played appropriate tunes for the romantic scenes and 'hurry' music for the Keystone Cops chases. By the 1920s the cinema had an orchestra of pianist, cellist and Signor Chiodini on violin; for the children's matinees the cashier rushed round from the box office to play the piano. During the First World War news flashes about the conflict and patriotic films were shown.

The Cottage Road Cinema's founders were G. R. Smith, a motor engineer, and Owen Brooks, a studio photographer and cinema pioneer, who had contact with Louis Le Prince in the 1880s and developed projection equipment at the Leeds Tivoli Theatre. When it was opened in 1912 it ran continuous performances from 6.00 p.m. to 10.30 p.m. Monday to Saturday, a matinee on Wednesdays and two children's matinees on Saturday. Ordinary seats cost sixpence and reserved seats one shilling – a night out within most people's budget.

By 1913 there were thirty-one 'electric theatres' in Leeds, and the Headingley Picture House, as the Cottage Road was originally known, was the first

In 1922 Owen Brooks and George Smith's widow, Ella, bought the building and formed The Headingley Picture House Ltd, with wealthy local builder Alfred Atkinson as co-director. In May 1931 it showed the first 'talkie' *On Approval*, a British comedy. In 1937, however, the company folded and the cinema was bought by Frank Thompson, the owner of Golden Acre Park. In 1938 he sold it to Leeds-based Associated Tower Cinemas.

Some modernisation was carried out in the 1950s, and its name was changed to the Cottage Road Cinema. With the rise of television, cinema audiences declined dramatically and in 1972 Associated Tower Cinemas, but after reviewing the future viability of the Cottage Road and the nearby Lounge Cinema on North Lane, decided to keep both cinemas open and modernise them. In 2005, though, the company decided to end its involvement with cinemas. The Lounge suddenly closed in January 2005, despite a protest campaign, but happily the Cottage Road was taken over at the last minute in July that year by Charles Morris, and became part of the Northern Morris Group of six independent cinemas.

The plaque is on the front of the cinema on Cottage Road (LS6 4DD), and was sponsored by Far Headingley Village Society with generous support from many local people. It was unveiled by Kay Mellor OBE on 29 July 2012.

The Majestic Cinema

Brought luxury and fantasy to everyday life when it opened in June 1922. Its fan-shaped auditorium, complete with classical dome and Parthenon-style frieze, seated 2,800 cinema-goers. Music was added to the pleasures of film by the Grand Organ, the Majestic Symphony Orchestra and dinner dances in its sumptuous restaurant. Architect: Pascal J. Stienlet.

Leeds' first purpose-built cinema, 'The Picture House', was opened on Briggate in 1911. Its popularity, like that of suburban cinemas such as the Cottage Road, was immense. By 1921 confidence in the future of the industry was so great that it encouraged the erection of a cinema in the city centre on an entirely new scale of size and opulence. The Majestic was designed by Newcastle architects Pascal J. Stienlet and J. C. Maxwell for Leeds Picture Playhouse Co. Ltd. The architects made good use of the site between Wellington Street and Quebec Street, designing a wide fan-shaped auditorium. The side entrances led to the cinema entrance halls and foyer, while the City Square entrance led to the restaurant. The building was faced with glazed 'Marmo' Burmantofts terracotta. Inside there was an astonishing ribbed and panelled 84-foot diameter dome with Grecian Ionic fluted columns and a classical frieze of beautifully modelled horse riders and chariots in high relief. The cinema had 'the most up-to-date equipment for picture displaying in an artistic manner in aesthetic surroundings'.

The opening film was D. W. Griffith's *Way Down East*, followed by Norma Talmadge in *The Sign on the Door*. The cinema-goers could also enjoy music provided by the Majestic Symphony Orchestra, directed by François Grandpierre, or listen to Harry Davidson on the Grand Organ with all its special effects – all this for between one shilling and two shillings and four pence! In 1926 the Majestic advertised its dinner dances in the Majestic Restaurant – for three shillings you could gain admission to Saturday's 'dansant'.

The sheer luxury of the 2,800-seat auditorium ensured its continued success. *South Pacific* opened in September 1958 and ran for 38 weeks, being seen by half a million people. But even that record was broken by *The Sound of Music* which was screened for two and a half years from 1967 to 1969.

But the competition from television and then multiplex cinemas sealed the Majestic's fate; in July 1969 the last film (Clint Eastwood's *The Good, the Bad and the Ugly*) was shown. The cinema then became a Top Rank Bingo Club. For a decade from 1996 the building enjoyed a fleeting revival as the 'Majestyk' nightclub, with a second club, 'Jumpin' Jaks', in the basement. But thereafter it stood empty and decaying until it was purchased by the property company Rushbond plc which aimed to give it new life as a first-rate leisure venue. The building underwent an immaculate extensive external refurbishment but, sadly, it was gutted by a fire in 2013. Nevertheless, there turned out to be a happy ending – in 2019 Channel Four television chose the cinema's re-renovated shell with a new interior as it new national headquarters.

The plaque on the City Square frontage (LS1 1PJ) was sponsored by Rushbond plc and unveiled on 12 July 2012 by Councillor Ann Castle, Lord Mayor of Leeds.

The Majestic renovated in 2012 before the fire.

BBC Radio in Leeds

In 1924 Lord Reith opened the Leeds-Bradford radio station. It broadcast national programmes and local talks on history, farming and humour, celebrity interviews, Children's Corner and religious services. The station closed in 1931 but local radio returned on 24th June 1968 with the launch of BBC Radio Leeds.

Mark Byford (left) and Phil Squire, managing director of BBC Radio Leeds.

The British Broadcasting Company began national radio broadcasts in 1922. In July 1924 its Leeds/ Bradford Relay Station, housed in offices and a studio in Cabinet Chambers, Basinghall Street, was officially opened by Lord Reith in the presence of the Lord Mayors of Leeds and Bradford and other distinguished guests. The Leeds and Bradford transmitters were replaced in 1931 by a regional transmitter at Slaithwaite, near Huddersfield, serving nineteen counties. Larger broadcasting studios for Leeds were soon required and 'New Broadcasting House' was opened in the former Friends Meeting House in Woodhouse Lane, which provided a large studio capable of holding a full-size orchestra, a talks studio, band room, artists' waiting room, control room and offices.

Programmes produced there included local talks: 'Bygone Yorkshire', 'Old Leeds', 'Old Bradford', 'Farmers' Corner', famous Yorkshire folk and local humour. Afternoon topics included contributions from theatrical stars visiting Leeds. 'Children's Corner' was run by two 'aunties', Nora and Doll, and a selection of 'uncles', Max, Bob, George, Jack and John. Religious services were transmitted from local churches and other outside broadcasts relayed concerts from cinemas, restaurants, Leeds Town Hall and even the bottom of Whitwood coal mine at Normanton! There were also special broadcasts during the Leeds Tercentenary Celebrations in 1926, including 'The Romance of Red Hall', 'The Battle of Briggate' and a band concert from Victoria Square.

Radio Leeds started at 5.30 p.m. on 24 June 1968, in new accessible studios in the Merrion Centre, the seventh of eight local radio stations being set up by the BBC. Many local and national celebrities, including Frankie Vaughan the famous singing star, attended the opening by Roy Mason, the Postmaster General at the time. Radio Leeds sought an informal atmosphere and aimed to cover the city in every aspect from the noisy world of show business to the quiet worlds of local poets, from factory to front room. It was the first local station to broadcast hourly news bulletins, pioneered the phone-in, and introduced the concept of 'walk-in and talk'. The station moved to the BBC premises in Woodhouse Lane in September 1978 and then to the new Broadcasting Centre in St Peter's Square with other branches of the local BBC.

The plaque is placed in the reception foyer of the BBC Broadcasting Centre in St Peter's Square (LS9 8AH). It was sponsored by the BBC and unveiled on 26 June 2008 by Mark Byford, Deputy Director-General of the BBC.

Ivy Benson (1913-1993)

Saxophonist, clarinettist and bandleader lived here 1919-1922. For over four decades from 1940 she led her famous 'all-girls' dance band, performing in prestige venues at home and abroad. Her appointment as the BBC's Resident Dance Band in 1943 confirmed her significant contribution to women's equality.

Ivy Benson was born in 1913 at the Malt Shovel on the Lower Headrow, her grandparents' public house. She was the only daughter of musician Douglas Benson and his wife Mary. Her father, trombonist at the Leeds Empire, started to teach her the piano when she was three, later teaching her to play the clarinet. He hoped she would choose a classical career but, on hearing a Benny Goodman record, Ivy knew she wanted to play swing. At 14 she left school and started work, saving up to buy a saxophone. At 15 she joined Edna Croudson's Rhythm Girls, playing summer seasons at Bridlington. Later she featured as a soloist on tour with Teddy Joyce and the Girlfriends.

In the late 1930s Ivy moved to London where she formed her own small groups and played for an all-girl revue. During the war, with male musicians disappearing into the armed forces, she and her 20-piece All Girls Band were increasingly in demand to play at dance halls. She got her big break in 1943 when her band was employed as a BBC Resident Dance Band based in Bristol; the girls were visited by Queen Mary, and broadcast at all hours to the troops overseas. This appointment caused outrage among male dance band leaders, apart from Joe Loss, who supported her throughout her career. Field Marshal Montgomery requested that the band play in the Victory in Europe celebrations in Berlin in 1946. Ivy spent most of the next twenty years touring the world, latterly for American troops in Germany, with summer seasons at Butlin's Holiday Camps.

Over 250 girls played with the band during its forty years, some starting at age 15, with Ivy

being employer, musical trainer and 'mother hen'. Ivy, helped by her father, did most of the work running the band: organising bookings, costumes, auditions, training and fighting discrimination. She continued to front the band for another twenty years, playing summer seasons on the Isle of Man. On retiring to Clacton-on-Sea, she continued to entertain holiday makers by playing the electric organ, introducing herself with the signature tune 'Lady be Good', which she had first used in 1944. Her success confounded critics who said that women could not sound as good as a male band, and brought untold enjoyment to countless people for over forty years.

The plaque is on the front of 59 Cemetery Road, Beeston (LS11 8SU). It was sponsored by the Beeston Ward Councillors, Jenna Bailey (Ivy's biographer), Doug Sandle and Veronica Lovell. It was unveiled by Councillor Angela Gabriel in the presence of six members of Ivy Benson's Band on 5 July 2011. Tricity Vogue sang Ivy's signature tune 'Lady be Good'.

Unveiling Singsong: Bob Tyrrell, Tricity Vogue and one of Ivy Benson's girls, Carol Gasser.

Live at Leeds

The University Refectory is a legendary concert venue. The Who's performance here on 14th February 1970 was recorded and released as 'Live at Leeds', the most celebrated live album of its generation.

Leeds Civic Trust's approach to Leeds University in 2005, suggesting more plaques to be placed on the campus, led in June 2006 to the biggest jamboree ever surrounding a Trust plaque unveiling. One of the university's ideas was to celebrate the University Refectory as a legendary concert venue. Trust Director Kevin Grady's memories of attending many rock band concerts in the 1970s as a student helped to make the decision to commemorate The Who's 'Live at Leeds' performance. The record which resulted is now regarded as the best ever live rock album. But could the surviving members of The Who, lead singer Roger Daltrey and guitarist Pete Townshend, be persuaded to unveil the plaque? By chance the University had recently awarded an honorary doctorate to Andy Kershaw, the well-known popular and world music broadcaster, who as a former student had been the Leeds University Union Entertainment Secretary. At the ceremony Vice Chancellor Michael Arthur mentioned the plaque to Andy and asked if he could persuade The Who to unveil it. They readily agreed, and were so pleased by the invitation that they arranged to return to the Refectory after thirty-six years to perform once more as the first date on their forthcoming world tour.

Pete Townshend and Roger Daltrey.

Clearly the unique combination of a blue plaque unveiling and a rock concert captured the media's imagination. Photos of the unveiling and the evening's concert appeared in local and national newspapers and on television. The unveiling was shown live on Sky News and BBC News 24. BBC2's Newsnight included a 10-minute feature, and Radio 4 broadcast a 30-minute programme about them in Andy Kershaw's 'School of Rock' series.

The Who were formed in Shepherd's Bush, London, in 1964, evolving out of local youth club band the Detours. Pete Townshend (guitar/vocals), Roger Daltrey (vocals) and John Entwistle (bass/vocals) (died 2002) were the founder members and soon recruited Keith Moon on drums (died 1978). They appeared on television's 'Ready, Steady Go!' and 'Top of the Pops', following the release of their first single 'I Can't Explain' in 1965. A succession of hit singles followed, leading to albums, world tours and continuing fame. The Who are unquestionably one of the finest acts of the rock generation. Alongside the Rolling Stones, they continue to be spoken of as the greatest rock 'n' roll band in the world.

The plaque is on the front of the University Refectory in Lifton Place (LS2 9JZ). It was sponsored by the University of Leeds and unveiled by Roger Daltrey and Pete Townshend on 17 June 2006.

Sport

The concept of leisure hardly existed for most ordinary working people until the later decades of the nineteenth century and beyond, when mills and factories began to reduce working hours and Saturday afternoons became available for people to enjoy themselves. Vast crowds, mainly men and boys, would watch cricket, football and rugby matches. Rugby League became one of the great northern sports. In 1907 the first Rugby League match played in this country by the touring New Zealanders took place at the Barley Mow ground in Bramley. In the same season Leeds' first rugby superstar Albert Goldthorpe and Hunslet Rugby League Football Club carried off all four Rugby League trophies.

Though then a minority sport, golf became much more popular in Leeds in the early twentieth century. The Leeds doctor, Alister McKenzie, began his career as a world-famous golf course designer in the city, creating Alwoodley and Moortown Golf Courses in 1907 and 1909 respectively. Meanwhile, the great summer game was cricket, and playing and watching it was hugely popular. The achievements of Yorkshire County Cricket Club are legendary. Three of Yorkshire and England's most celebrated cricketers in the inter-war period were Herbert Sutcliffe, Len Hutton and Hedley Verity.

In the twenty-first century Yorkshire has become one of the country's most important centres of cycling. But it was half a century earlier that the legendary cyclist Leeds-born Beryl Burton put Leeds on the cycling map. Between 1957 and 1988 she won a prodigious number of world and national titles.

Today the game of darts has become a mass spectator sport with its world championships held in arenas whilst being broadcast to millions on television. But it was not always so. Leeds was the birthplace of televised darts. In the 1980s a television programme called 'Indoor League', celebrating games played in pubs and introduced by the famous Yorkshire cricketer, Fred Trueman, was broadcast from the Irish Centre on York Road. It showed darts on television for the first time and led to a dramatic growth in the popularity of the game.

Legendary cyclist Beryl Burton in action.

Headingley Rugby Ground

Has been in constant use since 1890, the first game being Leeds v Manningham on 20th September. It was the venue for the first Challenge Cup Final, Batley v St. Helens, on 24th April 1897. The first ever Test Match between the Northern Union and New Zealand All Golds was played here on 25th January 1908.

The world's only dual Test arena, Headingley Emerald Stadium holds a unique place in the pantheon of world sporting venues. With legendary cricket deeds on one side of the North Stand and their rugby equivalents on the other, no other ground can boast adjacent facilities in two top-ranked sports.

Originally Lot 17a of the Cardigan estate, the land was purchased by a group of leading entrepreneurs, politicians and sports-minded citizens, with Lord Hawke as their chairman. They formed the Leeds Cricket, Football and Athletic Company in 1888 to bring top-class sport to the city. After levelling the ground and building the stands and pavilions, the stadium opened for its first rugby match just after the start of the 1890 season.

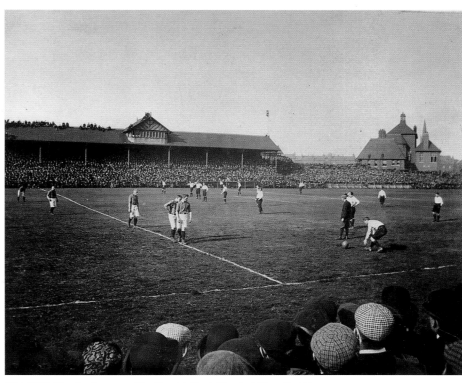

The 1901 Rugby League Challenge Cup Final at Headingley.

Under the visionary chairmanship of Sir Edwin Airey, who took the reins in 1923, major redevelopment took place, initially with the provision of extra terracing. The new South Stand of the rugby ground was completed and roofed in 1931. The North Stand burned down in 1931, but by the end of the following season a replacement with new seating, paddock facilities and press areas had been completed.

The record attendance at Headingley was set on 21 May 1947, when Leeds and Bradford Northern renewed their recent Challenge Cup Final rivalry — 40,175 fans crammed in for the drawn league game. The ground has hosted many famous games, most notably the first ever Test Match between the Northern Union and New Zealand All Golds in 1908, and Great Britain versus Australia Test Matches in 1921, 1948. 1956, 1959, 1970, and 1982.

Under-soil heating was installed in 1963 and floodlights three years later. New changing rooms were opened in 1991 in the middle of the North Stand. In late 2005 the first major construction for over seventy years took place with the building of the three-storey, cantilevered Carnegie Stand at the eastern end. In a ground-breaking initiative, the stand which has both seating and a terrace, included a community café and twelve class and lecture rooms for Leeds Metropolitan University. This increased the ground's capacity to 22,500.

In 2004, after a thirty-two year wait for a league championship, Leeds Rhinos won the Super League Grand Final — the start of a decade of great success. It culminated in the team attaining the modern-day Rugby League treble in 2015, winning the Challenge Cup, the League Leaders Shield and the Grand Final. This success finally initiated the construction of the new South Stand, completed in 2018, and the new North Stand, in partnership with Yorkshire County Cricket Club, completed in 2019.

The plaque is on the outside wall of the ground, next to the ticket office, on St Michael's Lane (LS6 3BR). It was unveiled on Friday, 8 November 2013 by Tony Iro, manager of the New Zealand Nation Rugby League Team.

Bramley RLFC

The Barley Mow Inn ground was the home of Bramley Rugby League Football Club (now Bramley Buffaloes) from 1891 until its move to McLaren Field in 1965. Bramley played New Zealand All Golds here in 1907 in the Northern Union's first ever tour game. Founded 1879.

Bramley Rugby League Club has a distinguished history. Formed in 1879, the team went through the 1880-81 season unbeaten. In 1893 it made the first challenge to the national rule that all rugby players should be amateurs, when it sought to reimburse its international player, Harry Bradshaw, for the time he would be missing from work for international duties. That challenge failed, but in 1895 the northern clubs broke away from Twickenham Rugby Football Union control, forming the Northern Union, over the issue of recompensing players for the time off work.

In March 1907, in Canterbury, New Zealand, postal clerk Albert Baskerville announced that a professional New Zealand rugby side would tour England to play the Northern Union Clubs. New Zealand Rugby Union players were not paid for playing but Baskerville was aware of the split in England by the northern clubs and that players there could be recompensed for time off work. An uproar ensued: there were calls to ban professional sport, Baskerville was banned by the New Zealand Rugby Union, and the English RFU also denounced the initiative. Despite this opposition, leading players supported Baskerville, who formed a 28-man squad. On their way to England the tourists stopped over in Australia, where the New South Wales Rugby Football League was created, and the most famous Australian player, H. H. (Dally) Messenger, joined the tour. On the voyage the tourists kept fit by stoking the ship's boilers. The team arrived in Leeds in October 1907 to be greeted by thousands of enthusiastic fans, who were then treated to a performance of the famous Maori war dance, the Haka. The crowds stopped the city traffic to escort the New Zealanders to their hotel.

The first game of the New Zealand All Golds tour was played at Bramley's Barley Mow Ground on 9 October 1907, the tourists winning 25-6 in front of a crowd of over 6,000. The dressing rooms were part of the pub, opening directly on to the pitch (now modern housing). The All Golds tour lasted five months and they won their first eight games but lost to England and Wales. They played 34 matches watched by over 300,000 people. The tour helped to establish Rugby League as we now know it in New Zealand and Australia, and pioneered the tradition of Rugby League tours. The Australian Rugby League Kangaroos toured England the following year.

The plaque is on the front of the Barley Mow pub, Town Street, Bramley (LS13 3EW). Sponsored by Bramley Rugby League Club, it was unveiled on 27 November 2007 by Tony Collins, Sports Professor at Leeds Metropolitan University.

Prof. Tony Collins (centre) with Bramley RFLC supporters.

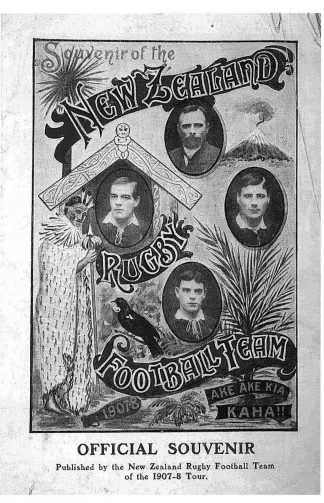

Kiwis 1907-08 Tour Souvenir.

Albert Goldthorpe (1871-1943)

Leeds' first sporting superstar. A supreme goal-kicker and talismanic captain of Hunslet Rugby Club, he made over 700 appearances during 22 seasons. His crowning glory was leading the team to the first ever 'grand slam' of all four Rugby League trophies in 1907/08.

Albert Edward Goldthorpe was a true sportsman. He played football and cricket, captaining Hunslet Cricket Club for many years, winning three Leeds League medals and four Hepworth Cup medals (1904-1913). But it was as a rugby player that he made his name. For well over forty years, 'Arh Albert' as he was affectionately known, served Hunslet Rugby Club as player, committee man and secretary-manager. He made his first team debut at full back, aged 16, in October 1888 and in the following year made his county debut at Hull against Durham, going on to captain Yorkshire for the first time at the age of 20 against Cheshire. He became captain and year after year was Hunslet's top scorer; he was a drop kick specialist, kicking 200 such goals in his career. He played for Yorkshire and was unlucky not to have had an England trial.

1907/08 was Hunslet's greatest season, when a squad of talented players, led by Albert Goldthorpe, won 37, drew 3 and lost just 6 matches, bringing home all four trophies: the Northern Union Challenge Cup, the Championship, the Yorkshire

Albert Goldthorpe with the 1907-8 cups.

Cup and the Yorkshire Senior Competition. The Hunslet team turned their Parkside ground into a fortress and their fearsome forward line would be forever known as the 'Terrible Six'. Not every game was a trail-blazing display – the team were also skilled at grinding out victories, often by narrow margins. Crowds of around 20,000 welcomed them home from their triumphs. On 25 April 1908 Leeds Railway Station and City Square were brought to a standstill as they returned from their 14-0 demolition of Hull in the Challenge Cup Final. The rejoicing became even more frenzied on 9 May when they sealed the unprecedented 'quadruple' of wins by beating Oldham 12-2 in the Championship Final replay.

Albert modestly attributed his success to taking care of himself and leading a hard-working and

open-air life as a farmer, a teetotaller and non-smoker. It was a mark of his popularity that upon the announcement of his marriage a public subscription was organised, and he and his wife were presented with a piano from the funds raised. On 8 January 1943 he died at the age of 71, two weeks before his wife, and they were buried in Hunslet Cemetery.

The plaque is by the main entrance to the John Charles Sports Centre, Middleton Grove, South Leeds (LS11 5DJ), near the former site of Hunslet's Parkside ground. It was sponsored by the McGrail family, Joan McGrail and her brother Geoffrey being Albert's grandchildren. It was unveiled on 2 December 2008 by David Oxley, former Secretary General of the Rugby League and trustee of the Rugby League Heritage Fund.

Dr Alister MacKenzie (1870-1934)

The great golf course architect lived here 1907-1929. His first designs were the courses at Alwoodley (1907) and Moortown (1909). His greatest achievements include Royal Melbourne (1926), Cypress Point, California (1928) and, most famous of all with Bobby Jones, Augusta National (1933-34).

Alexander 'Alister' MacKenzie was born in Normanton, Yorkshire in 1870. Educated at Cambridge, he studied medicine and served as a surgeon during the South African War. Returning to Britain, he held various senior medical posts in Yorkshire, including Consulting Surgeon at St Monica's Hospital, Easingwold, Honorary Medical Officer-in-Charge of surgical cases at Leeds Public Dispensary, and House Surgeon at Leeds General Infirmary.

MacKenzie was a member of Leeds Golf Club (Cobble Hall) from 1900-1910 and was a founder member of Alwoodley Golf Club in 1907; he was invited to collaborate in the course design by the golf architect, H. S. Colt, who was impressed with MacKenzie's models of greens and bunkers. Two years later MacKenzie designed the course at Moortown and later became involved in the design of the city's three municipal courses. Golf course design became his pre-occupation. He briefly returned as an army surgeon at the outbreak of the First World War. During this second spell of military service he quickly transferred to the Royal Engineers and developed camouflage techniques based on his knowledge gained in South Africa, where he had noticed and analysed the ability of Boer soldiers to hide effectively on treeless veldts. Camouflage techniques developed by MacKenzie are credited with saving thousands of lives.

He went on to design many golf courses in the UK and Ireland and in 1926 travelled to Australia and the United States where he designed some of the top courses in the world. He designed or advised on over three hundred courses, including the Royal & Ancient, St Andrews and Troon, and most famously, with Bobby Jones, Augusta National – the Home of the US Masters. He observed that golf course design, like camouflage, depended on utilising natural features to their fullest extent and creating artificial features that closely imitated nature. He believed that courses should be enjoyable, varied, scenic, interesting and challenging for both low handicap players and beginners. He was the author of *Golf Architecture* in 1920, and *The Spirit of St. Andrews* in 1934.

MacKenzie lived at Moor Allerton Lodge, Lidgett Lane, Leeds between 1907 and 1924, before embarking on his travels abroad. He died in Santa Cruz, California, in 1934. The annual MacKenzie Competition is an international event featuring clubs all over the world which were designed by him; in 2005 the event was jointly hosted by Alwoodley and Moortown Golf Clubs.

The plaque is on his former home, now the Corner House Club, 266 Lidgett Lane, Moortown (LS17 6QE). It was sponsored by Alwoodley and Moortown Golf Clubs and unveiled on 27 June 2005 by Olav Arnold, President of Leeds Civic Trust and a long-standing member of Alwoodley Golf Club.

MacKenzie's Home, Lidgett Lane.

Herbert Sutcliffe (1894-1978) & Sir Leonard Hutton (1916-1990)

These outstanding batsmen for Yorkshire and England learnt to play cricket on this ground. Sutcliffe holds the highest English career Test average of 60.73. Hutton, by scoring 364 v Australia in 1938, made the highest individual score by an Englishman in Test cricket.

Herbert Sutcliffe was born in Summerbridge, Nidderdale on 24 November 1894, but moved to Pudsey when he was a baby. Following the premature deaths of his parents he was cared for by his aunts. Aged 13 he began playing for Pudsey St Lawrence Cricket Club and it was not long before he made his First XI debut. Playing alongside him was Henry Hutton, the father of Len Hutton. In 1911, aged 16, he switched his allegiance to the rival Pudsey Britannia team, and in 1919 he made his Yorkshire First XI debut. A right-handed batsman, he was noted for his concentration and determination, qualities which made him invaluable to his teams in adverse batting conditions; he is remembered as one of the game's finest 'bad wicket batsmen'.

Soon becoming an opening batsman for England, his fame rests mainly on the great opening partnership he formed with Jack Hobbs between 1924 and 1930. He also formed notable opening partnerships at Yorkshire with Percy Holmes and, in his last few seasons, the young Len Hutton. During his career, Yorkshire won the County Championship twelve times. Meanwhile, he played in 54 Test matches for England and on four occasions toured Australia. His last tour in 1932-3 included the controversial 'bodyline series'. Statistically Sutcliffe was one of the most successful Test batsmen ever and the fourth-highest run scorer worldwide.

When his playing career ended in 1945, he became a successful businessman, and served on Yorkshire's club committee for twenty-one years, and for three years as an England Test selector. He died on 22 January 1978. Among the honours accorded to him have been his commemoration in the naming of a special set of gates at Headingley Cricket Ground and his induction into the International Cricket Council Cricket Hall of Fame.

Herbert Sutcliffe.

Len Hutton was born on 23 June 1916 in the Moravian community of Fulneck, Pudsey. Many of his family were local cricketers and he soon became immersed in the sport. He joined Pudsey St Lawrence as a junior and, aged 12, made his first appearance for the Second XI. By 1929 he reached the First Team. Sutcliffe was impressed by the young batsman and recommended him to Yorkshire as a good prospect. And so he turned out to be, playing as an opening batsman for Yorkshire from 1934 to 1955 and for England in 79 Test matches between 1937 and 1955.

He has been described in Wisden Cricketers' Almanack as one of the greatest batsmen in the history of cricket. He set a record in 1938 for the highest individual innings in a Test match in only his sixth test appearance, scoring 364 runs against Australia, a milestone that stood for nearly twenty years (and remains an England Test record). During the Second World War he received a serious injury to his arm while taking part in a commando training exercise. His arm never fully recovered, forcing him to alter his batting style.

Despite this, England depended on him and he remains statistically amongst the best batsmen to have played Test cricket. In 23 Tests as captain, he won 8 matches, lost 4, and drew 11. He retired from first-class cricket in 1955 and went on to be a Test selector, journalist and broadcaster. He was knighted for his contributions to cricket in 1956 and became president of Yorkshire CCC in 1990, but sadly died very shortly after on 6 September, aged 74.

Len Hutton.

John and Richard Hutton.

The plaque is on the pavilion at Pudsey St Lawrence Cricket Club, Tofts Road, Leeds LS28 7SQ. It was sponsored by Pudsey St Lawrence Cricket Club and unveiled on 30 October 2016 by Sir Len Hutton's sons, John and Richard.

Hedley Verity (1905-1943)

Yorkshire and England Cricketer was born here. An outstanding slow left-arm bowler, he dismissed Bradman on ten occasions, and took 1,956 wickets, including 144 in 40 test appearances for England (average 14.90). Yorkshire won the County Championship in 7 of his 10 seasons from 1930 to 1939.

Though born in Headingley, Hedley Verity's cricketing career began when his family moved to Rawdon. He attended Guiseley Secondary School, which had a strong cricket team, and in his first match for Rawdon Cricket Club, he scored 47 and took 7 cheap wickets. He persuaded his parents to support him as he set his sights on a cricket career with Yorkshire. Initially he bowled left-arm inswing at medium pace, but he found his forte as a bowler of quick left-arm spin. His success with Rawdon, and Horsforth Hall Park, earned him an invitation to the Yorkshire nets where he first met his mentor, the great George Hirst. As Wilfred Rhodes was still playing for Yorkshire, there was no immediate place for Verity and so, on Hirst's recommendation, he played as a professional with Accrington and later Middleton in the Lancashire League.

With Rhodes planning to retire at the end of the 1930 season, Verity seized the opportunity to claim his place in the Yorkshire First XI. Enjoying some helpful damp pitches, he finished top of the national bowling averages in his debut season and never looked back. Thanks to his countless hours of youthful practice, he had an easy action and superb control of length and flight, and was dangerous on bad or drying pitches.

In 1931 Verity claimed 35 wickets in his first 5 matches, including all 10 against Warwickshire at Headingley. He was selected for 2 Tests against New Zealand and was chosen by Wisden as one of their five cricketers of the year. He took all 10 wickets for just 10 runs against Nottinghamshire at Headingley on a rain-affected pitch, including a hat trick. His figures that day remain the best first-class figures ever.

Verity toured Australia on Douglas Jardine's infamous, and very successful, 'Bodyline' tour in 1932-33, where Bradman ranked him as his most dangerous foe. The Australian tour of England in 1934 was his greatest series, as he took 24 wickets at 24 apiece in the five high scoring Tests. His superb bowling on a wet pitch at Lord's won the match for England. He took Bradman's wicket twice in the match, and 15 wickets in all. When war broke out in September 1939, Verity enlisted in the Green Howards, joining the Allied invasion of Sicily in July 1943; sadly, he was seriously wounded and died at Caserta where he was buried in a military cemetery.

The plaque is on Hedley Verity's birthplace 4 Welton Grove, Headingley (LS6 1ES). It was unveiled on 19 August 2009 by his son Douglas Verity. A bugler from the Yorkshire Regiment played, and a poem about Hedley Verity was read by Lt Colonel David O'Kelly of the Yorkshire Regiment (formerly the Green Howards).

Douglas Verity (left) and Yorkshire and England cricket captain Brian Close at the unveiling.

Beryl Burton, OBE (1937-1996)

Was a cycling phenomenon. Born in Halton, Leeds and living in Morley for much of her married life, she became 3000 metre Track Pursuit World Champion in 1959 (the first of five victories). She was Road Racing World Champion twice and every year from 1959 to 1983 British Time Trials Best All Rounder.

Beryl Burton was born on 12 May 1937 at 3 Howard Avenue, Halton, Leeds, the daughter of John Henry Charnock, a motor engineer, and his wife, Jessie May. As a child she suffered chorea and rheumatic fever which kept her in hospital, and then in a convalescent home, for fifteen months. Her education suffered, and she left Stainbeck Secondary Modern School aged 15. While working as a clerk in a clothing factory, she met Charlie Burton and they married in 1955. He introduced her to club cycling and then competitive racing, a sport that she was to dominate for over a quarter of a century.

Her first season of serious competition was 1957, when she finished second in the national 100-mile time trial. Two years later, at Liège, she became World 3,000 metres Track Pursuit Champion. She successfully defended that title in 1960 in Leipzig and won it three more times, while domestically she won the national pursuit championship thirteen times.

Yet distance cycling on the road, either in bunched racing or time trials, as opposed to the shorter track events, was her real love. She became World Road-Racing Champion twice and national champion twelve times. In unpaced time trials her record was formidable. Although there were no World or European titles in this genre of the sport, she was British 25-mile champion twenty-five times, 50-mile champion twenty-three times, 100-mile champion eighteen times and the best all-rounder for twenty-five successive years. She was the first woman to beat one hour for 25 miles, two hours for 50 miles, and four hours for 100 miles. In 1967 she became the only woman ever to beat a men's record when in twelve hours she rode 277.25 miles.

Although she was awarded an MBE in 1964 and an OBE four years later, Burton justifiably never felt that her accomplishments were adequately recognized by the media. In Europe she was acclaimed, but in Britain the poor coverage given to women's cycling meant that few heard of her outstanding performances. The Burtons were never well off. Charlie Burton worked as an accounts clerk, but devoted much of his time to managing his wife's cycling career and acting

as her mechanic. Meanwhile, Beryl earned some income, and helped her physical fitness, by labouring in local market gardens and rhubarb farms. They had to finance many of her early trips abroad themselves, and Beryl refused to turn professional, despite the entreaties of Raleigh, the British cycle manufacturer.

Beryl won her last national title in 1988, but continued to ride in national championships for the sheer love of the sport. Sadly, out on a training ride on 5 May 1996, she died from a heart problem perhaps associated with her childhood illness. Her achievements had been formidable — she truly was a cycling phenomenon.

The plaque is in Queen Street, Morley (LS27 9BU). It was unveiled on 8 June 2014 by Maxine Peake, actress and writer of the theatre and radio play 'Beryl'.

The Crucible of Darts

Opened in 1970, Leeds Irish Centre has become the social and cultural heart of the city's Irish Community. Now drawing millions of viewers, televised darts was pioneered here in August 1973 when the Centre hosted Yorkshire Television's pub games series 'Indoor League' presented by Fred Trueman.

By the 1900s the Irish population, most of whom settled in East Leeds, had become a significant part of the rich tapestry of the city. Some six Irish clubs had developed, but a group with bigger ideas had by 1970 scraped together £6,000, and borrowed £114,000 from the brewers Tetley to build what would become the Irish Centre. They didn't want just a club for drinking but a family-friendly centre for the whole community. Traditional Irish music and football have been cornerstone activities of the centre; Irish dancing has blossomed, as have many arts and writing groups.

It is thought that the game of darts evolved from archery during the Middle Ages, perhaps beginning with soldiers hurling arrows at the covers of wine barrels. It maintained a strong appeal to the military and the world-wide spread of darts is credited to the British Army, which took it with them to every corner of the Empire. In the Victorian era legislation prohibited 'games of chance' (i.e. gambling) in pubs, and in 1908 a Leeds publican named Anakin was taken to court for permitting darts to be played on his premises. He offered to prove that darts was a game of skill and, having set up a board in the courtroom, he threw three darts in the 20. He challenged the magistrates to match his feat; they could not; so the court had to accept that darts was a game of skill and the laws were eventually changed.

In the early 1970s Yorkshire Television began broadcasting a new programme 'Indoor League' from the Leeds Irish Centre. It featured pub games (including shove ha'penny, bar billiards, table football, table skittles, arm wrestling and darts) and was hosted by Fred Trueman, the legendary Yorkshire and England cricketer. Darts was the big revelation of 'Indoor League' and soon took centre stage on TV, leading up to the first Darts World Championship in 1978. Today darts attracts vast audiences. In 2009, through the columns of The Times newspaper, sportswriter Giles Smith initiated an ultimately successful campaign for Leeds Civic Trust to erect a plaque at the Irish Centre to celebrate it as the birthplace of televised darts.

Sid Waddell and Nicola Cowell present Kevin Grady with the petition from The Times.

The plaque is on the Irish Centre on York Road (LS9 9NT). It was sponsored by the television sports company BSkyB and unveiled on 1 December 2010 by 'The Voice of Darts', Sid Waddell.

Sid Waddell unveils the plaque.

Leeds Civic Trust

Was founded on 25th October 1965 as a voluntary organisation devoted to conserving the heritage of the City of Leeds and promoting the improvement of its built-environment and amenities. Charles H. Crabtree, the Leeds printing press manufacturer, and his family endowed it with the magnificent gift of £50,000.

Leeds Civic Trust was founded in 1965 thanks to a gift of £50,000 by Charles H. Crabtree, whose firm manufactured printing presses on Water Lane, Holbeck. Crabtree's ambition was 'to see Leeds increase its prestige as far as possible'. John Hepper, the Trust's first chairman, and other influential friends successfully persuaded Mr Crabtree to endow an organisation which would campaign for the improvement of Leeds, primarily in the spheres of planning, architecture, heritage and city amenities. Their principal motivation came from seeing the wanton demolition of fine buildings in the city centre, and their rejection of the spirit of the 1960s and 1970s which favoured large areas of cities being torn down and replaced with modern concrete office blocks and high-rise flats. Leeds Civic Trust was born.

For the first three years, the Trust had offices at 10 East Parade, but in 1968 it moved to Claremont in Clarendon Road, which it shared with the Yorkshire Archaeological Society and the Thoresby Society. Between 1968 and 1978 its membership grew considerably from 150 to 350, but then declined sharply to 160 by 1986. The late 1980s produced a very strong revival with a renewed confidence in the importance of the organisation's role in the city. In 1992, with a steadily rising membership, it purchased its own premises in Wharf Street, placing it in the heart of the city centre. By the time it celebrated its 50th anniversary in 2015, it had over 500 individual and family members, more than 80 corporate members and 24 affiliated societies.

For many, the Trust's key role has been as a watchdog on planning and architecture. It has monitored every planning application in Leeds Metropolitan District for more than fifty years, commenting on many and encouraging improvements in the development projects brought forward. It has championed a variety of causes with enthusiasm: saving Barran's Moorish warehouse in Park Square, the Bank of England and Boar Lane from demolition; initiating and latterly promoting, with EYE on the Aire, the regeneration of the city centre waterfront; saving Kirkgate Market from conversion to a shopping centre; producing a variety of influential reports; and campaigning for Leeds to have major new city amenities including the Arena. Most pertinent to this book, part of its role in conserving and promoting interest in the city's heritage has been

achieved by establishing its historic plaques scheme in 1987 and erecting more than 150 blue plaques since then.

Major contributors to the Trust's development have been its chairmen and woman: John Hepper (1965-82), Olav Arnold (1982-92), Robert Collins (1992-98), John Richards (1998-2004), Peter Baker (2004-2010), and Lynda Kitching (2010-16). Outstanding contributors on the town planning side have included George Cox, Derek Linstrum, Brian Godward, Karen Lee, Peter Baker and Mike Piet. In the sphere of events and activities, other major contributors have been Linda Biran, Martin Staniforth and Meryll Wilford. Many more people could be named, including notable treasurers such as Peter Dyson, Trevor Kitson and Jeremy Burton; vice-chairmen Tony Moyes and Neville Rowell; and the queen of the Trust's blue plaques scheme, Valerie Ives. Most striking amongst its staff has been Dr Kevin Grady, who became the Trust's Director in 1987 and retired in 2016 after almost thirty years in the role. He was succeeded as Director by Martin Hamilton, and Jane Taylor became chair. The work of the Trust continues with great vigour.

Above all, the key to the Trust's success and longevity has been the successful passing on of the baton of responsibility for its work to a series of very capable and committed volunteers — indeed, the value of the role the Trust has played (and continues to play) in the city has been demonstrated by the willingness of literally hundreds of volunteers to support and continue its work for more than fifty years.

The plaque was erected at the Trust's headquarters, 17-19 Wharf Street, Leeds, LS2 97EQ on 21 October 2015. It was unveiled by Mrs Liz Dalziel, the granddaughter of Charles Crabtree.

Lynda Kitching, Liz Dalziel, Kevin Grady and Trust members at the unveiling.

Appendices

Select Bibliography

The information in this book is based on the published research of many authors and the research, carried out over many years, by this book's authors into primary source material held by Leeds City Libraries, the Thoresby Society, and the West Yorkshire Archive Service. Below are listed some of the principal published works relating to the subjects of the Trust's blue plaques.

General

Burt, S. and Grady, K., *The Illustrated History of Leeds* (2nd edn, Derby, 2002).

Fraser, D., ed., *A History of Modern Leeds* (Manchester, 1980).

Oxford Dictionary of National Biography.

Thornton, D., Leeds: *A Historical Dictionary of People, Places and Events* (Huddersfield, 2013).

Wrathmell, S., Leeds: *Pevsner Architectural Guide* (2005).

Early History

Bradford, E., *Headingley: 'This Pleasant Rural Village'* (2008).

Burt, S. and Grady, K., *A History of Kirkgate from Earliest Times to 1800* (Leeds, 2016).

Collinson, J. M., *Chapters in Headingley History* (J. M. Collinson, Leeds, 2016).

Hall, D., *Far Headingley, Weetwood and West Park* (Leeds, 2000).

Platt, G. M. and Morkill, J. W., *Records of the Parish of Whitkirk* (1892).

Sprittles, J. 'Links with Bygone Leeds' *Thoresby Society Publications Monograph*, LII (1969).

Thoresby, R., *Ducatus Leodiensis* (Leeds, 1715).

Wilson, B., *Our Village: A Sketch of the History and Progress of Bramley over Seven Centuries* (Bramley, 1860).

Industry and Invention

Burt, S. and Unsworth, R., *Leeds Cradle of Innovation* (Leeds, 2018).

Chartres, J., and Honeyman, K., eds., *Leeds City Business 1893-1993* (Leeds, 1993). Includes chapters on Leeds Permanent Building Society, Joshua Tetley and Son, and Montague Burton Ltd.

E. J. Arnold & Son Ltd, *A Service to Education, 1863-1963: The Story of E. J. Arnold & Son Ltd* (Leeds, 1963).

Hackett, D., *The History of the Future: The Bemrose Corporation, 1826-1976 (1976).* [Took over Alf Cooke's]

Honeyman, K., *Well Suited: A History of the Leeds Clothing Industry, 1850-1990* (Oxford, 2000).

Grace's Guide to British Industrial History [re Yorkshire Patent Steam Wagon Company], https://gracesguide.co.uk

Kitson Clark, E., *Kitsons of Leeds, 1837-1937* (London, 1938).

Lane, M. R., *The Story of the Steam Plough Works: Fowlers of Leeds* (1980).

North, A. C. T., *The Braggs and Astbury: Leeds and the Beginnings of Molecular Biology*, (2005). www.astbury.leeds.ac.uk

Pease, T., *The History of McLarens of Leeds* (Ashbourne, 2003). [Midland Engine Works]

Pease, T., *The History of Manns Patent Steam Cart & Wagon Company* (Ashbourne, 2005).

Pease, T., *The History of Thomas Green & Son Ltd* (Lydney, 2014).

Ryott, D., *John Barran's of Leeds, 1851-1951* (Leeds, 1951).

Sigsworth, E., *Montague Burton: The Tailor of Taste* (Manchester, 1990).

Skempton, A. W. ed., *John Smeaton, FRS* (1981).

Townsley, D. H., *The Hunslet Engine Works* (Norwich, 1998).

Turner, A. J., *The Crown Point Story* (Leeds, 1966).

Transport

Bate, D., *Samuel Ledgard: Beer and Blue Buses* (2005).

Jackson, A. J., *Blackburn Aircraft since 1909* (Putnam & Co. Ltd, 1968).

Joy, D., *A Regional History of the Railways of Great Britain, VIII, South and West Yorkshire* (Newton Abbot, 1975).

Middleton Railway Trust, *A History of the Middleton Railway* (Leeds, 2004).

Soper, J., *Leeds Transport* (Leeds Transport Historical Society, several volumes from 1985).

Tapper, O., *Roots in the Sky: A History of British Aerospace Aircraft* (1980).

Turton, A., *Horse-drawn Transport in Leeds: William Turton, Corn Merchant and Tramway Entrepreneur* (2015).

Commerce

Briggs, A., *Marks & Spencer 1884-1984* (1984).

Holyoake, G. J., *The Jubilee History of the Leeds Industrial Co-operative Society from 1847-1897* (Leeds, 1897).

Leeds Permanent Building Society, *A Survey of One Hundred Years, 1848-1948* (Leeds, 1948).

Linstrum, D., *Towers and Colonnades: The Architecture of Cuthbert Brodrick* (Leeds, 1999).

Houses

Beckett, L., ed., *City of Leeds Training College: Continuity and Change, 1907-2007* (Leeds, 2007).

Beresford, M. W. B., 'East End, West End: The Face of Leeds During Urbanisation, 1684-1842', *Thoresby Society Publications Monograph*, LX and LXI (1988).

Burt, S., *An Illustrated History of Roundhay Park* (Leeds, 2000).

Treen, C., 'The Process of Suburban Development in North Leeds, 1879-1914', in F. M. L. Thompson, ed. *The Rise of Suburbia* (Leicester, 1982).

Education

Benn, W., *Wortley-de-Leeds: A History of an Ancient Township* (Leeds, 1926).

Beresford, M. W., *Walks Round Red Brick* (2nd edn, Leeds, 2012).

Davies, J. G., *From Bridge to Moor: The History of Leeds Grammar School to 1854* (Otley, 2002).

Finnigan, R. E. and Bradley, G.T., eds. *Catholicism in Leeds: A Community of Faith, 1794-1994* (Leeds, 1994).

Gosden, P. H. J. H., and Taylor, A. J., *Studies in the History of a University – To Commemorate the Centenary of the University of Leeds 1874-1974* (Leeds, 1975).

Kennally, H., *Mount St. Mary's School, Leeds, 1853-2003* (Leeds, 2003).

Leeds Education Committee, *Education in Leeds: A backward Glance and A Present View* (Leeds, 1926).

Marshall, J. W. D., *Floreat Per Saecula: A History of Leeds Grammar School from 1854-1997* (Otley, 1997).

Health and Welfare

Anning, S. T., *The History of Medicine in Leeds* (Leeds, 1980)

Anning, S. T. and Walls, W. K. J., *A History of the Leeds School of Medicine* (Leeds, 1982).

Bateman, D., *Life of Berkeley Moynihan, Surgeon* (1940).

Beresford, M. W., *Walks Round Red Brick* (2nd edn, Leeds, 2012).

Reid, T. W., *A Memoir of John Deakin Heaton, M.D.* (1883).

Rolleston, H., *Sir Clifford Allbutt: A Memoir* (1929).

Weinberg, D., *The Oddfellows, 1810-2010* (Carnegie Publishing, 2010).

West, T., *Lady Sue Ryder of Warsaw: Single-minded Philanthropist* (2018).

Religion

Allott, W., 'Leeds Quaker Meeting', *Thoresby Society Publications*, L (1965).

Baker, A. M, and Frieze, S. A., eds., *United Hebrew Congregation, Leeds: The First 150 Years, 1846-1996* (1996).

Freedman, M., *Leeds Jewry: A History of its Synagogues* (1995).

Griffin, F., *Salem: A Short History,1784-1984* (Leeds, 1984).

Knott, K. and Kalsi, S. S., 'The Advent of Asian Religions', in Alistair Mason, ed., *Religion in Leeds* (Stroud, 1994).

Krausz, E., *Leeds Jewry: Its History and Social Structure* (Cambridge, 1964).

Mason, A., ed., *Religion in Leeds* (Stroud, 1994).

Medhurst, C. E., *The Life and Work of Lady Elizabeth Hastings* (Leeds, 1914).

The Methodist Church, *The Handbook of the Methodist Conference 1956 in Oxford Place Chapel, Leeds* (1956): The Story of Methodism in Leeds.

The Methodist Church – Leeds District, *Mission 200: Leeds and the Methodist Missionary Society, 1786-1986* (Leeds, 1986).

Shepherd, P., *The Making of a Northern Baptist College* (2004).

Politics and Society

Driver, C., *Tory Radical: The Life of Richard Oastler* (1946).

Hagerty, J. M., *Leeds at War 1914-18: 1939-1945* (Leeds, 1981).

Hammerton, H. J., *This Turbulent Priest: The Story of Charles Jenkinson, Parish Priest and Housing Reformer* (1952).

Hannam, J., *Isabella Ford* (Oxford, 1989).

Krausz, E., *Leeds Jewry: Its History and Social Structure* (Cambridge, 1964) [re. Leeds Trades Club/Leeds Jewish Institute Club].

Leeds City Council, *City of Leeds Civic Hall Golden Jubilee 1933-1983* (1983).

Liddington, J., *Rebel Girls: Their Fight for the Vote* (2006). [Includes Mary Gawthorpe, Isabella Ford and Leonora Cohen.]

McKenzie, P., *The Barnbow Story: A History of Armoured Vehicle Manufacture at Leeds* (Longhirst Press, 200).

Meadowcroft, M., 'The Years of Political Transition, 1914-39' in D. Fraser, ed., *Modern Leeds* (Manchester, 1980).

Meyer, W., 'Charles Henry Wilson: The Man Who Was Leeds', *Thoresby Society Publications*, 2nd ser., 8 (1998).

Payne, D., 'The Heatons of Claremont', in L Stevenson Tate, ed., *Aspects of Leeds*, vol 1 (Barnsley, 1998).

Podmore, A. J., *The Leeds Rifles*, 1859-1993.

Thornton, D. Leeds: *A Historical Dictionary of People, Places and Events* (Huddersfield, 2013).

Scott, W. H., *Leeds in the Great War, 1914-1918* (Leeds, 1923).

Steele, E. D., 'Imperialism and Leeds Politics, c. 1850-1914', in D. Fraser, ed., *Modern Leeds* (Manchester, 1980).

Towers, W., *City of Leeds Civic Hall* (Leeds City Council, 1933).

Art and Culture

Brears, P., *Of Curiosities and Rare Things: The Story of Leeds City Museums* (Leeds, 1989).

Carpenter, H., *J. R. R. Tolkien – A Biography* (1977).

Dyce, A., ed., *The Works of Richard Bentley.* (1836).

Frankmanis, J., 'The Roving Artist, Pioneer Song Collector [Frank Kidson]', *Folk Music Journal*, 8 (2001).

Kitson Clark, E., *The History of 100 Years of the Life of the Leeds Philosophical and Literary Society* (Leeds, 1924).

Monk, J. H., *The Life of Richard Bentley* (1833).

Robbins, R. and Webster, C., eds. *Through the Pages: 250 Years of The Leeds Library* (Leeds, 2018).

Steele, T., *Alfred Orage and the Leeds Arts Club, 1893-1923* (1990).

Entertainment

Brears, P. and Grady, K., *Briggate Yards and Arcades* (Leeds Civic Trust, 2007).

Holloway, L. C., *Adelaide Neilson: A Souvenir* (1885).

Lennon, P. and Joy, D., *Grand Memories: The Life and Times of the Grand Theatre and Opera House, Leeds* (Ilkley, 2006).

Oxford Dictionary of National Biography [re. Ivy Benson].

Preedy, R. E., *Leeds Cinemas* (Stroud, 2005).

Sport

Burton, B. and Kirkby, C., *The Autobiography of Beryl Burton* (2008).

Callaghan, D., *The Leeds Rugby League Story* (Derby, 1992).

Hill, A., *Hedley Verity: A Portrait of a Cricketer* (1986).

Hill, A., *Herbert Sutcliffe: Cricket Maestro* (1991).

Hodgson, D., *The Official History of Yorkshire County Cricket Club* (Marlborough, 1989).

Howatt, G., *Len Hutton: The Biography* (1988).

Smith, B., *Four Cups to Fame:1907-1908 Hunslet's Four Cup Winning Season* (Leeds, 1988).

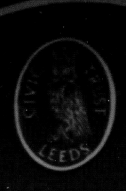

LOUIS LE PRINC

The pioneer of cinemat
had a workshop on thi
where he invented a one
camera and a projecting m
Le Prince produced what
believed to be the world's
moving pictures taken
Leeds Bridge in 19

Sir Richard Attenborough at the Louis Le Prince plaque unveiling 14 October 1988

Leeds Civic Trust Blue Plaques Erected November 1987 to March 2020

No	Title	Location	Unveiler	Date	Sponsor
1	Burley Bar Stone	Inside main entrance of Leeds Building Society, 105 Albion Street, LS1 5AS	Lord George Marshall of Leeds, President of Leeds Civic Trust, former Leader of Leeds City Council	27 Nov 1987	Leeds & Holbeck Building Society
2	Louis Le Prince (1st Plaque)	South-east corner of Leeds Bridge, Bridge End, LS10 1NB	Mr William Le Prince Huettle, great-grandson of Louis Le Prince	13 Oct 1988	British Waterways Board
3	Louis Le Prince (2nd Plaque)	Front of Broadcasting Place, 160 Woodhouse Lane, LS2 9EN	Sir Richard Attenborough, Actor, Broadcaster and Film Director	14 Oct 1988	British Broadcasting Corporation
4	Temple Mill	Marshall Street, Holbeck, LS11 9YJ	Mr Bruce Taylor, Managing Director of Kay & Co. Ltd	14 Feb 1989	Kay & Company Ltd
5	18 Park Place	18 Park Place, LS1 2SP	Sir Christopher Benson, Chairman, MEPC plc	24 Feb 1989	MEPC plc
6	The Victoria Hotel	28 Great George Street, LS1 3DL	Mr John Power MBE, Deputy Lord Lieutenant of West Yorkshire	25 Apr 1989	Joshua Tetley & Sons Ltd
7	The Assembly Rooms	Behind Leeds Corn Exchange in Crown Street, LS2 7DE	Mr Bettison (senior)	27 Apr 1989	Mr Bruce Bettison, then owner of Waterloo Antiques
8	Kemplay's Academy	The former Nash's Tudor Fish Restaurant, off New Briggate, LS2 8JE	Mr Lawrence Bellhouse, Proprietor, Nash's Tudor Fish Restaurant	May 1989	Mr Lawrence Bellhouse
9	Brodrick's Buildings	43-51 Cookridge Street, LS2 3AW	Mr John M. Quinlan, Director, Trinity Services	20 July 1989	Trinity Services (Developers)
10	The West Bar	34-38 Boar Lane, LS1 5HL	Councillor Les Carter, Lord Mayor of Leeds	19 Sept 1989	Bond Street Shopping Centre Merchants' Association
11	Park Square	45 Park Square, LS1 2NP	Mr Anthony Blackmore, Senior Partner, Simpson Curtis, Solicitors	21 Sept 1989	Simpson Curtis Solicitors
12	Leeds Manor House	Scarborough Hotel, Bishopsgate Street, LS1 5DY	Professor Maurice Beresford, Doyen of Leeds historians.	26 Sept 1989	Joshua Tetley & Sons Ltd
13	St Paul's House	St Paul's House, Park Square, LS1 2ND	Mr K. E. Reynolds, Branch Manager of the Fire Society	3 Oct 1989	Norwich Union Insurance Group
14	Leeds Charity School	Mark Lane, LS2 8JA	Professor Neville Rowell, Vice-Chairman, Leeds Civic Trust	30 Oct 1989	Professor Neville Rowell
15	Hotel Metropole	King Street, LS1 2HQ	Lord Strathclyde, Minister for Tourism	10 Nov 1989	Crown Hotels
16	Yorkshire Penny Bank	Yorkshire Bank plc (now Aspire event space), 2 Infirmary Street, LS1 2JP	Mr David Mortimer, Controller (Marketing), Yorkshire Bank	1 Feb 1990	Yorkshire Bank plc
17	William Hey's House	1 Albion Place, LS1 6JL	Private unveiling	March 1990	Leeds Law Society
18	Leeds Infirmary	Leeds General Infirmary, Great George Street, LS1 3EX	Professor Neville Rowell MD, FRCP, Vice-Chairman, Leeds Civic Trust	12 Mar 1990	Medical Faculty of the General Infirmary at Leeds

No	Title	Location	Unveiler	Date	Sponsor
19	Leeds School of Medicine	Thoresby Place, LS2 9NL	Professor M. S. Losowsky, Dean of the Faculty of Medicine and Professor of Medicine, University of Leeds	3 Apr 1990	Faculty of Medicine, University of Leeds
20	Queens Court	Queens Court, Lower Briggate, LS1 6LY	Mr Brian Prideaux, Property Developer	2 May 1990	Mr Brian Prideaux
21	Leeds & Liverpool Canal Warehouse	1 Canal Wharf, Water Lane, Leeds Canal Basin, LS11 5BB	Mr Len Davis, Leeds Canal Basin (Development) Ltd	3 May 1990	Mr Len Davis
22	Bank of England	1 South Parade, LS1 5QL	Councillor Les Carter, Lord Mayor of Leeds	11 May 1990	The Bank of England
23	A.S.L.E. & F.	The Commercial Inn, Sweet Street, LS11 9TE. Temporarily removed for safe keeping.	Mr Derrick Fullick, General Secretary, ASLEF	17 Jan 1991	ASLEF
24	The Great Synagogue	Belgrave Street, LS2 8DD	Rabbi Dr Solomon Brown	3 Feb 1991	The United Hebrew Congregation
25	Mill Hill Chapel and Joseph Priestley	Mill Hill Chapel, City Square, LS1 5DQ	Mrs Eila Forrester, President of the General Assembly of Victorian and Free Christian Churches	28 Mar 1991	Leeds & Holbeck Building Society
26	The Church Institute	9 Albion Place, LS1 6JL	No unveiling ceremony	1991	The British Deaf Association
27	Coloured Cloth Hall	Cloth Hall Court, Infirmary Street, LS1 2HT	Mr D .F .L. Sykes, Senior Partner, Hepworth & Chadwick, Solicitors	16 May 1991	Hepworth & Chadwick, Solicitors
28	Fairbairn House	71 Clarendon Road, LS2 9PJ	Col. Alan Roberts, Pro-Chancellor, University of Leeds	20 June 1991	University of Leeds
29	Atkinson Grimshaw	56 Cliff Road, Hyde Park, LS6 2EZ	Dr Tony Moyes at the request of Mrs Sandra Wood, great-granddaughter of Atkinson Grimshaw	18 July 1991	The Grimshaw family and North Hyde Park Neighbourhood Association
30	John Harrison	St John's Churchyard Wall New Briggate, LS2 8JA	Professor Neville Rowell, Vice-Chairman of Leeds Civic Trust	29 Aug 1991	Professor Neville Rowell
31	White Cloth Hall	Behind Leeds Corn Exchange, Crown Street, LS1 7RB	Mr David Houghton, Managing Director, Speciality Shops plc	24 Sept 1991	Speciality Shops plc
32	Joshua Tetley	The Brewery Gates, Hunslet Road, LS10 1JQ (now The Tetley gallery)	Mr Charles Tetley, Great-grandson of Joshua Tetley	29 Jan 1992	Joshua Tetley & Sons
33	Ralph Thoresby, FRS	15 Kirkgate, LS1 6BY	Mr Arthur Elton, President of The Thoresby Society	6 Oct 1992	The Thoresby Society
34	Arthur Ransome	6 Ash Grove, LS6 1AY	Mr Norman Willis, General Secretary of the Trades Union Congress and longstanding member of the Arthur Ransome Society	2 Mar 1993	Arthur Ransome Society

No	Title	Location	Unveiler	Date	Sponsor
35	Aire & Calder Navigation	Riverside Court, Call Lane, LS1 7BU	Mr Norman Stubbs, Chief Executive, Tay Homes	20 Apr 1993	Tay Homes and British Waterways
36	North-Eastern Railway Viaduct	Swinegate end of the Viaduct, Leeds, LS1 4AG	Mr Gerald Egan, Leeds City Station Manager	27 Apr 1993	Leeds Development Corporation and British Rail's Community Unit
37	Tower Works	Tower Works, Globe Road, LS11 5QU	Mr Martin Eagland, Chief Executive, Leeds Development Corporation	25 May 1993	Leeds Development Corporation
38	Samuel Smiles	Leeds City Museum, Cookridge Street, Leeds LS2 3AD	Mr J. Olav Arnold, President, Leeds Civic Trust	29 Mar 1994	Leeds & Holbeck Building Society
39	Fletland Mills	42 The Calls, LS2 7EW	Mr Keith Roberts, Secretary, The Bransby Agricultural Trading Association	25 May 1994	Leeds Development Corporation and Jonathan Wix, the owner of 42 The Calls
40	Joseph Aspdin	Packhorse Yard, between Lands Lane and Briggate, LS1 6AT	Sir George Mosley, Chairman, British Cement Association and the national Civic Trust	21 Oct 1994	British Cement Association
41	Yorkshire Ladies' Council of Education	18 Blenheim Terrace, LS2 9AR	Lady Grimthorpe DCVO, Past President, Yorkshire Ladies' Council of Education	2 Mar 1995	Mr & Mrs Peter Hartley, Hillards Charitable Trust
42	St Aidan's Church	St Aidan's Church, Roundhay Road, LS8 5QD	Mr Noel Squires, Landlord of the New Roscoe Inn	23 Apr 1995	Mr Noel Squires
43	East Bar	Leeds Parish Church boundary wall, Kirkgate, LS2 7DJ	Professor Neville Rowell. Vice-President of Leeds Civic Trust	23 May 1995	Professor Neville Rowell
44	Sir Leonard Hutton	On wall of the house at 5 Fulneck, Pudsey, LS28 8NT	Sir Lawrence Byford, President of Yorkshire County Cricket Club	14 Oct 1995	Yorkshire County Cricket Club
45	Leeds College of Art	Leeds College of Art, Vernon Street, LS2 9AQ	Sir Alan Bowness, former Director of The Henry Moore Foundation and former Director The Tate Gallery, son-in-law of Barbara Hepworth.	5 Mar 1996	The Henry Moore Foundation
46	First Leeds Synagogue	The Merrion Centre, Leeds LS2 8NG	Councillor Malcolm Bedford, Lord Mayor of Leeds	8 Dec 1996	Mr Edward Ziff, Town Centre Securities
47	City Varieties Music Hall	The City Varieties, Swan Street, LS1 6LW	Mr Paul Daniels, Magician and TV celebrity	27 Mar 1997	Friends of the City Varieties
48	Central Higher Grade School	2 Great George Street, LS2 8BA	Councillor Suzi Armitage, Chair of Community Benefits & Rights Committee of Leeds City Council.	16 Sept 1997	Leeds City Council
49	Leeds Union Workhouse	Thackray Medical Museum, Beckett Street, LS9 7LN	Mr Paul Thackray, Founder, Thackray Medical Museum	11 Feb 1998	Thackray Medical Museum
50	Oakwood Clock	498 Roundhay Road, LS8 2HU	Sir Jimmy Savile, TV Celebrity and local resident	7 Apr 1998	William H. Brown Estate Agents
51	Golden Acre Park	On the outside wall of the cafe in Golden Acre Park, Otley Road, LS16 8BQ	Professor Neville Rowell, Vice-President, Leeds Civic Trust	25 Aug 1998	Professor Neville Rowell
52	Leeds Burial Ground	Opposite St. James's Hospital, Beckett Street, LS9 7LS	Mrs Sylvia Barnard, Founder, Friends of Beckett Street Cemetery	11 Sept 1998	Mr & Mrs David Kaye, Publishers of the Funeral Services Journal
53	Leeds School Board	Civic Court, Calverley Street, LS1 3ED	Councillor Graham Kirkland, Lord Mayor of Leeds	2 Oct 1998	The Rushbond Group plc

No	Title	Location	Unveiler	Date	Sponsor
54	Moortown Golf Club	One plaque on the clubhouse and another on the entrance gates at Mootown Golf Club, Harrogate Road, LS11 7DB	Mr Malcolm Tain, Club Captain	11 Feb 1999	Moortown Golf Club
55	Bank Mills	Rose Wharf, 78-80 East Street, LS9 8EE	Mr Gordon Carey, RIBA, Chairman of Carey Jones Architects	12 Mar 1999	Caddick Developments and Carey Jones, Architects
56	Queen's Arcade	Briggate end of Queen's Arcade, LS1 6LF	Councillor Keith Wakefield, Chair, Leeds City Council Development Service Group Committee	28 Mar 1999	DTZ Debenham Thorpe
57	Meanwood Tannery	Mill Pond Road, Off Monkbridge Road, Meanwood, LS6 4ED	Mr Fred Casperson and Mr Arthur Hopwood, distinguished local historians	17 July 1999	Country & Metropolitan Homes Northern Ltd
58	Burmantofts Pottery	Gargrave Court, Gargrave Approach, Burmantofts, LS9 7ED	Mr George Mudie, MP	10 Dec 1999	Bramall Construction
59	Potternewton Mansion	Potternewton Mansion, Harehills Lane, LS7 4HB	Mr Fabian Hamilton, MP	1 Oct 1999	Park Lane College
60	Victoria Quarter	Between Briggate and Vicar Lane, LS1 6BE	Councillor Keith Parker, Lord Mayor of Leeds	2 May 2000	The Prudential Insurance Company
61	William Congreve	Bardsey Grange, Cornmill Lane, Bardsey, LS17 9EQ	Mrs Bridget Ely (nee Congreve) and Councillor David Congreve, relatives of William Congreve	8 July 2000	Councillor David Hudson representing Wetherby District on Leeds City Council
62	Leeds Town Hall	Inside the Calverley Street entrance of the Town Hall, LS1 3ADs	Councillor Bernard Atha OBE, Lord Mayor of Leeds	27 Nov 2000	Professor Neville Rowell
63	Kirkgate Market	The former Butchers' Row, Kirkgate Market, LS2 7HY	Mr Richard Wainwright, formerly Liberal MP for Colne Valley	14 Dec 2000	Richard Wainwright
64	Montague Burton	Hudson Road, LS9 7DN	Mr Arnold Burton and Mr Raymond Burton, the twin sons of Sir Montague Burton	30 Mar 2001	The Burton Family
65	Kirkstall Brewery	Broad Road, Kirkstall, LS5 3RX	No unveiling ceremony	2001	Leeds Metropolitan University
66	Cliff Tannery	Near the entrance to Sugarwell Court, Meanwood Road, LS7 2DZ. Restricted access.	No unveiling ceremony	2001	Leeds Metropolitan University

Plaques included in this book					
67	The Philosophical Hall	HSBC Bank, 33 Park Row, LS1 1LD	Dr Peter Evenett, President Leeds Philosophical and Literary Society	28 June 2001	Leeds Philosophical and Literary Society
68	Smithfield Ironworks	90-94 North Street, LS2 7PN	Councillor David Hudson, Lord Mayor of Leeds	15 July 2001	Road Roller Association
69	The Grange	Beckett Park, LS6 3QX	No unveiling ceremony when first erected	Oct 2001	Leeds Metropolitan University
70	Permanent House	Brown's Restaurant, The Light, The Headrow, LS1 8EQ	Mr Arnold Ziff, OBE, President of the Leeds Permanent Building Society	16 Jan 2002	Brown's Restaurant

No	Title	Location	Unveiler	Date	Sponsor
71	**Ellen Heaton**	Swarthmore Education Centre, 6 Woodhouse Square, LS3 1AD	Ms Rommi Smith, poet, performer and teacher.	27 Feb 2002	Friends of Swarthmore Education Centre and Little Woodhouse Community Association
72	**Leeds Civic Hall**	Millennium Square, Portland Crescent, LS1 1UR	Mr George Williamson, apprentice joiner, who worked on the construction of the Civic Hall	10 June 2002	Leeds City Council
73	**E. J. Arnold & Son Ltd**	3 Lower Briggate, LS1 4AF	Mr J. Olav Arnold and Mr Martin Arnold, great-grandsons of Edmund James Arnold	3 July 2002	J. Olav Arnold and family
74	**Leeds Grammar School**	Moorland Road, LS6 1AN	Councillor Bryan North, Lord Mayor of Leeds, with pupils Sam Best and Daniel Saffer	7 Oct 2002	Leeds Grammar School
75	**John Deakin Heaton**	Claremont, 23 Clarendon Road, LS2 9NZ	Professor Maurice Beresford, Emeritus Professor of Economic History, University of Leeds	30 Oct 2002	Yorkshire Archaeological Society and Mrs I. A. J. Moses
76	**Sir Berkeley Moynihan**	33 Park Square, LS1 2PF	Dr C. B. Wynn Parry, grandson of Sir Berkeley Moynihan	27 Jan 2003	The Faculty of the General Infirmary at Leeds
77	**Samuel Ledgard**	Nelson Inn, Armley Road, LS12 2LS	Councillor Michael Fox, Deputy Lord Mayor of Leeds	15 Apr 2003	Samuel Ledgard Society and the Ledgard family
78	**Frank Kidson**	5 Hamilton Avenue, LS7 4EG	Dr Vic Gammon, Chairman of Frank Kidson Memorial Fund and Senior Lecturer in Popular & World Music, University of Leeds	20 May 2003	Frank Kidson Memorial Fund
79	**Mann's Patent Steam Cart & Wagon Company Ltd**	Pepper Road, Hunslet, LS10 2RU	Councillor Neil Taggart, Lord Mayor of Leeds	15 June 2003	The Leeds & District Traction Engine Club
80	**Yorkshire Patent Steam Wagon Company**	Pepper Road, Hunslet, LS10 2RU	Councillor Neil Taggart, Lord Mayor of Leeds	15 June 2003	The Leeds & District Traction Engine Club
81	**Newton House**	54 Spencer Place, LS7 4BR	Mrs Jean White, former Deputy Lord Mayor of Leeds	10 Sept 2003	Angel Group plc
82	**The Hunslet Engine Company**	125 Jack Lane, Hunslet, LS10 1BJ	Councillor Neil Taggart, Lord Mayor of Leeds	21 Sept 2003	Don Townsley former General Sales Manager of the Company
83	**Dewhirst's and Marks & Spencer**	Harper Street, LS2 7EA	Mr Timothy Dewhirst, Chairman of Dewhirst Group Ltd, and great-grandson of Mr Isaac Dewhirst	21 Oct 2003	Urban Edge Group
84	**Bardon Hill Stables**	Bardon Hall Gardens, off Weetwood Lane, LS16 5TX. Restricted access.	Mrs Jacky Banyard, Sales and Marketing Director, CALA Homes (Yorkshire) Ltd.	20 Nov 2003	CALA Homes (Yorkshire) Ltd
85	**Cookridge Hall**	Cookridge Lane, LS16 7NL	Mr Don Cole, Cookridge historian	28 Nov 2003	Trustees of Kirke's Charity, Esporta Health and Fitness Club, and Leeds City Council.

No	Title	Location	Unveiler	Date	Sponsor
86	Sir John Barran, MP	Joseph's Well, Hanover Walk, LS3 1AB	Councillor Brian Walker, former Leader of Leeds City Council	4 Dec 2003	J Pullan & Sons Ltd
87	The Middleton Railway	Moor Road Station, Hunslet, LS10 2JQ	Councillor Neil Taggart, Lord Mayor of Leeds	27 Mar 2004	Middleton Railway Trust
88	Denison Hall	Hanover Square, Little Woodhouse, LS3 1BW	Mrs Freda Matthews, Little Woodhouse community campaigner	15 May 2004	Tandridge Investments Ltd
89	Olympia Works and Robert Blackburn	Tesco Supermarket, 361, Roundhay Road, LS8 4BU	Professor Robert Blackburn, grandson of Robert Blackburn	26 May 2004	Dr Philip Snaith
90	Leeds & County Liberal Club	Quebecs Hotel, Quebec Street, LS1 2HA	Mrs Joyce Wainwright, widow of Richard Wainwright, Liberal MP for the Colne Valley	13 July 2004	The Wainwright family
91	The Leeds Club	3 Albion Place, LS1 6JL	Councillor Christopher Townsley, Lord Mayor of Leeds	8 Dec 2004	Mr Bob Isle, Honorary Secretary of The Leeds Club
92	Mount St Mary's Convent, Orphanage & School	Mount St Mary's Catholic High School, Ellerby Road, LS9 8LA. Restricted access.	Mrs Helen Kennally, author of Mount St Mary's Schools Leeds 1853-2003	26 Jan 2005	Mount St Mary's Catholic High School
93	Headingley Hall	Headingley Hall, 5, Shire Oak Road, LS6 2DD	Councillor William S Hyde, Lord Mayor of Leeds and the Lady Mayoress, Mrs Patricia Hyde.	8 June 2005	Westward Care (Yorkshire) Ltd
94	Canal Gardens	Canal Gardens, on the archway leading to Tropical World, Princes Avenue, LS8 2ER	Mrs Marjorie Ziff, President of the Friends of Roundhay Park	21 June 2005	Friends of Roundhay Park
95	Dr Alister MacKenzie	The Corner House Club, 266 Lidgett Lane, LS17 6QE	Mr J. Olav Arnold, President of Leeds Civic Trust and playing member of Alwoodley Golf Club for over sixty years	27 June 2005	Alwoodley Golf Club and Moortown Golf Club
96	Richard Oastler	The Wardrobe, St Peter's Square, LS9 2AH	Councillor Andrew Carter, Deputy Leader, Leeds City Council, with the assistance of pupils from Fulneck School.	6 Sept 2005	Professor Neville Rowell
97	John Smeaton, FRS	On the towpath wall at Leeds Lock, Royal Armouries, LS10 1LT	Mr John McKenzie, President of the Smeatonian Society of Civil Engineers	6 Oct 2005	Smeatonian Society of Civil Engineers
98	Sir Clifford Allbutt	Lyddon Hall, University of Leeds Campus, LS2 9JT	Dr John Wales MD, FRCP, retired Consultant Physician and past Chairman of the Faculty at the General Infirmary at Leeds	7 Dec 2005	The Faculty at the General Infirmary at Leeds
99	Leeds General Cemetery	Gatehouse, St George's Field, University of Leeds campus, LS2 9JT	Dr Julie Rugg, a senior research fellow at York University and head of the Cemetery Research Group	24 Apr 2006	Mr and Mrs David Kaye
100	Whitelocks	Turks Head Yard, off Briggate, LS1 6HB	Ms Sarah Whitelock, great, great granddaughter of John Lupton Whitelock, landlord and licensee in 1867.	23 May 2006	Leeds Civic Trust
101	Richard Bentley FRS DD	Bentley Square, Calverley Rd, Oulton, LS26 8JH	Mr Malcolm Brocklesby, Vice-Chairman of the Oulton Society	7 June 2006	The Oulton Society

No	Title	Location	Unveiler	Date	Sponsor
102	Live at Leeds	University of Leeds Refectory, Lifton Place, LS2 9JZ	Mr Pete Townshend and Mr Roger Daltrey, surviving members of The Who's original line-up at their famous performance on 14 February 1970	17 June 2006	University of Leeds
103	The Leeds Rifles	Carlton Barracks, Carlton Gate, Lane, LS7 1HE	Dr Ingrid Roscoe, Lord Lieutenant of West Yorkshire	8 Nov 2006	Reserve Forces and Cadets Association for Yorkshire and the Humber
104	Leeds Co-operative Society	Gatepost at entrance to Leodis Court (opp. Temple Mill), LS11 5JJ	Mr David Schofield, past President of the Leeds Co-operative Society	1 Mar 2007	Leeds Co-operative Society
105	Leonora Cohen JP OBE	2 Claremont Villas, Clarendon Road, LS2 9NY	Mr Michael Meadowcroft, Chairman of the Electoral Reform Society 1989-1993	6 June 2007	Various individual sponsors
106	J & H McLaren's Midland Engine Works	Equinox Designs Ltd, 100 Jack Lane, Hunslet, LS10 1BN	Councillor Brian Cleasby, Lord Mayor of Leeds	17 June 2007	The Leeds & District Traction Engine Club
107	The Leeds Library	18 Commercial Street, LS1 6AL	Councillor Allan Taylor, Deputy Lord Mayor of Leeds	4 Sept 2007	The Leeds Library
108	William Turton	64 The Calls, LS2 7EF	Mr John Turton	28 Sept 2007	The Turton family
109	Bramley Rugby League Football Club	The Barley Mow Inn, Town Street, Bramley, LS13 3EW	Professor Tony Collins, Official Rugby League Historian	27 Nov 2007	Engineering Plastic Supplies Ltd, Bramley
110	Adelaide Neilson	Leeds Playhouse, Quarry Hill, LS2 7UP – by side entrance.	Josephine Tewson, actress	29 Jan 2008	Professor Neville Rowell
111	BBC Radio In Leeds	Foyer, BBC Broadcasting Centre, 2 St Peter's Square, Quarry Hill, LS9 8AH	Mr Mark Byford, Deputy Director-General of the BBC	26 June 2008	BBC Radio Leeds
112	Stocks Hill, Bramley	Stone wall adjacent to the pump, Stocks Hill, Town Street, Bramley LS13 3NA	Councillor Frank Robinson, Lord Mayor of Leeds	27 July 2008	Bramley History Society
113	Albert Goldthorpe	John Charles Centre for Sport, Middleton Grove, LS11 5DJ	Mr David Oxley, former Secretary General of the Rugby League and a Trustee of the Rugby League Heritage Foundation	2 Dec 2008	Stephen McGrail and family (Goldthorpe descendants)
114	Elmete Hall	Elmete Lane, Roundhay, LS8 2LJ	No unveiling ceremony	Dec 2008	Joe Hester
115	Gledhow Hall	On Gledhow Hall's boundary wall at the junction of Gledhow Ln, Lidgett Ln & Gledhow Wood Rd, LS8 1PG	Councillor Frank Robinson, Lord Mayor of Leeds	7 Feb 2009	Gledhow Valley Conservation Area Group and Tillasu Estates
116	The Yorkshire College	Textile Building, University Road, University of Leeds campus (next to the Great Hall), LS2 9JT	Mr John-Stoddart Scott, Chairman of Grants Committee, Clothworkers' Company	12 Feb 2009	University of Leeds
117	Lady Betty Hastings	By the main entrance to Holy Trinity, Boar Lane, LS1 6HW	Dr Ingrid Roscoe, Lord Lieutenant of West Yorkshire	20 Apr 2009	Land Securities, plc
118	Wortley Grammar School	69 Lower Wortley Road, LS12 4SL	Councillor Judith Elliott, Lord Mayor of Leeds	5 June 2009	Wortley Local History Group
119	Hedley Verity	4 Welton Grove, Headingley, LS6 1ES	Douglas Verity, son of Hedley Verity	19 Aug 2009	Yorkshire County Cricket Club

No	Title	Location	Unveiler	Date	Sponsor
120	Isabella Ford	Adel Grange Residential Home, Adel Grange Close, LS16 8HX	Frank Ford, representing the Ford family	6 Oct 2009	Adel Grange Residential Home
121	The Mansion	Mansion Lane, Roundhay Park, LS8 2HH	Councillor John Procter	27 Jan 2010	Daniel Gill of Dine
122	Rawdon College	Larchwood (the former Rawdon Baptist College), Woodlands Drive, Rawdon LS19 6JZ	Revd Ernie Whalley	4 Sept 2010	Residents of Larchwood
123	Carlton Hill Friends Meeting House	Old Broadcasting House, 160b Woodhouse Lane, LS2 9EN.	Mary Rowntree, daughter of the long-standing caretaker	9 Sept 2010	Leeds Area Meeting of the Religious Society of Friends (Quakers)
124	William Astbury	189 Kirkstall Lane, Headingley, LS6 3EJ	Adam Nelson, Professor of Chemical Biology and Director of the Astbury Centre, University of Leeds	26 Nov 2010	Thackray Medical Museum
125	The Crucible of Darts	The Leeds Irish Centre, York Road, LS9 9NT.	Mr Sid Waddell, 'The Voice of Darts'	1 Dec 2010	Sky Sports Publicity
126	The Leeds Odd Fellows	2 Queen Square, LS2 8AF	Brother Alan Cole	20 Jan 2011	Leeds Oddfellows
127	Sir Charles Wilson MP	The Northern School of Contemporary Dance, 98 Chapeltown Road, LS7 4BH	Councillor James McKenna, Lord Mayor of Leeds	18 May 2011	Chapeltown Heritage Advisory Group
128	Lady Sue Ryder of Warsaw	Scarcroft Grange, Wetherby Road, Scarcroft, LS14 3HJ	Elizabeth and Jeromy Cheshire (daughter and son of Sue Ryder and Leonard Cheshire)	25 June 2011	Sue Ryder Prayer Fellowship
129	Ivy Benson	59 Cemetery Road, Beeston, LS11	Councillor Angela Gabriel	5 July 2011	Beeston & Holbeck Ward Councillors, Adam Ogilvie, David Congreve and Angela Gabriel; and Ivy Benson fans Jenna Bailey, Veronica Lovell and Doug Sandle
130	Central Station Wagon Hoist	Wellington Place, Leeds LS1 4AJ	Councillor Revd Alan Taylor, Lord Mayor of Leeds	25 July 2011	MEPC
131	Gertrude Maretta Paul	Bracken Edge Primary School, Newton Road, Chapeltown, LS7 4HE	Gertrude's daughter Heather Paul and grandson Theo	21 Oct 2011	Chapeltown Heritage Advisory Group
132	Salem Chapel	At the back of the chapel, 11-15 Hunslet Road, LS10 1JW	Councillor Revd Alan Taylor, Lord Mayor of Leeds,	17 Nov 2011	aql Limited
133	The Revd Charles Jenkinson	St John & St Barnabas Church, Belle Isle Road, Belle Isle, LS10 3DN	Councillor Revd Alan Taylor, Lord Mayor of Leeds,	12 Feb 2012	Diocese of Ripon & Leeds
134	House of Faith	21 Leopold Street, Chapeltown, LS7 4DA	Councillor Mohammed Rafique and Ruth Sterne	14 Mar 2012	Unity Housing Association
135	The Leeds Arts Club	8 Blenheim Terrace, LS2 9HZ	Dr Ingrid Roscoe, Lord Lieutenant of West Yorkshire	15 May 2012	Ben Read (son of Herbert Read)
136	The Majestic Cinema	City Square, LS1 1PJ. Temporarily removed for safe keeping.	Councillor Ann Castle, Lord Mayor of Leeds,	12 July 2012	Rushbond plc
137	Cottage Road Cinema	Cottage Road, Far Headingley, LS6 4DD	Kay Mellor OBE	29 July 2012	Far Headingley Village Society

No	Title	Location	Unveiler	Date	Sponsor
138	J R R Tolkien CBE	2 Darnley Road, West Park, LS16 5JF	Dr Kersten Hall	1 Oct 2012	The Tolkien Society and the University of Leeds
139	The New Synagogue	Northern School of Contemporary Dance, Chapeltown Road, LS7 4BH	Judge Ian Dobkin	14 Oct 2012	The United Hebrew Congregation
140	The Railway Roundhouse	Wellington Road, LS12 1DR	Mr Paul Kirkman, Director National Railway Museum	20 Nov 2012	Leeds Commercial Limited
141	The ORT Technical Engineering School	New Horizons Community School, Newton Hill Road, Leeds, LS7 4JE	Sydney Sadler, former pupil of the school	14 Apr 2013	British ORT
142	Leeds Trades Club	Leeds Media Centre, 21 Savile Mount, Chapeltown, LS7 3HZ	Dick Banks, Chair Regional Committee, Unite; Brian Mulvey, Branch Secretary Unison Leeds Government Branch; Dave Noble, Regional President, GMB	1 May 2013	Unison, Unite, and GMB
143	Leeds Corn Exchange	Call Lane, LS1 7BR	Mark Cockerill, Corn Trader	16 July 2013	Zurich Assurance Ltd
144	Leeds Grand Theatre & Opera House	46 New Briggate, LS1 6NZ	Kay Mellor OBE	23 July 2013	Family and friends of the late Martin James Frazer
145	Leeds Methodist Pioneers	Leeds Playhouse, Quarry Hill, LS2 7UP – left side 10 metres from the front.	Rev. Ruth Gee, B.A. M.Litt., President of the Methodist Conference	6 Oct 2013	The Methodist Church Leeds District
146	Headingley Rugby Ground	On the wall near Leeds Rugby ticket office, St Michael's Lane, LS6 3BR	Tony Iro, New Zealand Team Manager	8 Nov 2013	Leeds Rugby Foundation
147	Weetwood Hall	Weetwood Hall Conference Centre & Hotel, Otley Road, LS16 5PS	Mrs Sheila Griffiths, former Warden of Weetwood Hall	7 May 2014	Weetwood Hall Conference Centre & Hotel
148	Gipton Board School	Shine, Harehills Road (between Conway Mount and Conway Street), LS8 5HS	Councillor Judith Blake, Leader of Leeds City Council	28 May 2014	The late Irene Revie, a former pupil
149	Beryl Burton OBE	Beryl Burton Gardens, Queen Street, Morley, LS27 9BU	Maxine Peake	8 June 2014	Morley Town Council, Morley Town Centre Management Board and Leeds City Council Outer South Area Committee Well-being Fund
150	Crown Point Printing Works	Leeds City College Printworks Campus, Hunslet Road, LS10 1JY	Councillor David Congreve, Lord Mayor of Leeds	25 June 2014	Leeds Civic Trust
151	John Fowler	Costco Car Park, Leathley Road, Hunslet, LS10 1BG	Councillor David Congreve, Lord Mayor of Leeds	4 Dec 2014	Leeds and District Traction Engine Club
152	Barnbow Royal Ordnance Factory	Former Factory Gates, Austhorpe Road, LS15 8FS	Mrs Val Orrell, former Barnbow employee	20 Apr 2015	Bellway Homes, East Leeds Historical & Archaeological Society and Leeds Civic Trust members

No	Title	Location	Unveiler	Date	Sponsor
153	Mary Gawthorpe	9 Warrel's Mount, Bramley, LS13 3NU	Dr Jill Liddington	30 April 2015	Members & friends of Leeds Civic Trust and Bramley Ward Councillors
154	The South Bar	South end of Leeds Bridge, LS10 1NB	Professor Neville Rowell	9 June 2015	Professor Neville Rowell
155	Whitkirk Manor House	Colton Road, Whitkirk, LS15 9AA	Mr Ed Anderson, High Sheriff of West Yorkshire	16 Oct 2015	Mrs Desi Abson and her late husband
156	Leeds Civic Trust	17-19 Wharf Street, off Kirkgate and The Calls, LS2 7EQ	Mrs Elizabeth Dalziel, granddaughter of Charles Crabtree.	21 Oct 2015	Leeds Civic Trust
157	Chapel Allerton Hall	Chapel Allerton Hall, Gledhow Lane, LS7 4NP	Councillor Judith Chapman, Lord Mayor of Leeds,	7 Nov 2015	Gledhow Valley Conservation Area Group
158	Thomas Edmund Harvey	Rydal House, 5 Grosvenor Terrace, Headingley, LS6 2DY	Michael Meadowcroft, former Liberal MP for Leeds West	6 July 2016	Dr Jon Wood & Dr Julia Kelly the owners of Rydal House
159	Hepper House	17A East Parade, LS1 2BH	Councillor Judith Blake, Leader of Leeds City Council	13 Sept 2016	Ibérica Restaurants Ltd
160	The New Penny	57-59 Call Lane, LS1 7BT	Councillor James Lewis, Deputy Leader of Leeds City Council	19 Oct 2016	Leeds City Council
161	Herbert Sutcliffe & Sir Leonard Hutton	Pudsey St Lawrence Cricket Club, Tofts Road LS28 7SQ	Richard and John Hutton (Sir Len Hutton's sons)	30 Oct 2016	Pudsey St Lawrence Cricket Club
162	St Michael's College	The Court, Clarendon Quarter, St John's Road, LS3 1EX	Mr Robin Smith, a former pupil	27 Apr 2017	AIG Global Real Estates
163	Kenneth Armitage	Mandela Gardens, Millennium Square, LS2 3AD	Robert Hiscox, Chair of the Kenneth Armitage Foundation	5 May 2017	The Kenneth Armitage Foundation
164	North Bar	The Old Red Bus Station, 101 Vicar Lane, LS2 7NL	James Bailey, General Manager, Victoria Quarter	30 Oct 2017	Professor Neville Rowell

Plaques erected since October 2017, not included in this book					
165	Benjamin Gott	Gotts Park Golf Club, Armley, LS12 2QX	Richard Gott, Great-great-great grandson	3 Mar 2018	Crowd-funded by members of the public
166	William Gascoigne	Patel Store, Town Street, Middleton, LS10 3PN	David Sellers, FRAS	23 Mar 2018	Leeds Philosophical & Literary Society; Morley Monday Club; Institute of Physics; Society for the History of Astronomy; Leeds Astronomical Society
167	Agnes Logan Stewart	Bridge Community Church, Rider Street, LS9 7BQ	The Rt Revd Paul Slater, Bishop of Kirkstall	10 Apr 2018	The Diocese of Leeds and Leeds Minster
168	Maurice Ellis FRCS	Leeds General Infirmary gatepost of principal entrance, Great George Street, LS1 3EX	Dr Taj Hassan, President of the Royal College of Emergency Medicine, and Consultant in Emergency Medicine at Leeds Teaching Hospitals NHS Trust	1 June 2018	Leeds Teaching Hospitals NHS Trust

No	Title	Location	Unveiler	Date	Sponsor
169	**Marshall's Mill**	Marshall Street, Holbeck, LS11 9YJ	Councillor Graham Latty, Lord Mayor of Leeds	10 Sept 2018	Workman LLP
170	**Titus Salt**	91 Queen Street, Morley, LS27 8EF	Colonel Alan Roberts	5 Oct 2018	Morley Town Centre Management & Morley Community Archives
171	**Charles Barker Howdill**	14 Hanover Square, LS3 1AP	Professor Duncan McCargo, owner of the house	27 Oct 2018	Professor Duncan McCargo
172	**Alice Bacon MP**	Leeds Corn Exchange, Call Lane, LS1 7BR (inside)	Rachel Reeves, MP for Leeds West	10 Jan 2019	Rushbond plc and University of Leeds
173	**Albert Johanesson**	Entrance to the East Stand, Elland Road Stadium, LS11 0ES	Samantha Jones, Albert's granddaughter, and Brian Deane, former Leeds United player	11 Jan 2019	Leeds United Supporters Trust, Leeds United, Leeds Civic Trust and Leeds City Council
174	**Catherine Mawer**	Starbucks, 48 Albion Street (junction with Commercial Street), LS1 6AB	Artists Pippa Hale and Jill McKnight as part of the Yorkshire Sculpture International Festival	11 July 2019	Linda O'Carroll and The Chambers (serviced apartments)
175	**The Mawer Group**	The Chambers, 30 Park Place, LS1 2SP (not yet erected)	Artists Pippa Hale and Jill McKnight as part of the Yorkshire Sculpture International Festival	11 July 2019	The Chambers (serviced apartments)
176	**Holbeck Working Men's Club**	HWMC, Jenkinson's Lawn, Holbeck, LS11 9QX	Terry Nicholls and Ian Pickup, long-standing club members	13 Sept 2019	Holbeck Working Men's Club and Slung Low theatre company
177	**R. A. H. Livett OBE**	76 Wykebeck Road, Gipton, LS9 6PB	Amanda Neville, granddaughter, and Vi and Jim Cooper, residents of the house	21 Sept 2019	Leeds City Council
178	**Morley Town Hall**	Queen Street, Morley, LS27 9DY	Councillor Andrew Hutchinson, Mayor of Morley	4 Oct 2019	Morley Town Centre Management and Morley Community Archives
179	**Keith Waterhouse**	Hunslet Library, Waterloo Street, LS10 2NS	Laura Collins, Editor of the Yorkshire Evening Post, and Anthony Clavane, author and journalist	6 March 2020	Leeds City Council and Hunslet and Riverside Ward councillors Elizabeth Nash, Paul Wray and Mohammed Iqbal
180	**Jim Bullock OBE**	Bowers Row Chapel, Bowers Row, Great Preston, LS26 8DF	Jim Bullock, Junior	21 May 2020	The Bullock Family

Roger Garnett erects the Crucible of Darts plaque at Leeds Irish Centre amidst the sudden snowfall.

Leeds city centre plaques

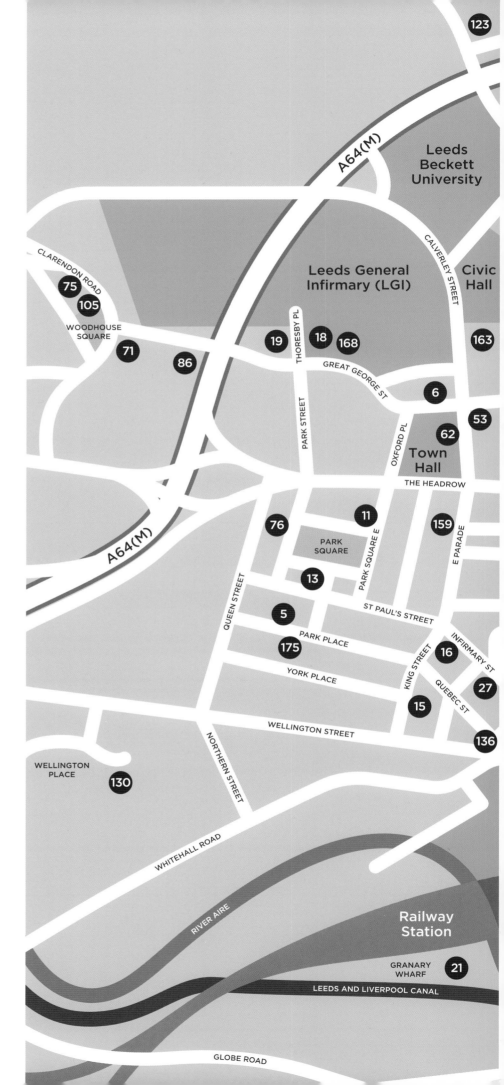

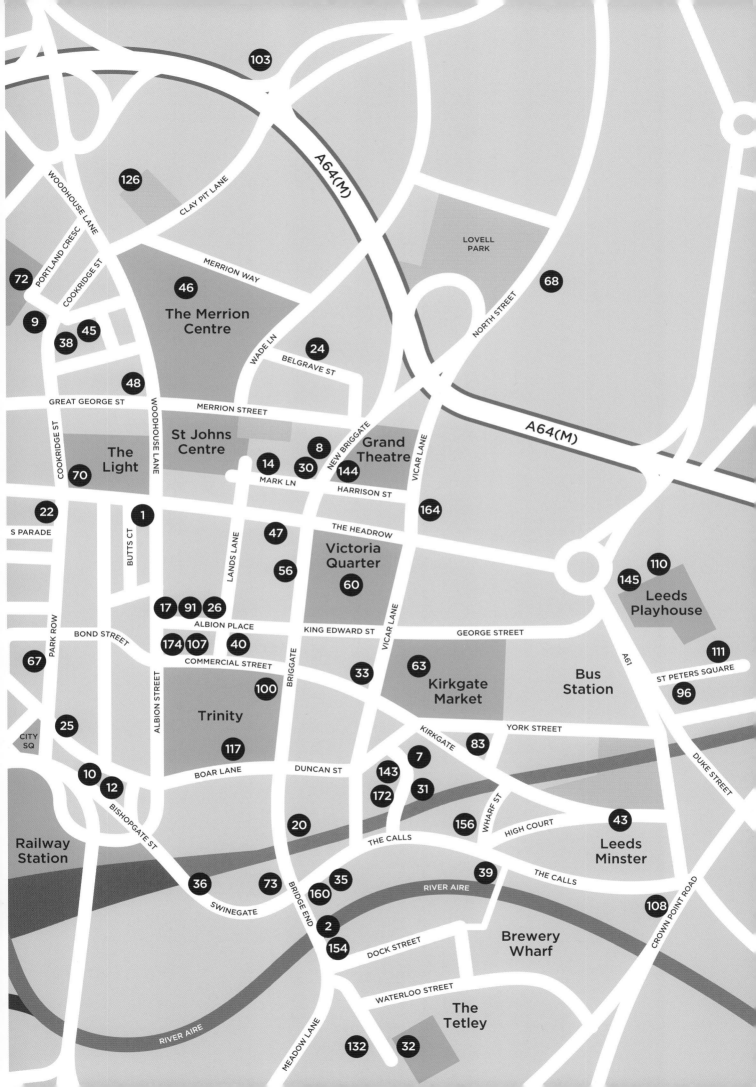

Beyond the city centre

Plaques beyond the boundaries of this map:

Bardsey: **61**

Belle Isle: **133**

Bramhope: **51**

Cookridge: **85**

Crossgates: **152**

Fulneck: **44**

Great Preston: **180**

Middleton: **113** **166**

Moortown: **54**

Morley: **149** **170** **178**

Oulton: **101**

Pudsey: **161**

Rawdon: **122**

Scarcroft: **128**

Whitkirk: **155**

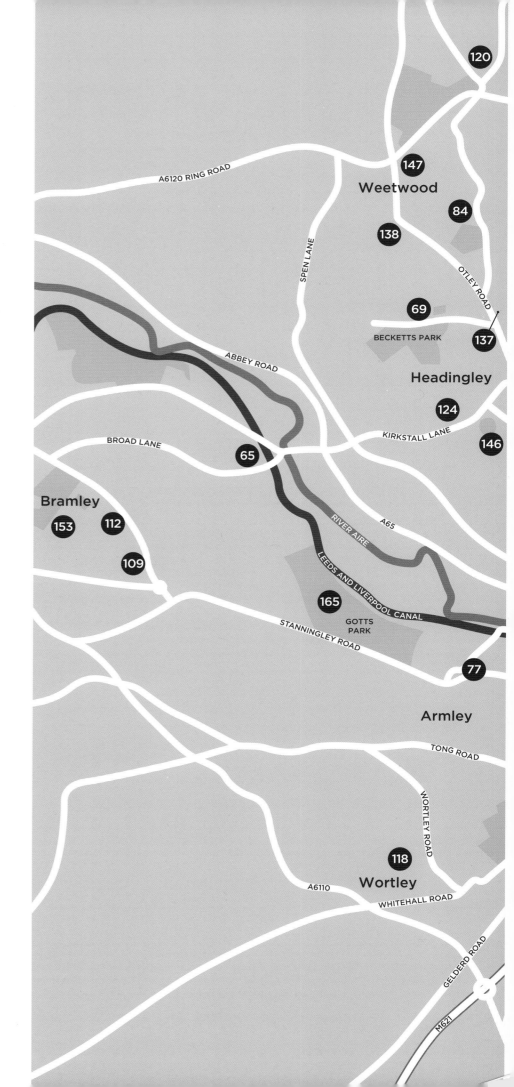

Moortown

A6120 RING ROAD

STONEGATE ROAD

STAINBECK ROAD

SCOTT HALL ROAD

HARROGATE ROAD

95

94 121

ROUNDHAY PARK

114

Meanwood

157

Chapel Allerton

115

Oakwood

GROVE LANE

57

POTTERNEWTON LANE

HAREHILLS LANE

50

89

ROUNDHAY ROAD

EASTERLY ROAD

93

MEANWOOD ROAD

66

141

131 59

Chapeltown

158

29

78

SPENCER LANE

81

A58

148

OTLEY ROAD

VICTORIA ROAD

119 34

Hyde Park

WOODHOUSE MOOR

139 134

142 127

42

Harehills

49

52

64

41

CLARENDON RD

99 135

3

123 103

74

162 102 98 116

BURLEY ROAD

28 75 105

71

58

88 171

BECKETT STREET

167

177

RIVER AIRE

CANAL STREET

130

140

See Leeds city centre map

125

YORK ROAD

Richmond Hill

55 92

97

WATER LN

169 104

MARSHALL ST

4

SWEET ST

23

A61

150

151

176

JACK LANE

82

Holbeck

106

Hunslet

129

173

79

ELLAND ROAD

BEESTON ROAD

Beeston

179

CHURCH ST

HUNSLET ROAD

RIVER AIRE

A63

87

BALM ROAD

PEPPER RD

80

M621

Index of Persons

Leeds Civic Trust

Leeds Civic Trust is a charity that was formed in 1965. We celebrate and stimulate public interest in and care for the beauty, history and importance of our city's unique heritage. We have an interest in sustainable development – promoting high standards of urban design, architecture and placemaking, championing world class amenities for Leeds citizens, and supporting the development and maintenance of green and public spaces and improvements to the city's waterfront.

Address: 17/19 Wharf Street, Leeds, LS2 7EQ
Telephone: 0113 2439594
Email: office@leedscivictrust.org.uk
Website: www.leedscivictrust.org.uk
Twitter: @leedscivictrust

Registered charity no: 1014362